2ND EDITION

Painting and Decorating

NVQ and Technical Certificate **Level 2**

www.heinemann.co.uk
✓ Free online support
✓ Useful weblinks
✓ 24 hour online ordering

01865 888118

D0452395

Heinemann is an imprint of Pearson Education Limited, a company incorporated in England and Wales, having its registered office at Edinburgh Gate, Harlow, Essex, CM20 2JE. Registered company number: 872828

www.heinemann.co.uk

Heinemann is a registered trademark of Pearson Education Limited

Text © Carillion Construction Ltd 2008

First published 2006
Second edition published 2008

12 11 10 09 08
10 9 8 7 6 5 4 3 2 1

British Library Cataloguing in Publication Data

A catalogue record for this book is available from the British Library

ISBN 978 0 435498 30 6

Copyright notice

Designed by HL Studios
Typeset by HL Studios
Original illustrations © Pearson Education Limited 2006, 2008
Illustrated by HL Studios
Cover design by GD Associates
Cover photo: © Pearson Education Limited/Gareth Boden
Printed in the UK by Scotprint

Acknowledgements

Every effort has been made to contact copyright holders of material reproduced in this book. Any omissions will be rectified in subsequent printings if notice is given to the publishers.

Websites

The websites used in this book were correct and up-to-date at the time of publication. There are links to relevant websites in this book. In order to ensure that the links are up-to-date, that the links work, and that the sites are not inadvertently linked to sites that could be considered offensive, we have made the links available on the Heinemann website at www. heinemann.co.uk/hotlinks. When you access the site, the express code is 3594P.

The information and activities in this book have been prepared according to the standards reasonably to be expected of a competent trainer in the relevant subject matter. However, you should be aware that errors and omissions can be made and that different employers may adopt different standards and practices over time. Therefore, before doing any practical activity, you should always carry out your own Risk Assessment and make your own enquiries and investigations into appropriate standards and practices to be observed.

Contents

Acknowledgements

Carillion would like to thank the following people for their contribution to this book: Stephen Olsen (lead author), Kevin Jarvis, Ralph Need, Arthur Carter and Derrick Thurlbeck.

Pearson Education Limited would like to thank the following for providing technical feedback: Michael Taylor from Hartlepool College and Brian Bibby and Nicole Simpson from Furness College.

Pearson Education Limited would like to thank everyone at the Carillion Construction Training Centre in Sunderland for all their help at the photo shoots.

Special thanks to Chris Ledson at Toolbank for supplying some photos. Visit the Toolbank website at www.toolbank.com.

Photo acknowledgements

The author and publisher would like to thank the following individuals and organisations for permission to reproduce photographs:

A1 Pix/Karl Thomas, p210;

Alamy Images/Elizabeth Whiting & Associates, p286 (top), p287 (top); Alamy Images/ David J. Green, p47 (bottom), p179 (bottom), p180 (top), p315 (bottom right); Alamy Images/Nic Hamilton, p33; Alamy Images/Ingram Publishing (Superstock Ltd), p274; Alamy Images/Jupiter Images, p165 (bottom); Alamy Images/Justin Kase, p36; Alamy Images/Osbornestock, p276; Alamy Images/PlainPicture GmbH & Co KG, p46; Alamy Images/SUNNYPhotography.com, p192 (middle); Alamy Images/The Photolibrary Wales, p56; Alamy Images/ V&A Museum, p286 (bottom); Caro Photo Agency, p315 (bottom left); Constructionphotography.com, p38, p63; Constructionphotography.com/Xavier de Canto, p213; Constructionphotography.com/DIY Photolibrary, p86; Constructionphotography. com/Chris Henderson, p77; Constructionphotography.com/Steven Miric, p313; Constructionphotography.com/Sally-Ann Norman, p71 (bottom); Constructionphotography. com/Ken Price, p71 (middle); Corbis, p1, p52 (top), p52 (bottom), p59, p62 (top), p111, p131, p161, p185, p233, p285; Corbis/Creasource, p129; Corbis/Yves Forestier, p278 (top); Corbis/Brigitte Sporrer/Zefa, p197; David Haggerton Photography, p316 (bottom); Dreamstime/Jason Stitt, p192 (bottom); Getty Images/Photodisc, p8, p9, p11, p13, p28, p31, p39, p42, p61, p91, p259, p270; Images courtesy of Graco Inc, p317 (all); iStock Photo, p181 (pliers); iStock Photo/Guy Erwood, p62 (bottom); Allen Miller, p315 (top right); Pearson Education Ltd, p191; Pearson Education Ltd/Chris Honeywell, p52 (goggles); Pearson Education Ltd/Jules Selmes, p54, p87, p162 (filling), p166 (pole); Pearson Education Ltd/Ginny Stroud Lewis, p53 (ear plugs, ear defenders, dust mask); Photographers Direct/Chris Batson, p192 (top); Photographers Direct/Bjorn Beheydt, p127; Photographers Direct/Rober Clare, p175 (top), p264 (top); Photographers Direct/Malcolm Farrow, p190; Photographers Direct/David Griffiths, p125; Science Photo Library/Scott Camazine, p47 (top); Science Photo Library/Garry Watson, p37 (safety sign for corrosive materials); Shout, p49 (foam fire extinguisher); Shutterstock.com, p3; Shutterstock.com/ Stephen Coburn, p75; Shutterstock.com/Frances A. Miller, p71 (top); Shutterstock.com/ Kaygorodov Yuriy, p221; Toolbank, p53 (top), p53 (bottom), p 167 (orbital), p170 (top), p181 (T-square), p264 (bottom), p315 (top left); Topham Picturepoint, p37 (safety signs for toxic and explosive materials); Warren McConnaughie Photography, p316 (top); Rachael Williams, p2, p95 (top), p189.

All other photos Pearson Education Ltd/Gareth Boden.

The contents of this book have been endorsed by Construction Skills.

Introduction

Painting and decorating combines many different practical and visual skills with knowledge of specialised materials and techniques. The information contained in these pages covers the painting and decorating trade as a whole and in particular the knowledge and skills needed for applying surface coatings and coverings, creating special effects and using high volume low pressure spray equipment. This book has been written based on a concept used with Carillion Training Centres for many years. The concept is about providing learners with the necessary information they need to support their studies and at the same time ensuring it is presented in a style which is both manageable and relevant.

This book has been produced to help you build a sound knowledge and understanding of all aspects of the NVQ and Technical Certificate requirements associated with painting and decorating. It has also been designed to provide assistance when revising for Technical Certificate end tests and NVQ job knowledge tests.

Each chapter of this book relates closely to a particular unit of the NVQ or Technical Certificate and aims to provide just the right level of information needed to form the required knowledge and understanding of that subject area.

This book provides a basic introduction to the tools, materials and methods of work required to complete work activities effectively and productively. Upon completion of your studies, this book will remain a valuable source of information and support when carrying out your work activities.

For further information on how the content of this student book matches to the unit requirements of the NVQ and Diploma, please see the mapping documents found on pages 325–328 of this book.

How this book can help you

You will discover a variety of features throughout this book, each of which has been designed and written to increase and improve your knowledge and understanding. These features are:

- **Photographs** – many photographs that appear in this book are specially taken and will help you to follow a step-by-step procedure or identify a tool or material.

- **Illustrations** – clear and colourful drawings will give you more information about a concept or procedure.

- **Definitions** – new or difficult words are picked out in **bold** in the text and defined in the margin.

- **Remember** – key concepts or facts are highlighted in these margin boxes.

- **Find out** – carry out these short activities and gain further information and understanding of a topic area.

- **Did you know?** – interesting facts about the building trade.

- **Safety tips** – follow the guidance in these margin boxes to help you work safely.

- **FAQs** – frequently asked questions appear in all chapters along with informative answers from the experts.

- **On the job scenarios** – read about a real-life situation and answer the questions at the end. What would you do? (Answers can be found in the Tutor Resource Disc that accompanies this book.)

- **Chapter opener module listings** – the technical certificate modules covered in each chapter are identified on the first page of the chapter. A detailed table defining each module can be found on page 325 of this book.

- **End of chapter knowledge checks** – test your understanding and recall of a topic by completing these questions.

- **Mapping grids for technical certificate** – a comprehensive list of the technical certificate module outcomes covered in this book can be found on pages 326-328 of this book.

- **Glossary** – at the end of this book you will find a comprehensive glossary that defines all the **bold** words and phrases found in the text. A great quick reference tool.

- **Links to useful websites** – any websites referred to in this book can be found at www.heinemann.co.uk/hotlinks. Just enter the express code 3594P to access the links.

chapter 1

The construction industry

OVERVIEW

Construction means creating buildings and services. These might be houses, hospitals, schools, offices, roads, bridges, museums, prisons, train stations, airports, monuments – and anything else you can think of that needs designing and building! What about an Olympic stadium? The 2012 London games will bring a wealth of construction opportunity to the UK and so it is an exciting time to be getting involved.

In the UK, 2.2 million people work in the construction industry – more than in any other – and it is constantly expanding and developing. There are more choices and opportunities than ever before and pay and conditions are improving all the time. Your career doesn't have to end in the UK either – what about taking the skills and experience you are developing abroad? Construction is a career you can take with you wherever you go. There's always going to be something that needs building!

This chapter will cover the following topics:

- Understanding the industry
- Communication
- General site paperwork
- Getting involved in the construction industry
- Sources of information and advice.

These topics can be found in the following modules:

CC 1001K	CC 1002K	CC 2002K
CC 1001S	CC 1002S	CC 2002S

Understanding the industry

Find out

Think of an example of a small, medium and large construction company. Do you know of any construction companies that have only one member of staff?

The construction industry is made up of countless companies and businesses that all provide different services and materials. An easy way to divide these companies into categories is according to their size.

- A small company is defined as having between 1 and 49 members of staff.
- A medium company consists of between 50 and 249 members of staff.
- A large company has 250 or more people working for it.

A business might only consist of one member of staff (a sole trader).

The different types of construction work

There are four main types of construction work:

1. New work – this refers to a building that is about to be or has just been built.

2. Maintenance work – this is when an existing building is kept up to an acceptable standard by fixing anything that is damaged so that it does not fall into disrepair.

3. Refurbishment/renovation work – this generally refers to an existing building that has fallen into a state of disrepair and is then brought up to standard by repair. It also refers to an existing building that is to be used for a different purpose, for example changing an old bank into a pub.

New work is just one type of construction area

4. Restoration work – this refers to an existing building that has fallen into a state of disrepair and is then brought back to its original condition or use.

These four types of work can fall into one of two categories depending upon who is paying for the work:

1. Public – the government pays for the work, as is the case with most schools and hospitals etc.

2. Private – work is paid for by a private client and can range from extensions on existing houses to new houses or buildings.

Job and careers

Jobs and careers in the construction industry fall mainly into one of four categories:

- building
- civil engineering
- electrical engineering
- mechanical engineering.

Building involves the physical construction (making) of a structure. It also involves the maintenance, restoration and refurbishment of structures.

Civil engineering involves the construction and maintenance of work such as roads, railways, bridges etc.

Electrical engineering involves the installation and maintenance of electrical systems and devices such as lights, power sockets and electrical appliances etc.

Mechanical engineering involves the installation and maintenance of things such as heating, ventilation and lifts.

The category that is the most relevant to your course is building.

Job types

The construction industry employs people in four specific areas:

1. professionals

2. technicians

3. building craft workers

4. building operatives.

Professionals

Professionals are generally of graduate level (i.e. people who have a degree from a university) and may have one of the following types of job in the construction industry:

- architect – someone who designs and draws the building or structure
- structural engineer – someone who oversees the strength and structure of the building
- surveyor – someone who checks the land for suitability to build on
- service engineer – someone who plans the services needed within the building, for example gas, electricity and water supplies.

Technicians

Technicians link professional workers with craft workers and are made up of the following people:

- architectural technician – someone who looks at the architect's information and makes drawings that can be used by the builder
- building technician – someone who is responsible for estimating the cost of the work and materials and general site management
- quantity surveyor – someone who calculates ongoing costs and payment for work done.

Definition

Trusses – prefabricated components of a roof which spread the load of a roof over the outer walls and form its shape

Plaster skim – a thin layer of plaster that is put on to walls to give a smooth and even finish

Coving – a decorative moulding that is fitted to the top of a wall where it meets the ceiling

Architrave – a decorative moulding, usually made from timber, that is fitted around door and window frames to hide the gap between the frame and the wall

Skirting – a decorative moulding that is fitted at the bottom of a wall to hide the gap between the wall and the floor

Building craft workers

Building craft workers are the skilled people who work with materials to physically construct the building. The following jobs fall into this category:

- carpenter or joiner – someone who works with wood but also other construction materials such as plastic and iron. A carpenter primarily works on site while a joiner usually works off site, producing components such as windows, stairs, doors, kitchens, and **trusses**, which the carpenter then fits into the building

- bricklayer – someone who works with bricks, blocks and cement to build the structure of the building

- plasterer – someone who adds finish to the internal walls and ceilings by applying a **plaster skim**. They also make and fix plaster **covings** and plaster decorations

- painter and decorator – someone who uses paint and paper to decorate the internal plaster and timberwork such as walls, ceilings, windows and doors, as well as **architrave** and **skirting**

- electrician – someone who fits all electrical systems and fittings within a building, including power supplies, lights and power sockets

- plumber – someone who fits all water services within a building, including sinks, boilers, water tanks, radiators, toilets and baths. The plumber also deals with lead work and rainwater fittings such as guttering

- slater and tiler – someone who fits tiles on to the roof of a building, ensuring that the building is watertight

- woodworking machinist – someone who works in a machine shop, converting timber into joinery components such as window sections, spindles for stairs, architraves and skirting boards, amongst other things. They use a variety of machines such as lathes, bench saws, planers and sanders.

Building operatives

There are two different building operatives working on a construction site.

1. Specialist building operative – someone who carries out specialist operations such as dry wall lining, asphalting, scaffolding, floor and wall tiling and glazing.

2. General building operative – someone who carries out non-specialist operations such as kerb laying, concreting, path laying and drainage. These operatives also support other craft workers and do general labouring. They use a variety of hand tools and power tools as well as **plant**, such as dumper trucks and JCBs.

Definition

Plant – industrial machinery

The building team

Constructing a building or structure is a huge task that needs to be done by a team of people who all need to work together towards the same goal. The team of people is often known as the building team and is made up of the following people.

Clients

The client is the person who requires the building or refurbishment. This person is the most important person in the building team because they finance the project fully and without the client there is no work. The client can be a single person or a large organisation.

Architect

The architect works closely with the client, interpreting their requirements to produce contract documents that enable the client's wishes to be realised.

Clerk of works

Selected by the architect or client to oversee the actual building process, the clerk of works ensures that construction sticks to agreed deadlines. They also monitor the quality of workmanship.

Local Authority

The Local Authority is responsible for ensuring that construction projects meet relevant planning and building legislation. Planning and building control officers approve and inspect building work.

Quantity surveyor

The quantity surveyor works closely with the architect and client, acting as an accountant for the job. They are responsible for the ongoing evaluation of cost and interim payments from the client, establishing whether or not the contract is on budget. The quantity surveyor will prepare and sign off final accounts when the contract is complete.

The building team is made up of many different people

Specialist engineers

Specialist engineers assist the architect in specialist areas, such as civil engineering, structural engineering and service engineering.

Health and safety inspectors

Employed by the Health and Safety Executive (HSE), health and safety inspectors ensure that the building contractor fully implements and complies with government health and safety legislation. For more information on health and safety in the construction industry, see Chapter 2 (page 31).

Building contractors

The building contractors agree to carry out building work for the client. Contractors will employ the required workforce based on the size of the contract.

Estimator

The estimator works with the contractor on the cost of carrying out the building contract, listing each item in the bill of quantities (e.g. materials, labour and plant). They calculate the overall cost for the contractor to complete the contract, including further costs as overheads, such as site offices, management administration and pay, not forgetting profit.

Site agent

The site agent works for the building contractor and is responsible for the day-to-day running of the site such as organising deliveries etc.

Suppliers

The suppliers work with the contractor and estimator to arrange the materials that are needed on site and ensure that they are delivered on time and in good condition.

General foreman

The general foreman works for the site manager and is responsible for co-ordinating the work of the ganger (see below), craft foreman and subcontractors. They may also be responsible for the hiring and firing of site operatives. The general foreman also liaises with the clerk of works.

Craft foreman

The craft foreman works for the general foreman organising and supervising the work of particular crafts. For example, the carpentry craft foreman will be responsible for all carpenters on site.

Ganger

The ganger supervises general building operatives.

Chargehand

The chargehand is normally employed only on large building projects, being responsible for various craftsmen and working with joiners, bricklayers, and plasterers.

Operatives

Operatives are the workers who carry out the building work, and are divided into three subsections:

1. Craft operatives are skilled tradesman such as joiners, plasterers, bricklayers.

2. Building operatives include general building operatives who are responsible for drain laying, mixing concrete, unloading materials and keeping the site clean.

3. Specialist operatives include tilers, pavers, glaziers, scaffolders and plant operators.

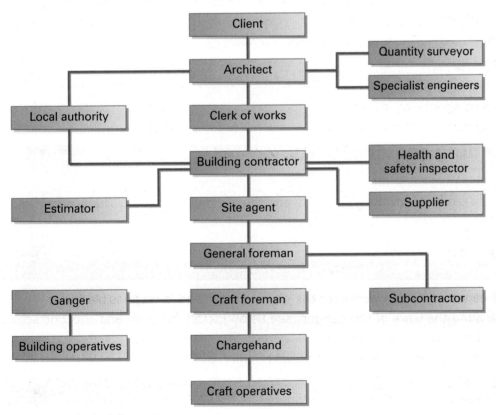

Figure 1.1 The building team

A low rise residential building

The different types of building

There are of course lots of very different types of building, but the main types are:

- residential – houses and flats etc.
- commercial – shops and supermarkets etc.
- industrial – warehouses and factories etc.

These types of building can be further broken down by the height or number of storeys that they have (one storey being the level from floor to ceiling):

- low rise – a building with one to three storeys
- medium rise – a building with four to seven storeys
- high rise – a building with seven storeys or more.

Buildings can also be categorised according to the number of other buildings they are attached to:

- detached – a building that stands alone and is not connected to any other building
- semi-detached – a building that is joined to one other building and shares a dividing wall, called a party wall
- terraced – a row of three or more buildings that are joined together, of which the inner buildings share two party walls.

Building requirements

Every building must meet the minimum requirements of the *Building Regulations*, which were first introduced in 1961 and then updated in 1985. The purpose of building regulations is to ensure that safe and healthy buildings are constructed for the public and that **conservation** is taken into account when they are being constructed. Building regulations enforce a minimum standard of building work and ensure that the materials used are of a good standard and fit for purpose.

Definition

Conservation
– preservation of the environment and wildlife

What makes a good building?

When a building is designed, there are certain things that need to be taken into consideration, such as:

- security
- safety
- privacy
- warmth
- light
- ventilation.

A well-designed building will meet the minimum standards for all of the considerations above and will also be built in line with building regulations.

The properties and principles of building work will be covered in greater detail in Chapter 4.

Communication

Communication, in the simplest of terms, is a way or means of passing on information from one person to another. Communication is very important in all areas of life and we often do it without even thinking about it. You will need to communicate well when you are at work, no matter what job you do. What would happen if someone couldn't understand something you had written or said? If we don't communicate well, how will other people know what we want or need and how will we know what other people want?

Companies that do not establish good methods of communicating with their workforce or with other companies, will not function properly and will end up with bad working relationships. Good working relationships can *only* be achieved with co-operation and good communication.

Methods of communication

There are many different ways of communicating with others and they all generally fit into one of these four categories:

1. speaking (verbal communication), for example talking face to face or over the telephone

2. writing, for example sending a letter or taking a message

3. body language, for example the way we stand or our facial expressions

4. electronic, for example email, fax and text messages.

Each method of communicating has good points (advantages) and bad points (disadvantages).

Verbal communication is probably the method you will use most

Verbal communication

Verbal communication is the most common method we use to communicate with each other. If two people don't speak the same language or if someone speaks very quietly or not very clearly, verbal communication cannot be effective. Working in the construction industry you may communicate verbally with other people face to face, over the telephone or by radio/walkie-talkie.

Advantages	Disadvantages
Verbal communication is instant, easy and can be repeated or rephrased until the message is understood.	Verbal communication can be easily forgotten as there is no physical evidence of the message. Because of this it can be easily changed if passed to other people. Someone's accent or use of slang language can sometimes make it difficult to understand what they are saying.

Written communication

Written communication can take the form of letters, faxes, messages, notes, instruction leaflets, text messages, drawings and emails, amongst others.

Advantages	Disadvantages
There is physical evidence of the communication and the message can be passed on to another person without it being changed. It can also be read again if it is not understood.	Written communication takes longer to arrive and understand than verbal communication and body language. It can also be misunderstood or lost. If it is handwritten, the reader may not be able to read the writing if it is messy.

Messages

To Andy Rodgers ....

Date Tues 10 Nov   Time 11.10 am   ..

Message: Mark from Stokes called with a query about the recent order. Please phone asap (tel 01234 567 890)

....

Message taken by: Lee Barber
....

Figure 1.2 A message is a form of written communication

Body language

It is said that, when we are talking to someone face to face, only 10 per cent of the communication is verbal. The rest of the communication is body language and facial expression. This form of communication can be as simple as the shaking of a head from left to right to mean 'no' or as complex as the way someone's face changes when they are happy or sad or the signs given in body language when someone is lying.

We often use hand gestures as well as words to get across what we are saying, to emphasise a point or give a direction. Some people communicate entirely through a form of body language called sign language.

Advantages

If you are aware of your own body language and know how to use it effectively, you can add extra meaning to what you say. For example, say you are talking to a client or a work colleague. Even if the words you are using are friendly and polite, if your body language is negative or unfriendly, the message that you are giving out could be misunderstood. By simply maintaining eye contact, smiling and not folding your arms, you have made sure that the person you are communicating with has not got a mixed or confusing message.

Body language is quick and effective. A wave from a distance can pass on a greeting without being close, and using hand signals to direct a lorry or a load from a crane is instant and doesn't require any equipment such as radios.

Disadvantages

Some gestures can be misunderstood, especially if they are given from very far away, and gestures that have one meaning in one country or culture can have a completely different meaning in another.

Try to be aware of your body language

Electronic communication

Electronic communication is becoming more and more common with the advances in technology allowing us to communicate more easily. Electronic communication can take many forms, such as email and fax. It is now even possible to send and receive emails via a mobile phone, which allows important information to be sent or received from almost anywhere in the world.

Advantages	Disadvantages
Electronic communication takes the best parts from verbal and written communication in as much as it is instant, easy and there is a record of the communication being sent. Electronic communication goes even further as it can tell the sender if the message has been received and even read. Emails in particular can be used to send a vast amount of information and can even give links to websites or other information. Attachments to emails allow anything from instructions to drawings to be sent with the message.	There are few disadvantages to electronic communication, the obvious ones being no signal or flat battery on a mobile phone and servers being down which prevent emails etc. Not every one is up to speed on the latest technology and some people are not comfortable using electronic communication. You need to make sure that the person receiving your message is able to understand how to access the information. Computer viruses can also be a problem as can security where hackers can tap into your computer and read your emails and other private information. A good security set-up and anti-virus software are essential.

Which type of communication should I use?

Of the many different types of communication, the type you should use will depend upon the situation. If someone needs to be told something formally, then written communication is generally the best way. If the message is informal, then verbal communication is usually acceptable.

The way that you communicate will also be affected by who it is you are communicating with. You should of course always communicate in a polite and respectful manner with anyone you have contact with, but you must also be aware of the need to sometimes alter the style of your communication. For example, when talking to a friend, it may be fine to talk in a very informal way and use slang language, but in a work situation with a client or a colleague, it is best to alter your communication to a more formal style in order to show professionalism. In the same way, it may be fine to leave a message or send a text to a friend that says 'C U @ 8 4 work', but if you wrote this down for a work colleague or a client to read, it would not look very professional and they may not understand it.

Communicating with other trades

Communicating with other trades is vital because they need to know what you are doing and when, and you need to know the same information from them. Poor communication can lead to delays and mistakes, which can both be costly. It is quite possible for poor communication to result in work having to be stopped or redone. Say you are decorating a room in a new building. You are just about to finish when you find out that the electrician, plumber and carpenter have to finish off some work in the room. This information didn't reach you and now the decorating will have to be done again once the other work has been finished. What a waste of time and money. A situation like this can be avoided with good communication between the trades.

Common methods of communicating in the construction industry

A career in construction means that you will often have to use written documents such as drawings, specifications and schedules. These documents can be very large and seem very complicated but, if you understand what they are used for and how they work, using such documents will soon become second nature.

You will work with people from other trades

General site paperwork

No building site could function properly without a certain amount of paperwork. Here is a brief, but not exhaustive, description of some of the other documents you may encounter. Some companies will have their own forms to cover such things as scaffolding checks.

Timesheet

Timesheets record hours worked, and are completed by every employee individually. Some timesheets are basic, asking just for a brief description of the work done each hour, but some can be complicated. In some cases timesheets may be used to work out how many hours the client will be charged for.

P. Gresford Building Contractors

Timesheet _____

Employee _____ **Project/site** _____

Date	Job no.	Start time	Finish time	Total time	Travel time	Expenses
M						
Tu						
W						
Th						
F						
Sa						
Su						
Totals						

Employee's signature _____

Supervisor's signature _____

Date _____

Figure 1.3 Timesheet

Day worksheets

Day worksheets are often confused with timesheets, but are different as they are used when there is no price or estimate for the work, to enable the contractor to charge for the work. Day worksheets record work done, hours worked and sometimes materials used.

P. Gresford Building Contractors

Day worksheet

Customer _Chris MacFarlane_   Date _____

Description of work being carried out _____
Hang internal door in kitchen.

Labour	Craft	Hours	Gross rate	TOTALS

Materials	Quantity	Rate	% addition	

Plant	Hours	Rate	% addition	

Comments

Signed _____   Date _____

Site manager/foreman signature _____

Figure 1.4 Day worksheet

P. Gresford Building Contractors

Job sheet

Customer   Chris MacFarlane

Address   1 High Street
          Any Town
          Any County

Work to be carried out

Hang internal door in kitchen

Special conditions/instructions

Fit with door closer
3 × 75mm butt hinges

Figure 1.5 Job sheet

Job sheet

A job sheet is similar to a day worksheet – it records work done – but is used when the work has already been priced. Job sheets enable the worker to see what needs to be done and the site agent or working foreman to see what has been completed.

```
VARIATION TO PROPOSED WORKS AT 123 A STREET

REFERENCE NO:

DATE _____

FROM _____

TO _____

POSSIBLE VARIATIONS TO WORK AT 123 A STREET

  ADDITIONS
  _____
  _____
  _____
  _____
  OMISSIONS
  _____
  _____
  _____
  _____

SIGNED ------------------------------------
```

Figure 1.6 Variation order

Variation order

This sheet is used by the architect to make any changes to the original plans, including omissions, alterations and extra work.

```
CONFIRMATION FOR VARIATION TO PROPOSED WORKS AT
123 A STREET

REFERENCE NO:

DATE _____

FROM _____

TO _____

I CONFIRM THAT I HAVE RECEIVED WRITTEN INSTRUCTIONS
FROM _____
POSITION _____
TO CARRY OUT THE FOLLOWING POSSIBLE VARIATIONS TO THE
ABOVE NAMED CONTRACT

  ADDITIONS
  _____
  _____
  _____
  OMISSIONS
  _____
  _____
  _____
  _____

SIGNED ------------------------------------
```

Figure 1.7 Confirmation notice

Confirmation notice

This is a sheet given to the contractor to confirm any changes made in the variation order, so that the contractor can go ahead and carry out the work.

Orders/requisitions

A requisition form or order is used to order materials or components from a supplier.

P. Gresford Building Contractors

Requisition form

Supplier _____   Order no. _____

_____   Serial no. _____

Tel no. _____   Contact _____

Fax no. _____   Our ref _____

Contract/Delivery address/Invoice address   **Statements/applications**

_____   **for payments to be sent to**

_____   _____

Tel no. _____   _____

Fax no. _____   _____

Item no.	Quantity	Unit	Description	Unit price	Amount

Total £ _____

Payment terms _____   Date

_____

Originated by

_____

Authorised by

_____

Figure 1.8 Requisition form

Bailey & Sons Ltd

Building materials supplier

Tel: 01234 567890

Your ref: AB00671

Our ref: CT020

Order no: 67440387

Date: 17 Jul 2006

Invoice address:
Carillion Training Centre,
Deptford Terrace, Sunderland

Delivery address:
Same as invoice

Description of goods	Quantity	Catalogue no.
OPC 25kg	10	OPC1.1

Comments:
Date and time of receiving goods:
Name of recipient (caps):
Signature:

Figure 1.9 Delivery note

Delivery notes

Delivery notes are given to the contractor by the supplier, and list all the materials and components being delivered. Each delivery note should be checked for accuracy against the order (to ensure what is being delivered is what was asked for) and against the delivery itself (to make sure that the delivery matches the delivery note). If there are any discrepancies or if the delivery is of a poor quality or damaged, you must write on the delivery note what is wrong *before* signing it and ensure the site agent is informed so that he/she can rectify the problem.

Invoices

Invoices come from a variety of sources such as suppliers or subcontractors, and state what has been provided and how much the contractor will be charged for it.

Remember

Invoices may need paying by a certain date – fines for late payment can sometimes be incurred – so it is important that they are passed on to the finance office or financial controller promptly

INVOICE			JARVIS BUILDING SUPPLIES		
			3rd AVENUE THOMASTOWN		
L Weeks Builders 4th Grove Thomastown					

Quantity	Description	Unit price	Vat rate	Total
30	Galvanised joint hangers	£1.32	17.5%	£46.53
			TOTAL	£46.53

To be paid within 30 days from receipt of this invoice

Please direct any queries to 01234 56789

Figure 1.10 Invoice

Delivery records

Delivery records list all deliveries over a certain period (usually a month), and are sent to the contractor's Head Office so that payment can be made.

JARVIS BUILDING SUPPLIES
3RD AVENUE
THOMASTOWN

Customer ref_____

Customer order date_____

Delivery date_____

Item no	Qty Supplied	Qty to follow	Description	Unit price
1	30	0	Galvanised joinst hangers	£1.32

Delivered to: L Weeks builders
4th Grove
Thomastown

Customer signature . . . .

Figure 1.11 Delivery record

Daily report/ site diary

This is used to pass general information (deliveries, attendance etc.) on to a company's Head Office.

DAILY REPORT/SITE DIARY

PROJECT_____
DATE_____

Identify any of the following factors, which are affecting or may affect the daily work activities and give a brief description in the box provided

WEATHER ( )   ACCESS ( )   ACCIDENTS ( )   SERVICES ( )
DELIVERIES ( )   SUPPLIES ( )   LABOUR ( )   OTHER ( )

SIGNED . . . .
POSITION . . . .

Figure 1.12 Daily report or site diary

Remember

You should always check a delivery note against the order and the delivery itself, then write any discrepancies or problems on the delivery note *before* signing it

Accident and near miss reports

It is a legal requirement that a company has an accident book, in which reports of all accidents must be made. Reports must also be made when an accident nearly happened, but did not in the end occur – known as a 'near miss'. It is everyone's responsibility to complete the accident book. If you are also in a supervisory position you will have the responsibility to ensure all requirements for accident reporting are met.

Safety tip

If you are involved in or witness an accident or near miss, make sure it is entered in the book – for your own safety and that of others on the site. If you don't report it, it's more likely to happen again

Report of an Accident, Dangerous Occurrence or Near Miss

Date of incident _____   Time of incident _____

Location of incident _____

Details of person involved in accident

Name _____   Date of birth _____

Address _____

_____

_____   Occupation _____

Date off work (if applicable) _____   Date returning to work _____

Nature of injury _____

Management of injury   ☐ First Aid only   ☐ Advised to see doctor

                         ☐ Sent to casualty   ☐ Admitted to hospital

Account of accident, dangerous occurrence or near miss
(Continued on separate sheet if necessary)

[   ]

Witnesses to the incident
(Names, addresses and occupations)

[   ]

Was the injured person wearing PPE? If yes, what PPE? _____

_____

Signature of person completing form _____

Occupation _____   Date _____

Figure 1.13 Accident/
near miss report

Drawings

Drawings are done by the architect and are used to pass on the client's wishes to the building contractor. Drawings are usually done to scale because it would be impossible to draw a full-sized version of the project. A common scale is 1:10, which means that a line 10 mm long on the drawing represents 100 mm in real life. Drawings often contain symbols instead of written words to get the maximum amount of information across without cluttering the page.

Specifications

Specifications accompany a drawing and give you the sizes that are not available on the drawing, as well as telling you the type of material to be used and the quality that the work has to be finished to.

Schedules

A schedule is a list of repeated design information used on big building sites when there are several types of similar room or house. For example, a schedule will tell you what type of door must be used and where. Another form of schedule used on building sites contains a detailed list of dates by which work must be carried out and materials delivered etc.

See Chapter 6 *Drawings* for more information.

Work programme

A work programme is a method of showing very easily what work is being carried out on a building and when. The most common form of work programme is a bar chart. Used by many site agents or supervisors, a bar chart lists the tasks that need to be done down the left side and shows a timeline across the top. A work programme is used to make sure that the relevant trade is on site at the correct time and that materials are delivered when needed. A site agent or supervisor can quickly tell from looking at the chart if work is keeping to schedule or falling behind.

Bar charts

The bar or Gantt chart is the most popular work programme as it is simple to construct and easy to understand. Bar charts have tasks listed in a vertical column on the left and a horizontal timescale running along the top.

Did you know?

The Gantt chart is named after the first man to publish it. This was Henry Gannt, an American engineer, in 1910.

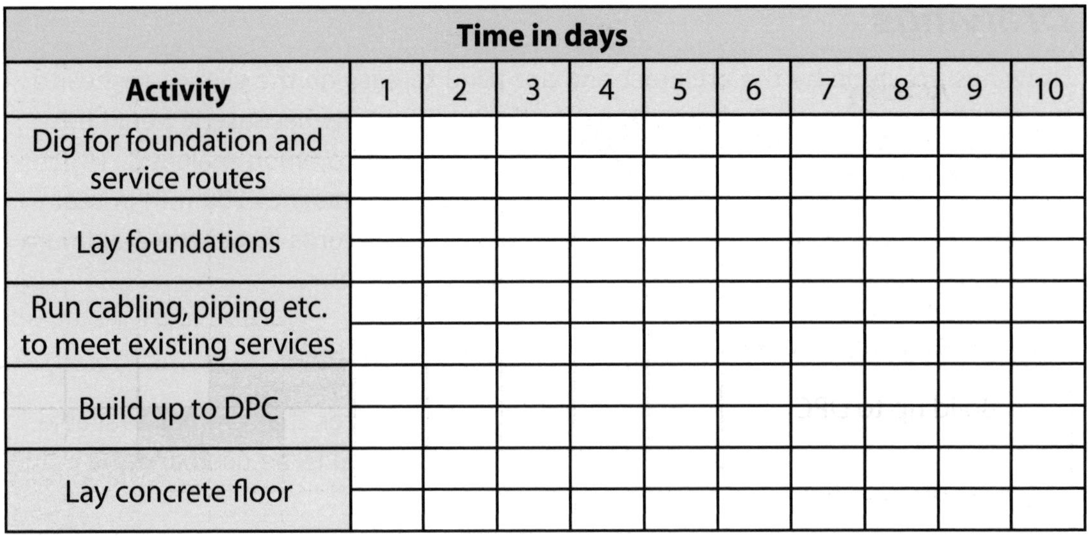

Time in days										
Activity	1	2	3	4	5	6	7	8	9	10
Dig for foundation and service routes										
Lay foundations										
Run cabling, piping etc. to meet existing services										
Build up to DPC										
Lay concrete floor										

Figure 1.14 Basic bar chart

Each task is given a proposed time, which is shaded in along the horizontal timescale. Timescales often overlap as one task often overlaps another.

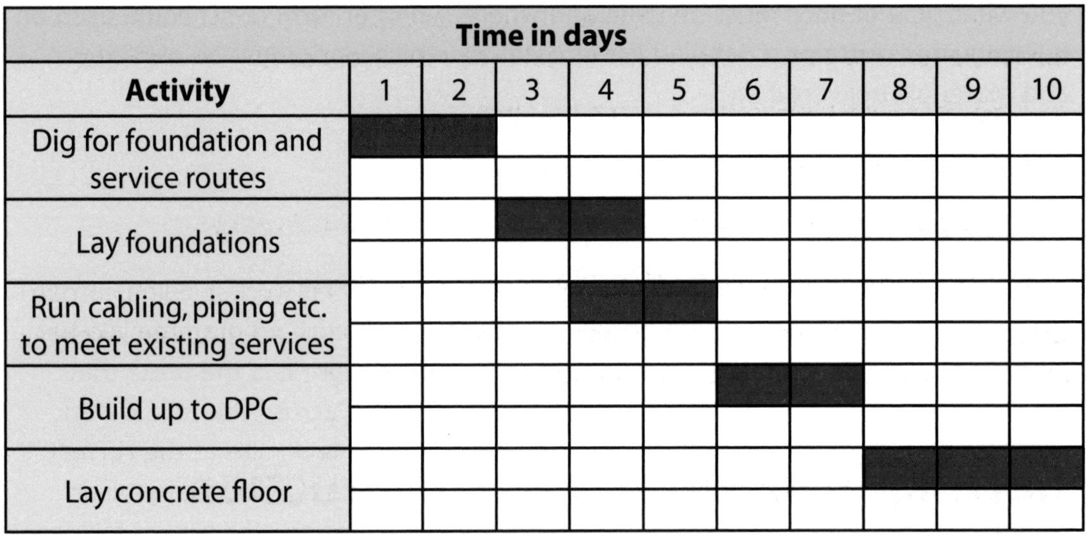

Time in days										
Activity	1	2	3	4	5	6	7	8	9	10
Dig for foundation and service routes	■	■								
Lay foundations			■	■						
Run cabling, piping etc. to meet existing services				■	■					
Build up to DPC						■	■			
Lay concrete floor								■	■	■

Figure 1.15 Bar chart showing proposed time for a contract

The bar chart can then be used to check progress. Often the actual time taken for a task is shaded in underneath the proposed time (in a different way or colour to avoid confusion). This shows how what *has* been done matches up to what *should have* been done.

As you can see, a bar chart can help you plan when to order materials or plant, see what trade is due in and when, and so on. A bar chart can also tell you if you are behind on a job; if you have a penalty clause written into your contract, this information is vital.

Time in days										
Activity	1	2	3	4	5	6	7	8	9	10
Dig for foundation and service routes	■	■								
	■	■								
Lay foundations			■	■						
			■	■						
Run cabling, piping etc. to meet existing services				■	■					
				■	■	■				
Build up to DPC						■	■			
							■	■		
Lay concrete floor								■	■	■
									■	■

■ Proposed time   ■ Actual time

Figure 1.16 Bar chart showing actual time half way through a contract

When creating a bar chart, you should build in some extra time to allow for things such as bad weather, labour shortages, delivery problems or illness. It is also advisable to have contingency plans to help solve or avoid problems, such as:

- capacity to work overtime to catch up time
- bonus scheme to increase productivity
- penalty clause on suppliers to try to avoid late or poor deliveries
- source of extra labour (e.g. from another site) if needed.

Good planning, with contingency plans in place, should allow a job to run smoothly and finish on time, leading to the contractor making a profit.

Getting involved in the construction industry

There are many ways of entering the construction industry, but the most common way is as an apprentice.

Apprenticeships

You can become an apprentice by:

1. being employed directly by a construction company who will send you to college
2. being employed by a training provider, such as Carillion, which combines construction training with practical work experience.

Did you know?

Bad weather is the main external factor responsible for delays on building sites in the UK. A Met Office survey showed that the average UK construction company experiences problems caused by the weather 26 times a year

On 1 August 2002, the construction industry introduced a mandatory induction programme for all apprentices joining the industry. The programme has four distinct areas:

1. apprenticeship framework requirements

2. the construction industry

3. employment

4. health and safety.

Apprenticeship frameworks are based on a number of components designed to prepare people for work in a particular construction occupation.

Construction frameworks are made up of the following mandatory components:

● NVQs

● technical certificates (construction awards)

● key skills.

However, certain trades require additional components. Bricklaying, for example, requires abrasive wheels certification.

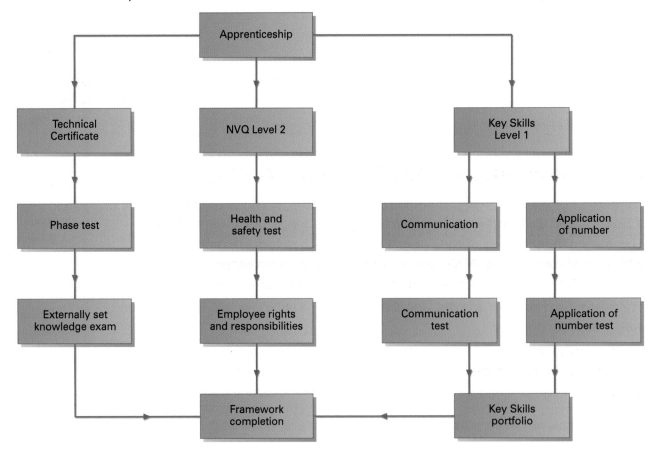

Figure 1.17 Apprenticeship framework

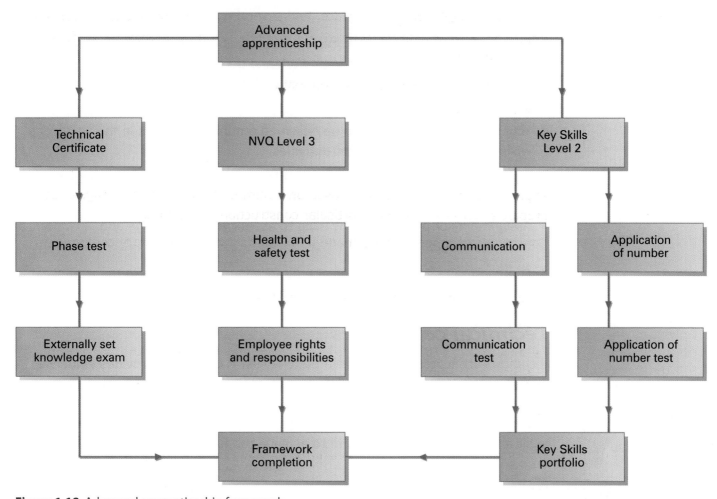

Figure 1.18 Advanced apprenticeship framework

National Vocational Qualifications (NVQs)

NVQs are available to anyone, with no restrictions on age, length or type of training, although learners below a certain age can only perform certain tasks. There are different levels of NVQ (e.g. 1, 2, 3), which in turn are broken down into units of competence. NVQs are not like traditional examinations in which someone sits an exam paper. An NVQ is a 'doing' qualification, which means it lets the industry know that you have the knowledge, skills and ability to actually 'do' something.

The Construction Industry Training Board (CITB) is the national training organisation for construction in the UK and is responsible for setting training standards. NVQs are made up of both mandatory and optional units and the number of units that you need to complete for an NVQ depends on the level and the occupation.

NVQs are assessed in the workplace, and several types of evidence are used:

- Witness testimony consists of evidence provided by various individuals who have first-hand knowledge of your work and performance relating to the NVQ. Work colleagues, supervisors and even customers can provide evidence of your performance.

- Your natural performance can be observed a number of times in the workplace while carrying out work-related activities.

- The use of historical evidence means that you can use evidence from past achievements or experience, if it is directly related to the NVQ.

- Assignments or projects can be used to assess your knowledge and understanding of a subject.

- Photographic evidence showing you performing various tasks in the workplace can be used, providing it is authenticated by your supervisor.

Technical certificates

Technical certificates are often related to NVQs. A certificate provides evidence that you have the underpinning knowledge and understanding required to complete a particular task. An off-the-job training programme, either in a college or with a training provider, may deliver technical certificates. You generally have to sit an end-of-programme exam to achieve the full certificate.

Key skills

Some students have key skills development needs, so learners and apprentices must achieve key skills at Level 1 or 2 in both Communications and Application of number. Key skills are signposted in each level of the NVQ and are assessed independently, so you will need to be released from your training to attend a key skills test.

Employment

Conditions of employment are controlled by legislation and regulations. The Department of Trade and Industry (DTI) publishes most of this legislation. To find out more about your working rights, visit the DTI website. A quick link has been made available at www.heinemann.co.uk/hotlinks – just enter the express code 3594P.

The main pieces of legislation that will apply to you are:

- The Employment Act 2002 which gives extra rights to working parents and gives new guidance on resolving disputes, amongst other things.

- The Employment Relations Act 1999 covers areas such as trade union membership and disciplinary and grievance proceedings.

- The Employment Rights Act 1996 details the rights an employee has by law, including the right to have time off work and the right to be given notice if being dismissed.

- The Sex Discrimination Acts of 1975 and 1986 state that it is illegal for an employee to be treated less favourably because of their sex, for example paying a man more than a woman or offering a woman more holiday than a man, even though they do the same job.

- The Race Relations Act 1976 states that it is against the law for someone to be treated less favourably because of their skin colour, race, nationality or ethnic origin.

- The Disability Discrimination Act 2005 makes it illegal for someone to be treated less favourably just because they have a physical or mental disability.

- The National Minimum Wage Act 1998 makes sure that everyone in the UK is paid a minimum amount. How much you must be paid depends on how old you are and whether or not you are on an Apprenticeship Scheme. The national minimum wage is periodically assessed and increased so it is a good idea to make sure you know what it is. At the time of writing, under 18s and those on Apprenticeship Schemes do not qualify for the minimum wage. For those aged 18–21, the minimum wage is £4.60 per hour and for adult workers aged 22 or over, the minimum wage is £5.52 per hour.

Men and women must be treated equally at work

Contract of employment

Within two months of starting a new job, your employer must give you a contract of employment. This will tell you the terms of your employment and should include the following information:

- job title
- place of work
- hours of work
- rates of pay
- holiday pay
- overtime rates
- statutory sick pay
- pension scheme
- discipline procedure

Find out

What is the national minimum wage at the moment? You can find out from lots of different places, including the DTI website. You can find a link to the site at www.heinemann.co.uk/hotlinks – just enter the express code 3594P

- termination of employment
- dispute procedure.

If you have any questions about information contained within your contract of employment, you should talk to your supervisor before you sign it.

When you start a new job, you should also receive a copy of the safety policy and an employee handbook containing details of the general policy, procedures and disciplinary rules.

Discrimination in the workplace

Discrimination means treating someone unjustly, and in the workplace it can range from bullying, intimidation or harassment to paying someone less money or not giving them a job. Discriminating against people within the working environment is against the law. This includes discrimination on the grounds of:

- sex, gender or sexual orientation
- race, colour, nationality or ethnic origin
- religious beliefs
- disability.

The law states that employment, training and promotion should be open to all employees regardless of any of the above. Pay should be equal for men and women if they are required to do the same job.

The Race Relations Act protects people of all skin colours, races and nationalities

Sources of information and advice

There are many places you can go to get information and advice about a career in the construction industry. If you are already studying, you can speak to your tutor, your school or college careers adviser or you can get in touch with Connexions for careers advice especially for young people. Visit www.heinemann. co.uk/hotlinks and enter the express code 3594P for a link to Connexions' website. You can also find their telephone number in your local phone book.

Organisations such as those listed below are very good sources of careers advice specific to the construction industry.

- CITB (Construction Industry Training Board) – the industry's national training organisation
- City and Guilds – a provider of recognised vocational qualifications
- The Chartered Institute of Building Services Engineers
- The Institute of Civil Engineers

- Trade unions such as GMB (Britain's General Union), UCATT (Union of Construction, Allied Trades and Technicians), UNISON (the public services union), Amicus (the manufacturing union, previously MSF).

Links to all these organisations' websites can be found by visiting www.heinemann.co.uk/hotlinks and entering the express code 3594P.

FAQ

Why do I need to learn about different trades?

It is very important that you have some basic knowledge of what other trades do. This is because you will often work with people from other trades and their work will affect yours and vice versa.

What options do I have once I have gained my NVQ Level 2 qualification?

Once you are qualified, there is a wide range of career opportunities available to you. For example, you could progress from a tradesman to a foreman and then to a site agent. There may also be the opportunity to become a clerk of works, an architect or a college lecturer. Some tradesmen are happy to continue as tradesmen and some start up their own businesses.

Knowledge check

1. How many members of staff are there in a small company, a medium company and a large company?

2. Give an example of a public construction project. Who pays for public work?

3. Name a job in each of the four construction employment areas: professional; technician; building craft worker; building operative.

4. Why is the client the most important member of the building team?

5. Explain the meaning of the following building types: residential; low rise; semi-detached.

6. What are the four different methods of communication?

7. What information might a schedule give you?

8. What does NVQ stand for?

9. What information must be in your contract of employment?

chapter 2

Health and safety

OVERVIEW

Every year in the construction industry over 100 people are killed and thousands more are seriously injured as a result of the work that they do. There are thousands more who suffer from health problems, such as dermatitis, asbestosis, industrial asthma, vibration white finger and deafness. You can therefore see why learning as much as you can about health and safety is very important.

This chapter will cover the following topics:

- Health and safety legislation
- Health and welfare in the construction industry
- Manual handling
- Hazards
- Fire and fire-fighting equipment
- Safety signs
- Personal protective equipment (PPE)
- Emergencies
- First aid
- Reporting accidents
- Risk assessments.

These topics can be found in the following modules:

CC 1001K	CC 1001S

Health and safety legislation

While at work, whatever your location or type of work, you need to be aware that there is important legislation you must comply with. Health and safety legislation is there not just to protect you, but also states what you must and must not do to ensure that no workers are placed in a situation **hazardous** to themselves or others.

Each piece of legislation covers your own responsibilities as an employee and those of your employer – it is vital that you are aware of both. As a Level 2 candidate, you not only have to think of your responsibilities for you own actions, but must also consider your supervisory responsibilities for others. These may involve ensuring that others are aware of legislation and considering such legislation when you are overseeing others' work.

What is legislation?

Legislation means a law or set of laws passed by Parliament, often called an Act. There are hundreds of Acts covering all manner of work from hairdressing to construction. Each Act states the duties of the **employer** and **employee**. If an employer or employee does something they shouldn't – or doesn't do something they should – they can end up in court and be fined or even imprisoned.

Approved code of practice, guidance notes and safety policies

As well as Acts, there are two sorts of codes of practice and guidance notes: those produced by the **Health and Safety Executive (HSE)**, and those created by companies themselves. Most large construction companies – and many smaller ones – have their own guidance notes, which go further than health and safety law. For example, the law states that that everyone must wear safety boots in a hazardous area, but a company's code may state that everyone must wear safety boots at all times. This is called taking a **proactive** approach, rather than a **reactive** one.

Most companies have some form of safety policy outlining the company's commitment and stating what they plan to do to ensure that all work is carried out as safely as possible. As an employee, you should make sure you understand the company's safety policy as well as their codes of practice. If you act against company policy you may not be prosecuted in court, but you could still be disciplined by the company or even fired.

Health and safety legislation you need to be aware of

There are some 20 pieces of legislation you will need to be aware of, each of which sets out requirements for employers and often employees. One phrase often comes up here – *'so far as is reasonably practicable'*. This means that health and safety must be adhered to at all times, but must take a common sense, practical approach.

For example, the Health and Safety at Work Act 1974 states that an employer must *so far as is reasonably practicable* ensure that a safe place of work is provided. Yet employers are not expected to do everything they can to protect their staff from lightning strikes, as there is only a 1 in 800,000 chance of this occurring – this would not be reasonable!

We will now look at the regulations that will affect you most.

The Health and Safety at Work Act 1974 (HASAW)

HASAW applies to all types and places of work and to employers, employees, the self-employed, subcontractors and even suppliers. The Act is there to protect not only the people at work but also the general public, who may be affected in some way by the work that has been or will be carried out.

The main objectives of the Health and Safety at Work Act are to:

- ensure the health, safety and welfare of all persons at work
- protect the general public from all work activities
- control the use, handling, storage and transportation of explosives and highly flammable substances
- control the release of noxious or offensive substances into the atmosphere.

Legislation is there to protect employees and the public alike

To ensure that these objectives are met there are duties for all employers, employees and suppliers.

Employer's duties

Employers must:

- provide safe **access** and **egress** to and within the work area
- provide a safe place to work
- provide and maintain plant and machinery that is safe and without risks to health

Definition

Access – entrance, a way in

Egress – exit, a way out

- provide information, instruction, training and supervision to ensure the health and safety at work of all employees

- ensure safety and the absence of risks to health in connection with the handling, storage and transportation of articles and substances

- have a written safety policy that must be revised and updated regularly, and ensure all employees are aware of it

- involve trade union safety representatives, where appointed, in all matters relating to health and safety

- provide and not charge for **personal protective equipment (PPE)**.

Employee's duties

The employee must:

- take reasonable care for his/her own health and safety

- take reasonable care for the health and safety of anyone who may be affected by his/her acts or **omissions**

- co-operate with his/her employer or any other person to ensure legal **obligations** are met

- not misuse or interfere with anything provided for their health and safety

- use any equipment and safeguards provided by his/her employer.

Employees cannot be charged for anything that has been done or provided for them to ensure that legal requirements on health and safety are met. The self-employed and subcontractors have the same duties as employees – and if they have employees of their own, they must obey the duties set down for employers.

Supplier's duties

Persons designing, manufacturing, importing or supplying articles or substances for use at work must ensure that:

- articles are designed and constructed so that they will be safe and without risk to health at all times while they are being used or constructed

- substances will be safe and without risk to health at all times when being used, handled, transported and stored

- tests on articles and substances are carried out as necessary

- adequate information is provided about the use, handling, transporting and storing of articles or substances.

Definition

PPE – personal protective equipment, such as gloves, a safety harness or goggles

Omission – something that has not been done or has been missed out

Obligation – something you have a duty or a responsibility to do

HASAW, like most of the other Acts mentioned, is enforced by the Health and Safety Executive (HSE). HSE inspectors visit sites and have the power to:

- enter any premises at any reasonable time

- take a police constable with them

- examine and investigate anything on the premises

- take samples

- take possession of any dangerous article or substance

- issue improvement notices giving a company a certain amount of time to sort out a health and safety problem

- issue a prohibition notice stopping all work until the site is deemed safe

- **prosecute** people who break the law including employers, employees, self-employed, manufacturers and suppliers.

Provision and Use of Work Equipment Regulations 1998 (PUWER)

These regulations cover all new or existing work equipment – leased, hired or second-hand. They apply in most working environments where the HASAW applies, including all industrial, offshore and service operations.

PUWER covers starting, stopping, regular use, transport, repair, modification, servicing and cleaning.

'Work equipment' includes any machinery, appliance, apparatus or tool, and any assembly of components that are used in non-domestic premises. Dumper trucks, circular saws, ladders, overhead projectors and chisels would all be included, but substances, private cars and structural items all fall outside this definition.

The general duties of the Act require equipment to be:

- suitable for its intended purpose and only to be used in suitable conditions

- maintained in an efficient state and maintenance records kept

- used, repaired and maintained only by a suitably trained person, when that equipment poses a particular risk

- able to be isolated from all its sources of energy

- constructed or adapted to ensure that maintenance can be carried out without risks to health and safety

- fitted with warnings or warning devices as appropriate.

In addition, the Act requires:

- all those who use, supervise or manage work equipment to be suitably trained

Definition

Prosecute – to accuse someone of committing a crime which usually results in being taken to court and, if found guilty being punished

- access to any dangerous parts of the machinery to be prevented or controlled
- injury to be prevented from any work equipment that may have a very high or low temperature
- suitable controls to be provided for starting and stopping the work equipment
- suitable emergency stopping systems and braking systems to be fitted to ensure the work equipment is brought to a safe condition as soon as reasonably practicable
- suitable and sufficient lighting to be provided for operating the work equipment.

Control of Substances Hazardous to Health Regulations 2002 (COSHH)

These regulations state how employees and employers should work with, handle, store, transport and dispose of potentially hazardous substances (substances that might negatively affect your health) including:

- substances used directly in work activities (e.g. adhesives or paints)
- substances generated during work activities (e.g. dust from sanding wood)
- naturally occurring substances (e.g. sand dust)
- biological agents (e.g. bacteria).

These substances can be found in nearly all work environments. All are covered by COSHH regulations except asbestos and lead paint, which have their own regulations.

To comply with COSHH regulations, eight steps must be followed:

Hazardous substances

Step 1 Assess the risks to health from hazardous substances used or created by your activities.

Step 2 Decide what precautions are needed.

Step 3 Prevent employees from being exposed to any hazardous substances. If prevention is impossible, the risk must be adequately controlled.

Step 4 Ensure control methods are used and maintained properly.

Step 5 Monitor the exposure of employees to hazardous substances.

Step 6 Carry out health surveillance to ascertain if any health problems are occurring.

Step 7 Prepare plans and procedures to deal with accidents such as spillages.

Step 8 Ensure all employees are properly informed, trained and supervised.

Identifying a substance that may fall under the COSHH regulations is not always easy, but you can ask the supplier or manufacturer for a COSHH data sheet, outlining the risks involved with a substance. Most substance containers carry a warning sign stating whether the contents are corrosive, harmful, toxic or bad for the environment.

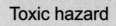

Toxic hazard

Risk of explosion

Common safety signs for corrosive, toxic and explosive materials

Safety tip

Not all substances are labelled, and sometimes the label may not match the contents. If you are in any doubt, do not use or touch the substance

The Personal Protective Equipment at Work Regulations 1992 (PPER)

These regulations cover all types of PPE, from gloves to breathing apparatus. After doing a risk assessment and once the potential hazards are known, suitable types of PPE can be selected. PPE should be checked prior to issue by a trained and competent person and in line with the manufacturer's instructions. Where required, the employer must provide PPE free of charge along with a suitable and secure place to store it.

The employer must ensure that the employee knows:

- the risks the PPE will avoid or reduce
- its purpose and use
- how to maintain and look after it
- its limitations.

The employee must:

- ensure that they are trained in the use of the PPE prior to use
- use it in line with the employer's instructions
- return it to storage after use
- take care of it, and report any loss or defect to their employer.

Remember

PPE must only be used as a last line of defence

Noise at work

The Control of Noise at Work Regulations 2005

At some point in your career in construction, you are likely to work in a noisy working environment. These regulations help protect you against the consequences of being exposed to high levels of noise, which can lead to permanent hearing damage.

Damage to hearing has a range of causes, from ear infections to loud noises, but the regulations deal mainly with the latter. Hearing loss can result from one very loud noise lasting only a few seconds, or from relatively loud noise lasting for hours, such as a drill.

The regulations state that the employer must:

- assess the risks to the employee from noise at work
- take action to reduce the noise exposure that produces these risks
- provide employees with hearing protection or, if this is impossible, reduce the risk by other methods
- make sure the legal limits on noise exposure are not exceeded
- provide employees with information, instruction and training
- carry out health surveillance where there is a risk to health.

The Work at Height Regulations 2005

Construction workers often work high off the ground, on scaffolding, ladders or roofs. These regulations make sure that employers do all that they can to reduce the risk of injury or death from working at height.

The employer has a duty to:

- avoid work at height where possible
- use any equipment or safeguards that will prevent falls
- use equipment and any other methods that will minimise the distance and consequences of a fall.

As an employee, you must follow any training given to you, report any hazards to your supervisor and use any safety equipment made available to you.

The Electricity at Work Regulations 1989

These regulations cover any work involving the use of electricity or electrical equipment. An employer has the duty to ensure that the electrical systems their employees come into contact with are safe and regularly maintained. They must also have done everything the law states to reduce the risk of their employees coming into contact with live electrical currents.

The Manual Handling Operations Regulations 1992

These regulations cover all work activities in which a person does the lifting rather than a machine. They state that, wherever possible, manual handling should be avoided, but where this is unavoidable, a risk assessment should be done.

In a risk assessment, there are four considerations:

- *Load* – is it heavy, sharp-edged, difficult to hold?
- *Individual* – is the individual small, pregnant, in need of training?
- *Task* – does the task require holding goods away from the body, or repetitive twisting?
- *Environment* – is the floor uneven, are there stairs, is it raining?

After the assessment, the situation must be monitored constantly and updated or changed if necessary.

The Reporting of Injuries, Diseases and Dangerous Occurrences Regulations 1995 (RIDDOR)

Under RIDDOR, employers have a duty to report accidents, diseases or dangerous occurrences. The HSE use this information to identify where and how risk arises and to investigate serious accidents.

Other Acts to be aware of

You should also be aware of the following pieces of legislation:

- The Fire Precautions (Workplace) Regulations 1997
- The Fire Precautions Act 1991
- The Highly Flammable Liquids and Liquid Petroleum Gases Regulations 1972
- The Lifting Operations and Lifting Equipment Regulations 1998
- The Construction (Health, Safety and Welfare) Regulations 1996
- The Environmental Protection Act 1990
- The Confined Spaces Regulations 1997
- The Working Time Regulations 1998
- The Health and Safety (First Aid) Regulations 1981
- The Construction (Design and Management) Regulations 1994.

You can find out more at the library or online.

Find out

Look into the other regulations listed here via the Government website www.hse.gov.uk

Health and welfare in the construction industry

Jobs in the construction industry have one of the highest injury and accident rates and as a worker you will be at constant risk unless you adopt a good health and safety attitude. By following the rules and regulations set out to protect you and by taking reasonable care of yourself and others, you will become a safe worker and thus reduce the chance of any injuries or accidents.

The most common risks to a construction worker

What do you think these might be? Think about the construction industry you are working in and the hazards and risks that exist.

The most common health and safety risks a construction worker faces are:

- accidents
- ill health.

Accidents

We often hear the saying 'accidents will happen', but when working in the construction industry, we should not accept that accidents just happen sometimes. When we think of an accident, we quite often think about it as being no one's fault and something that could not have been avoided. The truth is that most accidents are caused by human error, which means someone has done something they shouldn't have done or, just as importantly, not done something they should have done.

Accidents often happen when someone is hurrying, not paying enough attention to what they are doing or they have not received the correct training.

If an accident happens, you or the person it happened to may be lucky and will not be injured. More often, an accident will result in an injury which may be minor (e.g. a cut or a bruise) or possibly major (e.g. loss of a limb). Accidents can also be fatal. The most common causes of fatal accidents in the construction industry are:

- falling from scaffolding
- being hit by falling objects and materials
- falling through fragile roofs
- being hit by forklifts or lorries
- cuts
- infections
- burns
- electrocution.

Remember

Health and safety laws are there to protect you and other people. If you take shortcuts or ignore the rules, you are placing yourself and others at serious risk

Accidents can happen if your work area is untidy

Ill health

While working in the construction industry, you will be exposed to substances or situations that may be harmful to your health. Some of these health risks may not be noticeable straight away and it may take years for **symptoms** to be noticed and recognised.

Ill health can result from:

- exposure to dust (such as asbestos), which can cause breathing problems and cancer
- exposure to solvents or chemicals, which can cause **dermatitis** and other skin problems
- lifting heavy or difficult loads, which can cause back injury and pulled muscles
- exposure to loud noise, which can cause hearing problems and deafness
- exposure to sunlight, which can cause skin cancer
- using vibrating tools, which can cause **vibration white finger** and other problems with the hands.

Everyone has a responsibility for health and safety in the construction industry but accidents and health problems still happen too often. Make sure you do what you can to prevent them.

Substance abuse

Substance abuse is a general term and mainly covers things such as drinking alcohol and taking drugs.

Taking drugs or inhaling solvents at work is not only illegal, but is also highly dangerous to you and everyone around you as reduced concentration problems can lead to accidents. Drinking alcohol is also dangerous at work; going to the pub for lunch and having just one drink can lead to slower reflexes and reduced concentration.

Although not a form of abuse as such, drugs prescribed by your doctor as well as over the counter painkillers can be dangerous. Many of these medicines carry warnings such as 'may cause drowsiness' or 'do not operate heavy machinery'. It is better to be safe than sorry, so always ensure you follow any instructions on prescriptions and, if you feel drowsy or unsteady, then stop work immediately.

Definition

Symptom – a sign of illness or disease (e.g. difficulty breathing, a sore hand or a lump under the skin)

Dermatitis – a skin condition where the affected area is red, itchy and sore

Vibration white finger – a condition that can be caused by using vibrating machinery (usually for very long periods of time). The blood supply to the fingers is reduced which causes pain, tingling and sometimes spasms (shaking)

Always wash your hands to prevent ingesting hazardous substances

Staying healthy

As well as keeping an eye out for hazards, you must also make sure that you look after yourself and stay healthy. One of the easiest ways to do this is to wash your hands on a regular basis. By washing your hands you are preventing hazardous substances from entering your body through ingestion (swallowing). You should always wash your hands after going to the toilet and before eating or drinking.

Other precautions that you can take are ensuring that you wear **barrier cream**, the correct PPE and only drink water that is labelled as drinking water. Ensure that you are protected from the sun with a good sunscreen, and ensure your back, arms and legs are covered by suitable clothing. Remember that some health problems do not show symptoms straight away and what you do now can affect you much later in life.

Welfare facilities

Welfare facilities are things such as toilets, which must be provided by your employer to ensure a safe and healthy workplace. There are several things that your employer must provide to meet welfare standards and these are:

- Toilets – the number of toilets provided depends upon the amount of people who are intended to use them. Males and females can use the same toilets providing there is a lock on the inside of the door. Toilets should be flushable with water or, if this is not possible, with chemicals.

- Washing facilities – employers must provide a basin large enough to allow people to wash their hands, face and forearms. Washing facilities must have hot and cold running water as well as soap and a means of drying your hands. Showers may be needed if the work is very dirty or if workers are exposed to **corrosive** and **toxic** substances.

- Drinking water – there should be a supply of clean drinking water available, either from a tap connected to the mains or from bottled water. Taps connected to the mains need to be clearly labelled as drinking water and bottled drinking water must be stored in a separate area to prevent **contamination**.

- Storage or dry room – every building site must have an area where workers can store the clothes that they do not wear on site, such as coats and motorcycle helmets. If this area is to be used as a drying room then adequate heating must also be provided in order to allow clothes to dry.

Definition

Barrier cream – a cream used to protect the skin from damage or infection

Definition

Corrosive – a substance that can damage things it comes into contact with (e.g. material, skin)

Toxic – poisonous

Contamination – when harmful chemicals or substances pollute something (e.g. water)

- Lunch area – every site must have facilities that can be used for taking breaks and lunch well away from the work area. These facilities must provide shelter from the wind and rain and be heated as required. There should be access to tables and chairs, a kettle or urn for boiling water and a means of heating food, such as a microwave.

When working in an occupied house, you can make arrangements with the client to use the facilities in their house.

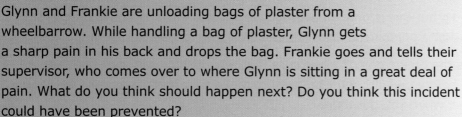

On the job: Manual handling

Glynn and Frankie are unloading bags of plaster from a wheelbarrow. While handling a bag of plaster, Glynn gets a sharp pain in his back and drops the bag. Frankie goes and tells their supervisor, who comes over to where Glynn is sitting in a great deal of pain. What do you think should happen next? Do you think this incident could have been prevented?

Poor manual handling techniques can lead to serious permanent injury

Manual handling

Manual handling means lifting and moving a piece of equipment or material from one place to another without using machinery. Lifting and moving loads by hand is one of the most common causes of injury at work. Most injuries caused by manual handling result from years of lifting items that are too heavy, are awkward shapes or sizes, or from using the wrong technique. However, it is also possible to cause a lifetime of back pain with just one single lift.

Poor manual handling can cause injuries such as muscle strain, pulled ligaments and hernias. The most common injury by far is spinal injury. Spinal injuries are very serious because there is very little that doctors can do to correct them and, in extreme cases, workers have been left paralysed.

What you can do to avoid injury

The first and most important thing you can do to avoid injury from lifting is to receive proper manual handling training. Kinetic lifting is a way of lifting objects that reduces the chance of injury and is covered in more detail on the next page.

Before you lift anything you should ask yourself some simple questions:

- Does the object need to be moved?

- Can I use something to help me lift the object? A mechanical aid such as a forklift or crane or a manual aid such as a wheelbarrow may be more appropriate than a person.

- Can I reduce the weight by breaking down the load? Breaking down a load into smaller and more manageable weights may mean that more journeys are needed, but it will also reduce the risk of injury.

- Do I need help? Asking for help to lift a load is not a sign of weakness and team lifting will greatly reduce the risk of injury.

- How much can I lift safely? The recommended maximum weight a person can lift is 25 kg but this is only an average weight and each person is different. The amount that a person can lift will depend on their physique, age and experience.

- Where is the object going? Make sure that any obstacles in your path are out of the way before you lift. You also need to make sure there is somewhere to put the object when you get there.

- Am I trained to lift? The quickest way to receive a manual handling injury is to use the wrong lifting technique.

Lifting correctly (kinetic lifting)

When lifting any load it is important to keep the correct posture and to use the correct technique.

The correct posture before lifting:

- feet shoulder width apart with one foot slightly in front of the other

- knees should be bent

- back must be straight

- arms should be as close to the body as possible

- grip must be firm using the whole hand and not just the finger tips.

The correct technique when lifting:

- approach the load squarely facing the direction of travel

- adopt the correct posture (as opposite)

- place hands under the load and pull the load close to your body

- lift the load using your legs and not your back.

When lowering a load you must also adopt the correct posture and technique:

- bend at the knees, not the back
- adjust the load to avoid trapping fingers
- release the load.

Think before lifting

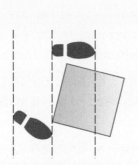

Adopt the correct posture before lifting

Get a good grip on the load

Adopt the correct posture when lifting

Move smoothly with the load

Adopt the correct posture and technique when lowering

Hazards

The building industry can be a very dangerous place to work and there are certain hazards that all workers need to be aware of.

The main types of hazards that you will face are:

- falling from height
- tripping
- chemical spills
- burns
- electrical
- fires.

Falling from height will be covered in detail in Chapter 3 *Working at height* so here we will look at the remaining hazards.

An untidy work site can present many trip hazards

Tripping

The main cause of tripping is poor housekeeping. Whether working on scaffolding or on ground level, an untidy workplace is an accident waiting to happen. All workplaces should be kept tidy and free of debris. All offcuts should be put either in a wheelbarrow (if you are not near a skip) or straight into the skip. Not only will this prevent trip hazards, but it will also prevent costly clean-up operations at the end of the job and will promote a good professional image.

Chemical spills

Chemical spillages can range from minor inconvenience to major disaster. Most spillages are small and create minimal or no risk. If the material involved is not hazardous, it simply can be cleaned up by normal operations such as brushing or mopping up the spill. However, on some occasions the spill may be on a larger scale and may involve a hazardous material. It is important to know what to do before the spillage happens so that remedial action can be prompt and harmful effects minimised. Of course, when a hazardous substance is being used a COSHH or risk assessment will have been made, and it should include a plan for dealing with a spillage. This in turn should mean that the materials required for dealing with the spillage should be readily available.

Burns

Burns can occur not only from the obvious source of fire and heat but also from materials containing chemicals such as cement or painter's solvents. Even electricity can cause burns. It is vital when working with materials that you are aware of the hazards it may present and take the necessary precautions.

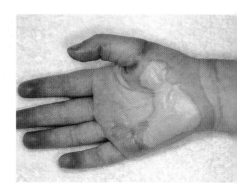

Fire, heat, chemicals and electricity can cause burns

Electricity

Electricity is a killer. Around 30 workers a year die from electricity related accidents, with over 1000 more being seriously injured (source: HSE). One of the main problems with electricity is that it is invisible. You don't even have to be working with an electric tool to be electrocuted. Working too close to live overhead cables, plastering a wall with electric sockets, carrying out maintenance work on a floor, or drilling into a wall can all lead to an electric shock.

Electric shocks may not always be fatal; electricity can also cause burns, muscular problems and cardiac (heart) problems. The level of voltage is not a direct guide to the level of injury or danger of death, despite this common misconception; a small shock from static electricity may contain thousands of volts but has very little current behind it. Generally, the lower the voltage, the less chance of death occurring.

There are two main types of voltage in use in the UK. These are 230 V and 110 V. 230 V is the standard UK power supply and this is what all the sockets in your house are. Contained within the wiring there should be three wires: the live and neutral, which carry the alternating current, and the earth wire, which acts as a safety device. The three wires are colour-coded as follows:

Live – Brown

Neutral – Blue

Earth – Yellow and green

These have been changed recently to comply with European colours. Some older properties will have the following colours:

Live – Red

Neutral – Black

Earth – Yellow and green

230 V has been deemed as unsafe on construction sites so 110 V must be used here. 110 V, identified by a yellow cable and different style plug, works from a transformer which converts the 230 V to 110 V.

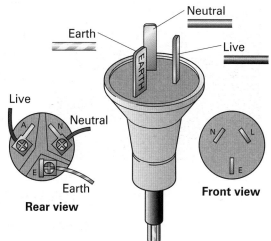

Figure 2.1 Colour coding of the wires in a 230 V plug

A 110 V plug

Dealing with electric shocks

In helping a victim of an electric shock, the first thing you must do is disconnect the power supply, if it is safe to do and will not take long to find; touching the power source may put you in danger. If the victim is in contact with something portable, such as a drill, attempt to move it away using a non-conductive object such as a wooden broom. Time is precious and separating the victim from the source can prove an effective way to speed the process. Do not attempt to touch the affected person until they are free and clear of the supplied power. Don't even touch the victim until you are sure the power supply is turned off. Be especially careful in wet areas, such as bathrooms, since most water will conduct electricity and electrocuting yourself is also possible.

People 'hung up' in a live current flow may think they are calling out for help but most likely no sound will be heard from them. When the muscles contract under household current (most electrocutions happen from house current at home), the person affected will appear in locked-up state, unable to move or react to you. Using a wooden object, swiftly and strongly knock the person free, trying not to injure them, and land them clear of the source. The source may also be lifted or removed, if possible, with the same wooden item. This is not recommended on voltages that exceed 500 V. Do not attempt any of this without rubber or some form of insulated sole shoes; bare or socked feet will allow the current to flow to ground through your body as well.

First aid procedures for an electric shock victim

- Check if you are alone. If there are other people around, instruct them to call an ambulance right away.

- Check for a response and breathing.

- If the area is safe for you to be in, and you have removed the object or have cut off its power supply, yell to the person to see if they are conscious. At this stage, do not touch the victim.

- Check once again to see if the area is safe. If you are satisfied that it is safe, start resuscitating the victim. If you have no first aid knowledge, call emergency services for an ambulance.

Fire and fire-fighting equipment

Fires can start almost anywhere and at any time but a fire needs three things to burn. These are:

1. fuel

2. heat

3. oxygen.

Figure 2.2 The triangle of fire

This can be shown in what is known as 'the triangle of fire'. If any of the sides of the triangle are removed, the fire cannot burn and it will go out.

Remember:

- Remove the fuel and there is nothing to burn so the fire will go out.
- Remove the heat and the fire will go out.
- Remove the oxygen and the fire will go out as fire needs oxygen to survive.

Fires can be classified according to the type of material that is involved:

- Class A – wood, paper, textiles etc.
- Class B – flammable liquids, petrol, oil etc.
- Class C – flammable gases, liquefied petroleum gas (**LPG**), propane etc.
- Class D – metal, metal powder etc.
- Class E – electrical equipment.

Fire-fighting equipment

There are several types of fire-fighting equipment, such as fire blankets and fire extinguishers. Each type is designed to be the most effective at putting out a particular class of fire and some types should never be used in certain types of fire.

Fire extinguishers

A fire extinguisher is a metal canister containing a substance that can put out a fire. There are several different types and it is important that you learn which type should be used on specific classes of fires. This is because if you use the wrong type, you may make the fire worse or risk severely injuring yourself.

Fire extinguishers are now all one colour (red) but they have a band of colour which shows what substance is inside.

Water

The coloured band is red and this type of extinguisher can be used on Class A fires. Water extinguishers can also be used on Class C fires in order to cool the area down.

A water fire extinguisher should *never* be used to put out an electrical or burning fat/oil fire. This is because electrical current can carry along the jet of water back to the person holding the extinguisher, electrocuting them. Putting water on to burning fat or oil will make the fire worse as the fire will 'explode', potentially causing serious injury.

Find out

What fire risks are there in the construction industry? Think about some of the materials (fuel) and heat sources that could make up two of the sides of 'the triangle of fire'

Water fire extinguisher

Foam fire extinguisher

Foam

The coloured band is cream and this type of extinguisher can also be used on Class A fires. A foam extinguisher can also be used on a Class B fire if the liquid is not flowing and on a Class C fire if the gas is in liquid form.

Carbon dioxide (CO_2)

The coloured band is black and the extinguisher can be used on Class A, B, C and E fires.

Dry powder

The coloured band is blue and this type of extinguisher can be used on all classes of fire. The powder puts out the fire by smothering the flames.

Carbon dioxide (CO_2) extinguisher

Dry powder extinguisher

Fire blankets

Fire blankets are normally found in kitchens or canteens as they are good at putting out cooking fires. They are made of a fireproof material and work by smothering the fire and stopping any more oxygen from getting to it, thus putting it out. A fire blanket can also be used if a person is on fire.

It is important to remember that when you put out a fire with a fire blanket, you need to take extra care as you will have to get quite close to the fire.

A fire blanket

What to do in the event of a fire

During **induction** to any workplace, you will be made aware of the fire procedure as well as where the fire assembly points (also known as **muster points**) are and what the alarm sounds like. On hearing the alarm you must stop what you are doing and make your way to the nearest muster point. This is so that everyone can be accounted for. If you do not go to the muster point or if you leave before someone has taken your name, someone may risk their life to go back into the fire to get you.

When you hear the alarm, you should not stop to gather any belongings and you must not run. If you discover a fire, you must only try to fight the fire if it is blocking your exit or if it is small. Only when you have been given the all-clear can you re-enter the site or building.

Definition

Induction – a formal introduction you will receive when you start any new job, where you will be shown around, shown where the toilets and canteen etc. are, and told what to do if there is a fire

Muster points – fire assembly points

Remember

Fire and smoke can kill in seconds so think and act clearly, quickly and sensibly

Safety signs

Safety signs can be found in many areas of the workplace and they are put up in order to:

- warn of any **hazards**
- prevent accidents
- inform where things are
- tell you what to do in certain areas.

Types of safety sign

There are many different safety signs but each will usually fit into one of four categories:

1. Prohibition signs – these tell you that something *must not* be done. They always have a white background and a red circle with a red line through it.

2. Mandatory signs – these tell you that something *must* be done. They are also circular but have a white symbol on a blue background.

3. Warning signs – these signs are there to alert you to a specific hazard. They are triangular and have a yellow background and a black border.

4. Information signs – these give you useful information like the location of things (e.g. a first aid point). They can be square or rectangular and are green with a white symbol.

Most signs only have symbols that let you know what they are saying. Others have some words as well, for example a no smoking sign might have a cigarette in a red circle, with a red line crossing through the cigarette and the words 'No smoking' underneath.

Figure 2.5 A warning sign

Figure 2.6 An information sign

Figure 2.7 A safety sign with both symbol and words

Definition

Hazard – a danger or risk

Figure 2.3 A prohibition sign

Figure 2.4 A mandatory sign

Remember

Make sure you take notice of safety signs in the workplace – they have been put up for a reason!

Personal protective equipment (PPE)

Personal protective equipment (PPE) is a form of defence against accidents or injury and comes in the form of articles of clothing. This is not to say that PPE is the only way of preventing accidents or injury. It should be used together with all the other methods of staying healthy and safe in the workplace (i.e. equipment, training, regulations and laws etc.).

PPE must be supplied by your employer free of charge and you have responsibility as an employee to look after it and use it whenever it is required.

Types of PPE

There are certain parts of the body that require protection from hazards during work and each piece of PPE must be suitable for the job and used properly.

Head protection

There are several different types of head protection but the one most commonly used in construction is the safety helmet (or hard hat). This is used to protect the head from falling objects and knocks and has an adjustable strap to ensure a snug fit. Some safety helmets come with attachments for ear defenders or eye protection. Safety helmets are meant to be worn directly on the head and must not be worn over any other type of hat.

Eye protection

Eye protection is used to protect the eyes from dust and flying debris. The three main types are:

1. Safety goggles – made of a durable plastic and used when there is a danger of dust getting into the eyes or a chance of impact injury.

2. Safety spectacles – these are also made from a durable plastic but give less protection than goggles. This is because they don't fully enclose the eyes and so only protect from flying debris.

3. Facemasks – again made of durable plastic, facemasks protect the entire face from flying debris. They do not, however, protect the eyes from dust.

A safety helmet

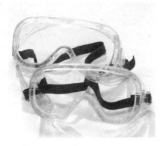

Safety goggles

Safety spectacles

Foot protection

Safety boots or shoes are used to protect the feet from falling objects and to prevent sharp objects such as nails from injuring the foot. Safety boots should have a steel toe-cap and steel mid-sole.

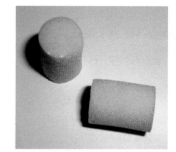
Safety boots

Hearing protection

Hearing protection is used to prevent damage to the ears caused by very loud noise. There are several types of hearing protection available but the two most common types are ear-plugs and ear defenders.

1. Ear-plugs – these are small fibre plugs that are inserted into the ear and used when the noise is not too severe. When using ear-plugs, make sure that you have clean hands before inserting them and never use plugs that have been used by somebody else.

2. Ear defenders – these are worn to cover the entire ear and are connected to a band that fits over the top of the head. They are used when there is excessive noise and must be cleaned regularly.

Ear-plugs

Respiratory protection

Respiratory protection is used to prevent the worker from breathing in any dust or fumes that may be hazardous. The main type of respiratory protection is the dust mask.

Dust masks are used when working in a dusty environment and are lightweight, comfortable and easy to fit. They should be worn by only one person and must be disposed of at the end of the working day. Dust masks will only offer protection from non-toxic dust, so if the worker is to be exposed to toxic dust or fumes, a full respiratory system should be used.

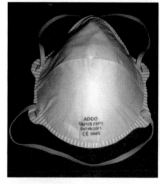
Ear defenders

Hand protection

There are several types of hand protection and each type must be used for the correct task. For example, wearing lightweight rubber gloves to move glass will not offer much protection so leather gauntlets must be used. Plastic–coated gloves will protect you from certain chemicals and Kevlar® gloves offer cut resistance. To make sure you are wearing the most suitable type of glove for the task, you need to look first at what is going to be done and then match the type of glove to that task.

A dust mask

Safety gloves

Emergencies

We have so far covered most of the emergencies that occur on site, such as accidents and fires, but there are other emergencies that you need to be aware of, such as security alerts and bomb scares.

At your site induction, it should be made perfectly clear to you what you should do in the event of an emergency. You also should be made aware of any sirens or warning noises that accompany each and every type of emergency such as bomb scares or fire alarms. Some sites may have different variations on sirens or emergency procedures, so it is vital that you pay attention and listen to all instructions. If you are unsure always ask.

First Aid

In the unfortunate event of an accident on site, first aid may have to be administered. If there are more than five people on a site, then a qualified first aider must be present at all times. On large building sites there must be several first aiders. During your site induction you will be made aware of who the first aiders are and where the first aid points are situated. A first aid point must have the relevant first aid equipment to deal with the types of injuries that are likely to occur. However, first aid is only the first step and, in the case of major injuries, the emergency services should be called.

A good first aid box should have plasters, bandages, antiseptic wipes, latex gloves, eye patches, slings, wound dressings and safety pins. Other equipment, such as eye wash stations, must also be available if the work being carried out requires it.

Remember

Health and safety is everyone's duty. If you receive first aid treatment and notice that there are only two plasters left, you should report it to your line manager.

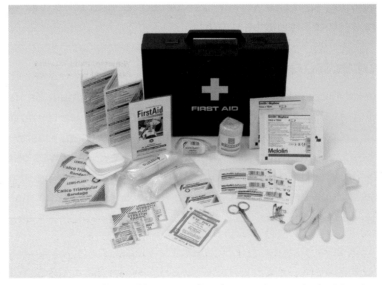

A first aid box provides the supplies to deal with minor injuries

Reporting accidents

When an accident occurs, there are certain things that must be done. All accidents need to be reported and recorded in the accident book and the injured person must report to a trained first aider in order to receive treatment. Serious accidents must be reported under the Reporting of Injuries, Diseases and Dangerous Occurrences Regulations 1995 (RIDDOR). Under RIDDOR your employer must report to the HSE any accident that results in:

- death
- major injury
- an injury that means the injured person is not at work for more than three consecutive days.

The accident book

The accident book is completed by the person who had the accident or, if this is not possible, someone who is representing the injured person.

The accident book will ask for some basic details about the accident, including:

- who was involved
- what happened
- where it happened
- the day and time of the accident
- any witnesses to the accident
- the address of the injured person
- what PPE was being worn
- what first aid treatment was given.

As well as reporting accidents, 'near misses' must also be reported. This is because near misses are often the accidents of the future. Reporting near misses might identify a problem and can prevent accidents from happening in the future. This allows a company to be **proactive** rather than **reactive**.

Report of an Accident, Dangerous Occurrence or Near Miss

Date of incident _____ Time of incident _____
Location of incident _____
Details of person involved in accident
Name _____ Date of birth _____ Sex _____
Address _____
_____
_____ Occupation _____
Date off work (if applicable) _____ Date returning to work _____
Nature of injury _____
Management of injury ☐ First Aid only ☐ Advised to see doctor
☐ Sent to casualty ☐ Admitted to hospital

Account of accident, dangerous occurrence or near miss
(Continued on separate sheet if necessary)

Witnesses to the incident
(Names, addresses and occupations)

Was the injured person wearing PPE? If yes, what PPE? _____

Signature of person completing form _____
Occupation _____ Date _____

Figure 2.8 A typical accident book page

Even an everyday task like cutting the grass has its own dangers

Risk assessments

You will have noticed that most of the legislation we have looked at requires risk assessments to be carried out. The Management of Health and Safety at Work Regulations 1999 require every employer to make suitable and sufficient assessment of:

- the risks to the health and safety of his/her employees to which they are exposed while at work
- the risks to the health and safety of persons not in his/her employment arising out of or in connection with his/her work activities.

As a Level 2 candidate, it is vital that you know how to **carry out a risk assessment**. Often you may be in a position where you are given direct responsibility for this, and the care and attention you take over it may have a direct impact on the safety of others. You must be aware of the dangers or hazards of any task, and know what can be done to prevent or reduce the risk.

There are five steps in a risk assessment – here we use cutting the grass as an example:

Step 1 Identify the hazards

When cutting the grass the main hazards are from the blades or cutting the wire, electrocution and any stones that may be thrown up.

Step 2 Identify who will be at risk

The main person at risk is the user but passers-by may be struck by flying debris.

Step 3 Calculate the risk from the hazard against the likelihood of an accident taking place

The risks from the hazard are quite high: the blade or wire can remove a finger, electrocution can kill and the flying debris can blind or even kill. The likelihood of an accident happening is medium: you are unlikely to cut yourself on the blades, but the chance of cutting through the cable is medium, and the chance of hitting a stone high.

Step 4 Introduce measures to reduce the risk

Training can reduce the risks of cutting yourself; training and the use of an **RCD** can reduce the risk of electrocution; and raking the lawn first can reduce the risk of sending up stones.

Step 5 Monitor the risk

Constantly changing factors mean any risk assessment may have to be modified or even changed completely. In our example, one such factor could be rain.

On the job: Scaffold safety

Ralph and Vijay are working on the second level of some scaffolding clearing debris. Ralph suggests that, to speed up the task, they should throw the debris over the edge of the scaffolding into a skip below. The building Ralph and Vijay are working on is on a main road and the skip is not in a closed off area. What do you think of Ralph's idea? What are your reasons for this answer?

FAQ

How do I find out what safety legislation is relevant to my job?

Ask your employer or manager, or contact the HSE at www.hse.gov.uk.

When do I need to do a risk assessment?

A risk assessment should be carried out if there is any chance of an accident happening as a direct result of the work being done. To be on the safe side, you should make a risk assessment before starting each task.

Do I need to read and understand every regulation?

No. It is part of your employer's duty to ensure that you are aware of what you need to know.

Knowledge check

1. Name five pieces of health and safety legislation that affect the construction industry.

2. What does HSE stand for? What does it do?

3. What does COSHH stand for?

4. What does RIDDOR stand for?

5. What might happen to you or your employer if a health and safety law is broken?

6. What are the two most common risks to construction workers?

7. State two things that you can do to avoid injury when lifting loads using manual handling techniques.

8. What are the two main types of voltage in use in the UK?

9. What three elements cause a fire and keep it burning?

10. What class(es) of fire can be put out with a carbon dioxide (CO_2) extinguisher?

11. What does a prohibition sign mean?

12. Describe how you would identify a warning sign.

13. Name the six different types of PPE.

14. Name five items that should be included in a first aid kit.

15. Who fills in an accident report form?

16. Why is it important to report 'near misses'?

17. Briefly explain what a risk assessment is.

Working at height

OVERVIEW

Most construction trades require frequent use of some type of working platform or access equipment. Working off the ground can be dangerous and the greater the height the more serious the risk of injury. This chapter will give you a summary of some of the most common types of access equipment and provide information on how they should be used, maintained and checked to ensure that the risks to you and others are minimal.

This chapter will cover the following topics:

- General safety considerations
- Stepladders and ladders
- Roof work
- Trestle platforms
- Hop-ups
- Scaffolding
- Fall protection.

These topics can be found in the following modules:

CC 1001K   CC 1001S

General safety considerations

You will need to be able to identify potential hazards associated with working at height, as well as hazards associated with equipment. It is essential that access equipment is well maintained and checked regularly for any deterioration or faults, which could compromise the safety of someone using the equipment and anyone else in the work area. Although obviously not as important as people, equipment can also be damaged by the use of faulty access equipment. When maintenance checks are carried out they should be properly recorded. This provides very important information that helps to prevent accidents.

Risk assessment

Before any work is carried out at height, a thorough risk assessment needs to be completed. Your supervisor or someone else more experienced will do this while you are still training, but it is important that you understand what is involved so that you are able to carry out an assessment in the future.

For a working at height risk assessment to be valid and effective a number of questions must be answered:

1. How is access and egress to the work area to be achieved?

2. What type of work is to be carried out?

3. How long is the work likely to last?

4. How many people will be carrying out the task?

5. How often will this work be carried out?

6. What is the condition of the existing structure (if any) and the surroundings?

7. Is adverse weather likely to affect the work and workers?

8. How competent are the workforce and their supervisors?

9. Is there a risk to the public and work colleagues?

Duties

Your employer has a duty to provide and maintain safe plant and equipment, which includes scaffold access equipment and systems of work.

You have a duty:

- to comply with safety rules and procedures relating to access equipment
- to take positive steps to understand the hazards in the workplace and report things you consider likely to lead to danger, for example a missing handrail on a working platform
- not to tamper with or modify equipment.

Did you know?

Only a fully trained and competent person is allowed to erect any kind of working platform or access equipment. You should therefore not attempt to erect this type of equipment unless this describes you!

Stepladders and ladders

Stepladders

A stepladder has a prop, which when folded out allows the ladder to be used without having to lean it against something. Stepladders are one of the most frequently used pieces of access equipment in the construction industry and are often used every day. This means that they are not always treated with the respect they demand. Stepladders are often misused – they should only be used for work that will take a few minutes to complete. When work is likely to take longer than this, a sturdier alternative should be found.

When stepladders are used, the following safety points should be observed:

- Ensure the ground on which the stepladder is to be placed is firm and level. If the ladder rocks or sinks into the ground it should not be used for the work.

- Always open the steps fully.

- Never work off the top tread of the stepladder.

- Always keep your knees below the top tread.

- Never use stepladders to gain additional height on another working platform.

- Always look for the kitemark, which shows that the ladder has been made to British Standards.

A number of other safety points need to be observed depending on the type of stepladder being used.

Wooden stepladder

Before using a wooden stepladder:

- Check for loose screws, nuts, bolts and hinges.

- Check that the tie ropes between the two sets of **stiles** are in good condition and not frayed.

- Check for splits or cracks in the stiles.

- Check that the treads are not loose or split.

Never paint any part of a wooden stepladder as this can hide defects, which may cause the ladder to fail during use, causing injury.

Figure 3.1 British Standards Institution kitemark

Definition

Stiles – the side pieces of a stepladder into which the steps are set

Wooden stepladder

Safety tip

If any faults are revealed when checking a stepladder, it should be taken out of use, reported to the person in charge and a warning notice attached to it to stop anyone using it

Find out

What are the advantages and disadvantages of each type of stepladder?

Did you know?

Stepladders should be stored under cover to protect from damage such as rust or rotting

Safety tip

Ladders must *never* be repaired once damaged and must be disposed of

Aluminium stepladder

Before using an aluminium stepladder:

- check for damage to stiles and treads to see whether they are twisted, badly dented or loose
- avoid working close to live electricity supplies as aluminium will conduct electricity.

Fibreglass stepladder

Before using a fibreglass stepladder, check for damage to stiles and treads. Once damaged, fibreglass stepladders cannot be repaired and must be disposed of.

Aluminium stepladder

Ladders

A ladder, unlike a stepladder, does not have a prop and so has to be leant against something in order for it to be used. Together with stepladders, ladders are one of the most common pieces of equipment used to carry out work at heights and gain access to the work area.

As with stepladders, ladders are also available in timber, aluminium and fibreglass and require similar checks before use.

Ladder types

Pole ladder

These are single ladders and are available in a range of lengths. They are most commonly used for access to scaffolding platforms. Pole ladders are made from timber and must be stored under cover and flat, supported evenly along their length to prevent them sagging and twisting. They should be checked for damage or defects every time before being used.

Extension ladder

Extension ladders have two or more interlocking lengths, which can be slid together for convenient storage or slid apart to the desired length when in use.

Pole ladder

Extension ladders are available in timber, aluminium and fibreglass. Aluminium types are the most favoured as they are lightweight yet strong and available in double and triple extension types. Although also very strong, fibreglass versions are heavy, making them difficult to manoeuvre.

Aluminium extension ladder

Erecting and using a ladder

The following points should be noted when considering the use of a ladder:

- As with stepladders, ladders are not designed for work of long duration. Alternative working platforms should be considered if the work will take longer than a few minutes.

- The work should not require the use of both hands. One hand should be free to hold the ladder.

- You should be able to do the work without stretching.

- You should make sure that the ladder can be adequately secured to prevent it slipping on the surface it is leaning against.

Pre-use checks

Before using a ladder check its general condition. Make sure that:

- no rungs are damaged or missing

- the stiles are not damaged

- no **tie-rods** are missing

- no repairs have been made to the ladder.

In addition, for wooden ladders ensure that:

- they have not been painted, which may hide defects or damage

- there is no decay or rot

- the ladder is not twisted or warped.

Erecting a ladder

Observe the following guidelines when erecting a ladder:

- Ensure you have a solid, level base.

- Do not pack anything under either (or both) of the stiles to level it.

- If the ladder is too heavy to put it in position on your own, get someone to help.

- Ensure that there is at least a four-rung overlap on each extension section.

Definition

Tie-rods – metal rods underneath the rungs of a ladder that give extra support to the rungs

Did you know?

On average in the UK, 14 people a year die at work falling from ladders; nearly 1,200 suffer major injuries (source: Health and Safety Executive)

- Never rest the ladder on plastic guttering as it may break, causing the ladder to slip and the user to fall.

- Where the base of the ladder is in an exposed position, ensure it is adequately guarded so that no one knocks it or walks into it.

- The ladder should be secured at both the top and bottom. The bottom of the ladder can be secured by a second person, however this person must not leave the base of the ladder whilst it is in use.

- The angle of the ladder should be a ratio of 1:4 (or 75°). This means that the bottom of the ladder is 1 m away from the wall for every 4 m in height (see Figure 3.2).

- The top of the ladder must extend at least 1 m, or 5 rungs, above its landing point.

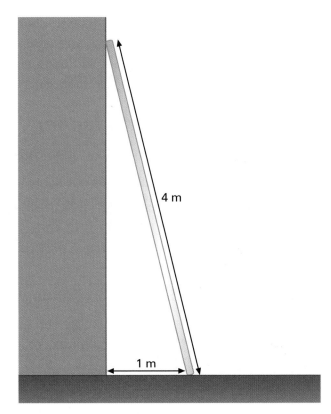

Figure 3.2 Correct angle for a ladder

Roof work

When carrying out any work on a roof, a roof ladder or **crawling board** must be used. Roof work also requires the use of edge protection or, where this is not possible, a safety harness.

The roof ladder is rolled up the surface of the roof and over the ridge tiles, just enough to allow the ladder to be turned over and the ladder hook allowed to bear on the tiles on the other side of the roof. This hook prevents the roof ladder sliding down the roof once it is accessed.

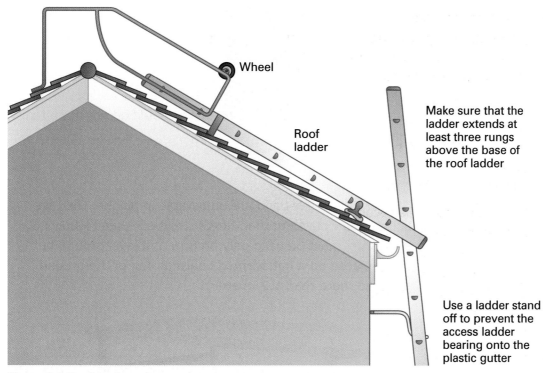

Wheel

Roof
ladder

Make sure that the
ladder extends at
least three rungs
above the base of
the roof ladder

Use a ladder stand
off to prevent the
access ladder
bearing onto the
plastic gutter

Figure 3.3 Roof work equipment

Trestle platforms

A trestle is a frame upon which a platform or
other type of surface (e.g. a table top) can
be placed. A trestle should be used rather
than a ladder for work that will take longer
than a few minutes to complete. Trestle
platforms are composed of the frame and
the platform (sometimes called a stage).

Frames

A-frames

These are most commonly
used by carpenters and painters. As the
name suggests, the frame is in the shape
of a capital A and can be made from timber,
aluminium or fibreglass. Two are used
together to support a platform (a scaffold or
staging board). See Figure 3.4.

Figure 3.4 A-frame trestles
with scaffold board

When using A-frames:

- they should always be opened fully and, in the same way as stepladders, must be placed on firm, level ground
- the platform width should be no less than 450 mm
- the overhang of the board at each end of the platform should be not more than four times its thickness.

Steel trestles

These are sturdier than A-frame trestles and are adjustable in height. They are also capable of providing a wider platform than timber trestles – see Figure 3.5. As with the A-frame type, they must be used only on firm and level ground but the trestle itself should be placed on a flat scaffold board on top of the ground. Trestles should not be placed more than 1.2 m apart.

Figure 3.5 Steel trestle with staging board

Platforms

Scaffold boards

To ensure that scaffold boards provide a safe working platform, before using them check that they:

- are not split
- are not twisted or warped
- have no large knots, which cause weakness.

Staging boards

These are designed to span a greater distance than scaffold boards and can offer a 600 mm wide working platform. They are ideal for use with trestles.

Hop-ups

Also known as step-ups, these are ideal for reaching low-level work that can be carried out in a relatively short period of time. A hop-up needs to be of sturdy construction and have a base of not less than 600 mm by 500 mm. Hop-ups have the disadvantage that they are heavy and awkward to move around.

Scaffolding

Tubular scaffold is the most commonly used type of scaffolding within the construction industry. There are two types of tubular scaffold:

1. Independent scaffold – free-standing scaffold that does not rely on any part of the building to support it (although it must be tied to the building to provide additional stability).

2. Putlog scaffold – scaffolding that is attached to the building via the entry of some of the poles into holes left in the brickwork by the bricklayer. The poles stay in position until the construction is complete and give the scaffold extra support.

No one other than a qualified **carded scaffolder** is allowed to erect or alter scaffolding. Although you are not allowed to erect or alter this type of scaffold, you must be sure it is safe before you work on it. You should ask yourself a number of questions to assess the condition and suitability of the scaffold before you use it:

- Are there any signs attached to the scaffold which state that it is incomplete or unsafe?
- Is the scaffold overloaded with materials such as bricks?
- Are the platforms cluttered with waste materials?
- Are there adequate guardrails and scaffold boards in place?
- Does the scaffold actually *look* safe?
- Is there the correct access to and from the scaffold?
- Are the various scaffold components in the correct place (see Figure 3.6)?
- Have the correct types of fittings been used (see Figure 3.7)?

Safety tip

Do not use items as hop-ups that are not designed for the purpose (e.g. milk crates, stools or chairs). They are usually not very sturdy and can't take the weight of someone standing on them, which may result in falls and injury

Definition

Carded scaffolder – someone who holds a recognised certificate showing competence in scaffold erection

Did you know?

It took 14 years of experimentation to finally settle on 48 mm as the diameter of most tubular scaffolding poles

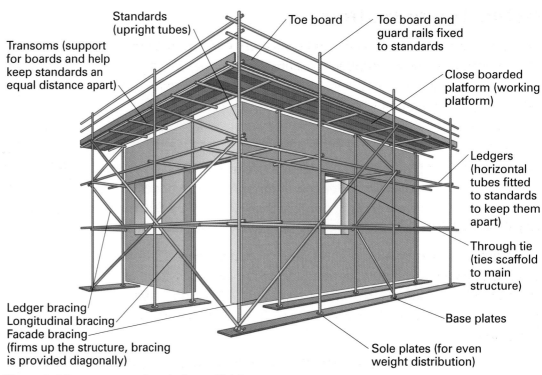

Standards (upright tubes)

Toe board

Toe board and guard rails fixed to standards

Transoms (support for boards and help keep standards an equal distance apart)

Close boarded platform (working platform)

Ledgers (horizontal tubes fitted to standards to keep them apart)

Through tie (ties scaffold to main structure)

Ledger bracing
Longitudinal bracing
Facade bracing
(firms up the structure, bracing is provided diagonally)

Base plates

Sole plates (for even weight distribution)

Figure 3.6 Components of a tubular scaffolding structure

Right angle coupler – load bearing; used to join tubes at right angles

Universal coupler – load bearing; also used to join tubes at right angles

Swivel coupler – load bearing; used to join tubes at various angles, e.g. diagonal braces

Adjustable base plate or base plate used at the base of standards to allow even weight distribution

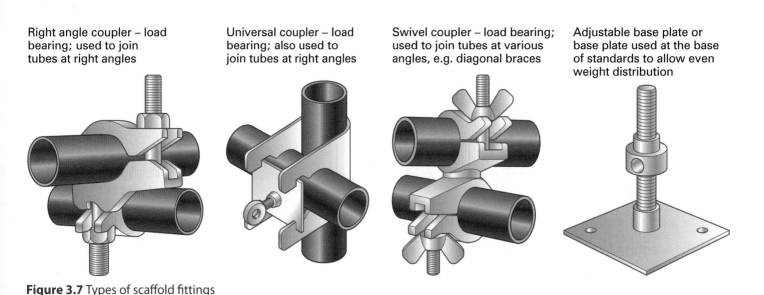

Figure 3.7 Types of scaffold fittings

Mobile tower scaffolds

Mobile tower scaffolds are so called because they can be moved around without being dismantled. Lockable wheels make this possible and they are used extensively throughout the construction industry by many different trades. A tower can be made from either traditional steel tubes and fittings or aluminium, which is lightweight and easy to move. The aluminium type of tower is normally specially designed and is referred to as a 'proprietary tower'.

Low towers

These are a smaller version of the standard mobile tower scaffold and are designed specifically for use by one person. They have a recommended working height of no more than 2.5 m and a safe working load of 150 kg. They are lightweight and easily transported and stored.

These towers require no assembly other than the locking into place of the platform and handrails. However, you still require training before you use one and you must ensure that the manufacturer's instructions are followed when setting up and working from this type of platform.

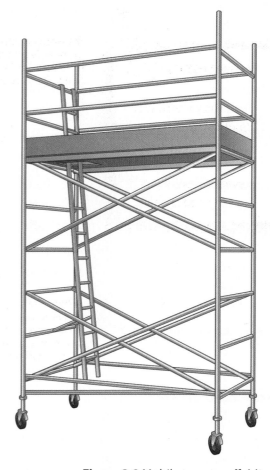

Figure 3.8 Mobile tower scaffold

Figure 3.9 Low tower scaffold

Definition

Proportionately – in relation to the size of something else

Safety tip

Mobile towers must *only* be moved when they are free of people, tools and materials

Safety tip

Never climb a scaffold tower on the outside as this can cause it to tip over

Erecting a tower scaffold

It is essential that tower scaffolds are situated on a firm and level base. The stability of any tower depends on the height in relation the size of the base:

- For use inside a building, the height should be no more than three-and-a-half times the smallest base length.

- For outside use, the height should be no more than three times the smallest base length.

The height of a tower can be increased provided the area of the base is increased **proportionately**. The base area can be increased by fitting outriggers to each corner of the tower.

For mobile towers, the wheels must be in the locked position while they are in use and unlocked only when they are being repositioned.

There are several important points you should observe when working from a scaffold tower:

- Any working platform above 2 m high must be fitted with guardrails and toe boards. Guard rails may also be required at heights of less than 2 m if there is a risk of falling onto potential hazards below, for example reinforcing rods. Guardrails must be fitted at a minimum height of 950 mm.

- If guardrails and toe boards are needed, they must be positioned on all four sides of the platform.

- Any tower higher than 9 m must be secured to the structure.

- Towers must not exceed 12 m in height unless they have been specifically designed for that purpose.

- The working platform of any tower must be fully boarded and be at least 600 mm wide.

- If the working platform is to be used for materials then the minimum width must be 800 mm.

- All towers must have their own access and this should be by an internal ladder.

Fall protection

With any task that involves working at height, the main danger to workers is falling. Although scaffolding, etc. should have edge protection to prevent falls, there are certain tasks where edge protection or scaffolding simply cannot be used.

In these instances some form of fall protection must be in place to prevent the worker falling, keep the fall distance to a minimum or ensure the landing point is cushioned.

There are various different types of fall protection available but the most common used are:

- harness and lanyards
- safety netting
- air bags.

Harness and lanyards

Harness and lanyards are a type of fall-arrest system, which means that, in the event of a slip or fall, the worker will only fall a few feet at most.

The system works with a harness that is attached to the worker and a lanyard attached to a secure beam/eyebolt. If the worker slips, then they will only fall as far as the length of cord/lanyard and will be left hanging, rather than falling to the ground.

A harness and lanyard can prevent a worker from falling to the ground

Safety netting

Safety netting is also a type of fall-arrest system but is used mainly on the top floor where there is no higher point to attach a lanyard.

Primarily used when decking roofing, the nets are attached to the joists/beams and are used to catch any worker who may slip or fall. Safety netting is also used on completed buildings where there is a fragile roof.

Safety netting is used when working at the highest point

Safety netting can be used under fragile roofs

Air bags

An airbag safety system is a form of soft fall-arrest and is comprised of interlinked modular air mattresses. The modules are connected by push connectors and/or flexible couplings and are inflated by a pump-driven fan, which can be electric, petrol, or butane gas powered. As the individual airbags fill with low-pressure air, they expand together to form a continuous protective safety surface, giving a cushioned soft fall and preventing serious injury.

The system must be kept inflated and, if it is run on petrol or gas, should be checked regularly to ensure that it is still functioning. This system is ideal for short fall jobs, but should not be used where a large fall could occur.

FAQ

Am I protected from electrocution if I am working on a wooden stepladder?

No. If you are working near a live current on a wooden stepladder, if any metal parts of the ladder, such as the tie rods, come into contact with the current, they will conduct the flow of electricity and you may be electrocuted. Take every precaution possible in order to avoid the risk of electrocution – the simplest precaution is turning off the electricity supply.

What determines the type of scaffolding used on a job?

As you will have read in this chapter, only a carded scaffolder is allowed to erect or alter scaffolding. They will select the scaffolding to be used according to the ground condition at the site, whether or not people will be working on the scaffolding, the types of materials and equipment that will be used on the scaffolding and the height to which access will be needed.

On the job: Attending to fascia boards

Pete has been asked by a client to take a look at all the fascia boards on a two-storey building. Depending on the condition of the fascia boards, they will need either repairing or replacing. The job will probably take Pete between two and six hours, depending on what he has to do.

What types of scaffolding do you think might be suitable for Pete's job? Can you think of anything Pete will have to consider while he prepares for and carries out this task? Think about things like egress and exit points, whether or not the area is closed off to the public and how long Pete will be working at height etc.

Knowledge check

1. Name four different methods of gaining height while working.

2. What must be done before any work at height is carried out?

3. What are your three health and safety duties when working at height?

4. As a rule, what is the maximum time you should work from a ladder or stepladder?

5. How should a wooden stepladder be checked before use?

6. When storing a wooden pole ladder, why does it need to be evenly supported along its length?

7. Explain the 1:4 (or 75°) ratio rule which should be observed when erecting a ladder.

8. When should a trestle platform be used?

9. What two types of board can be used as a platform with a trestle frame?

10. Why should you only use a specially designed hop-up?

11. There are two types of tubular scaffolding – what are they and how do they differ?

12. What are the eight questions you should ask yourself before using scaffolding?

13. In order to increase the height of a tower scaffold, what else has to be increased and by how much?

14. How high should scaffold guardrails be?

15. What is the only way you should access scaffolding?

16. When can safety netting be used?

17. How does an airbag safety system work?

Principles of building

OVERVIEW

Whatever type of building is being constructed there are certain principles/elements that must be included, for example a block of flats and a warehouse will all have foundations, a roof, etc.

In Chapter 1, you learned about different types of building. In this chapter, you will have a more in-depth look at the elements behind the main principles of building work.

This chapter will cover the following topics:

- Structural loading
- Substructure
- Superstructure
- Primary elements
- Secondary elements
- Finishing elements
- Services.

These topics can be found in the following modules:

CC 1003K	CC 2003K
CC 1003S	CC 2003S

This chapter will only look briefly at the components contained within buildings. For more detailed information on carpentry components, check the relevant chapter in this book. For all other components, check the relevant book from Heinemann's Carillion Construction series.

Structural loading

The main parts of a building that are in place to carry a load are said to be in a constant state of **stress**.

There are three main types of stress:

- Tension pulls or stretches a material and can have a lengthening effect.
- Compression squeezes the material and can have a shortening effect.
- Shear occurs when one part of a component slips or slides over another causing a slicing effect.

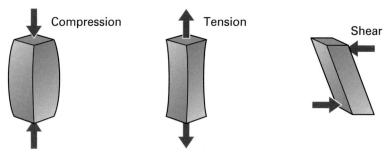

Figure 4.1 The three types of stress

To cause one of these types of stress a component or member must be under the strain of a load. Within construction there are two main types of loading:

- Dead load – the weight of the building itself and the materials used to construct the building, covering components such as floors and roofs.
- Imposed loads – any moveable loads like furniture as well as natural forces such as wind, rain and snow.

To cope with the loads that a building must withstand there are load-bearing structural members strategically placed throughout the building.

There are three main types of load bearing members:

- Horizontal members – One of the most common type of horizontal members is a floor joist, which carries the load and transfers it back to its point of support. The horizontal member, when under loading, can bend and be in all three types of stress, with the top in compression, the bottom in tension and the ends in shear.

Definition

stress – a body that has a constant force or system of forces exerted upon it resulting in strain or deformation

Remember

Where you are in the country will determine what materials you use for constructing. For example, some places with a lot of snowfall will require stronger structures to deal with the extra load from the snow

The bending can be contained by using correctly stress-graded materials or by adding a load-bearing wall to support the floor.

- Vertical members – Any walls or columns that are in place to transfer the loads from above (including horizontal members) down to the substructure and foundations have vertical members. Vertical members are usually in a compression state.

- Bracing members – Bracing members are usually fitted diagonally to form a triangle which stiffens the structure. Bracing members can be found in roofs and even on scaffolding. Bracing is usually in compression or tension.

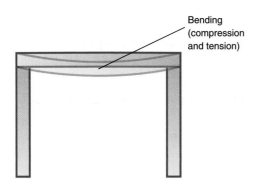
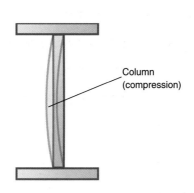
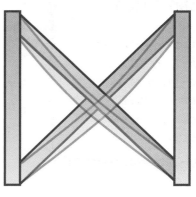

Figure 4.2 Horizontal structural members   **Figure 4.3** Vertical structural members   **Figure 4.4** Bracing structural members

Substructure

All buildings will start with the substructure – that is, all of the structure below ground and up to and including the damp proof course (DPC). The purpose of the substructure is to receive the loads from the main building (superstructure) and transfer them safely down to a suitable load-bearing layer of ground.

The main part of the substructure is the foundations. When a building is at the planning stage, the entire area – including the soil – will be surveyed to check what depth, width and size of foundation will be required. This is vital: the wrong foundation could lead to the building subsiding or even collapsing.

All buildings have a substructure

Did you know?

During the surveying of the soil, the density and strength of the soil are tested and laboratory tests check for harmful chemicals contained within the soil

The main type of foundation is a strip foundation. Depending on the survey reports and the type of building, one of four types of foundation will usually be used.

- Narrow strip foundation - the most common foundation used for most domestic dwellings and low-rise structures.

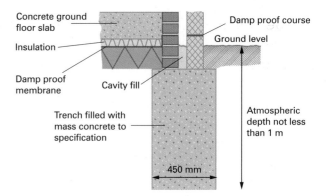

Figure 4.5 Narrow strip foundation

- Wide strip foundation – used for heavier structures or where weak soil is found.

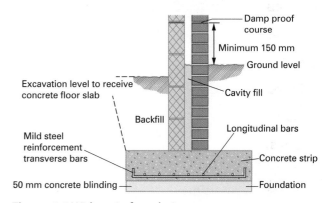

Figure 4.6 Wide strip foundation

- Raft foundation – used where very poor soil is found. This is basically a slab of concrete that is thicker around the edges.

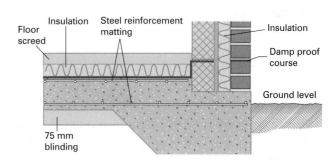

Figure 4.7 Raft foundation

- Pad foundation – where pads are placed at strategic points, with concrete beams placed across the pad to spread the load.

Once the substructure is in place, the building is then built on top of it.

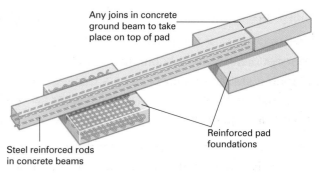

Figure 4.8 Pad foundation

Superstructure

The superstructure covers everything above the substructure, from walls to floors to roofing. The purpose of the superstructure is to enclose and divide space, as well as spread loads safely into the substructure.

Within the superstructure, you will find the primary, secondary and finishing elements, as well as the services.

Primary elements

The primary elements are the main supporting, enclosing and protecting elements of the superstructure. They divide space and provide floor-to-floor access.

The main primary elements are:

- walls
- floors
- roofs
- stairs.

Walls

There are two main types of wall within a building: external and internal.

External walls

External walls come in a variety of styles, but the most common is cavity walling. Cavity walling is simply two brick walls built parallel to each other, with a gap between acting as the cavity. The cavity wall acts as a barrier to weather, with the outer leaf preventing rain and wind penetrating the inner leaf. The cavity is usually filled with insulation to prevent heat loss.

Timber kit houses are becoming more and more common as they can be erected to a wind and watertight stage within a few days. The principle is similar to a cavity wall: the inner skin is a timber frame clad in timber sheet material, covered in a breathable membrane to prevent water and moisture penetrating the timber. The outer skin is usually face brickwork.

There are also other types of exterior walling, such as solid stone or log cabin style. Industrial buildings may have steel walls clad in sheet metal.

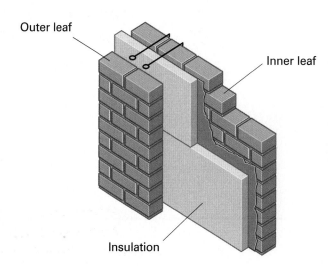

Figure 4.9 A cavity wall

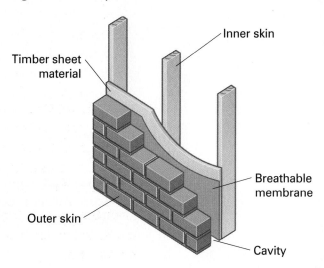

Figure 4.10 A timber and cavity wall

Internal walls

Internal walls are either load bearing – meaning they support any upper floors or roof – or are in place to divide rooms into shapes and sizes.

Internal walls also come in a variety of styles. Here is a list of the most common types.

- Solid block walls – simple block work, either covered with plasterboard or plastered over to give a smooth finish, to which wallpaper or paint is applied. Solid block walls offer low thermal and sound insulation qualities but advances in technology and materials means that blocks such as thermalite blocks can give better sound and heat insulation.

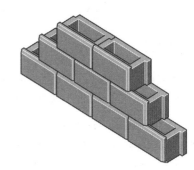

Figure 4.11 Solid block wall

- Solid brick walling – usually made with face brickwork as a decorative finish. It is unusual for all walls within a house to be made from brickwork.

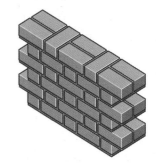

Figure 4.12 Solid brick wall

- Timber stud walling – more common in timber kit houses and newer buildings. Timber stud walling is also preferred when dividing an existing room, as it is quicker to erect. Clad in plasterboard and plastered to a smooth finish, timber stud partitions can be made more fire resistant and sound/thermal qualities can be improved with the addition of insulation or different types of plasterboard. Another benefit of timber stud walling is that timber noggins can be placed within the stud to give additional fixings for components such as radiators or wall units. Timber stud walling can also be load bearing, in which case thicker timbers are used.

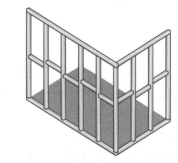

Figure 4.13 Timber stud wall

- Metal stud walling – similar to timber stud, except metal studs are used and the plasterboard is screwed to the studding.

Figure 4.14 Metal stud wall

- Grounds lats – timber battens that are fixed to a concrete or stone wall to provide a flat surface, to which plasterboard is attached and a plaster finish applied.

Floors

There are two main types of floor: ground and upper.

Ground floors

There are a few main types of ground floor. These are the ones you will most often come across.

- Suspended timber floor – a floor where timber joists are used to span the floor. The size of floor span determines the depth and thickness of the timbers used. The joists are either built into the inner skin of brickwork, sat upon small walls (dwarf/sleeper wall), or some form of joist hanger is used. The joists should span the shortest distance and sometimes dwarf/sleeper walls are built in the middle of the span to give extra support or to go underneath load-bearing walls. The top of the floor is decked with a suitable material (usually chipboard or solid pine tongue and groove boards). As the floor is suspended, usually with crawl spaces underneath, it is vital to have air bricks fitted, allowing air to flow under the floor, preventing high moisture content and timber rot.

- Solid concrete floor – concrete floors are more durable and are constructed on a sub-base incorporating hardcore, damp proof membranes and insulation. The depth of the hardcore and concrete will depend on the building and will be set by the *Building Regulations* and the local authority. Underfloor heating can be incorporated into a solid concrete floor. Great care must be taken when finishing the floor to ensure it is even and level.

- Floating floor – basic timber floor constructions that are laid on a solid concrete floor. The timbers are laid in a similar way to joists, though they are usually 50 mm thick maximum as there is no need for support. The timbers are laid on the floor at predetermined centres, and are not fixed to the concrete base (hence floating floor); the decking is then fixed on the timbers. Insulation or underfloor heating can be placed between the timbers to enhance the thermal and acoustic properties.

Figure 4.15 Ground lats

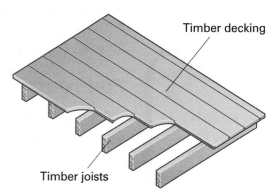

Timber decking

Timber joists

Figure 4.16 Suspended timber floor

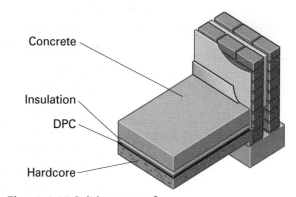

Concrete

Insulation

DPC

Hardcore

Figure 4.17 Solid concrete floor

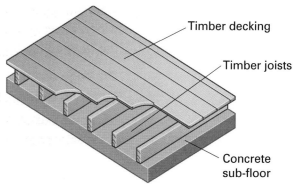

Timber decking

Timber joists

Concrete sub-floor

Figure 4.18 Floating floor

Upper floors

Again, solid concrete slabs can be used in larger buildings, but the most common type of upper floor is the suspended timber floor. As before, the joists are either built into the inner skin of brickwork or supported on some form of joist hanger. Spanning the shortest distance, with load-bearing walls acting as supports, it is vital that **regularised joists** are used as a level floor and ceiling are required. The tops of the joists are again decked out, with the underside being clad in plasterboard and insulation placed between the joists to help with thermal and sound properties.

Roofs

Although there are several different types of roofing, all roofs will either technically be a flat roof or a pitched roof.

Flat roofs

A flat roof is a roof with a pitch of 10° or less. The pitch is usually achieved through laying the joists at a pitch, or by using **firring pieces**.

The main construction method for a flat roof is similar to that for a suspended timber floor, with the edges of the joists being supported either via a hanger or built into the brickwork, or even a combination of both. Once the joists are laid and firring pieces are fitted (if required), insulation and a vapour barrier are put in place. The roof is then decked on top and usually plasterboarded on the underside. The decking on a flat roof must be waterproof, and can be made from a wide variety of materials, including fibreglass or bitumen-covered boarding with felt layered on it.

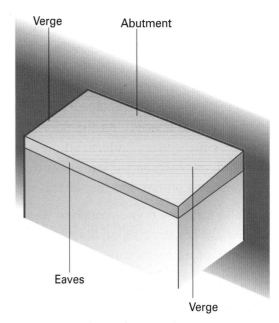

Figure 4.19 Flat roof terminology

Drainage of flat roofs is vital. The edge where the fall leads to must have suitable guttering to allow rainwater to run away, and not down the face of the wall.

Pitched roofs

There are several types of pitch roof, from the basic gable roof to more complex roofs such as mansard roofs. Whichever type of roof is being fitted to a building, it will most likely be constructed in one of the following ways.

- Prefabricated truss roof – as the name implies, this is a roof that has prefabricated members called trusses. Trusses are used to spread the load of the roof and to give it the required shape. Trusses are factory-made, delivered to site and lifted into place, usually by a crane. They are also easy and quick to fit: either they are nailed to a wall plate or held in place by truss clips. Once fitted, bracing is attached to keep the trusses level and secure from wind. Felt is then fixed to the trusses and tiles or slate are used to keep the roof and dwelling waterproof.

Figure 4.20 Duo pitch roof with gable ends

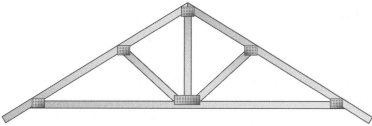

Figure 4.21 Prefabricated wooden roof truss

- Traditional/cut roof – an alternative to trusses, the cut roof uses loose timbers that are cut in-situ to give the roof its shape and spread the relevant load. More time-consuming and difficult to fit than trusses, the cut roof uses rafters that are individually cut and fixed in place, with two rafters forming a sort of truss. Once the rafters are all fixed, the roof is finished with felt and tiles or slate.

Metal trusses can also be used for industrial or more complex buildings.

To finish a roof where it meets the exterior wall (eaves), you must fix a vertical timber board (fascia) and a horizontal board (soffit) to the foot of the rafters/trusses. The fascia and soffit are used to close off the roof space from insects and birds.

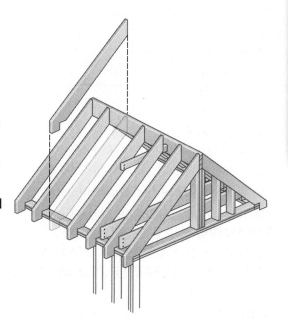

Figure 4.22 Individually cut rafters

Did you know?

Due to the fact that heat rises, the majority of heat loss that occurs is through a building's roof. Insulation such as mineral wool or polystyrene must be fitted to roof spaces and ideally any intermediate floors

Ventilators are attached to the soffits to allow air into the roof space, preventing rot, and guttering is attached to the fascia board to channel the rainwater into a drain.

Stairs

Stairs are used to provide access between different floors of a dwelling or to gain access to a higher/lower area. Stairs are made up of a number of steps, and each continuous set of steps running in the same direction is known as a flight. Steps are made of vertical boards called risers and horizontal boards called treads.

There are various types of stair, ranging from spiral staircases(often fitted where there is a lack of space) to multi-flight staircases, such as dog-leg or half-turn stairs.

Stairs are strictly governed by the *Building Regulations*, and there are numerous requirements that must be adhered to when constructing and installing them.

Stairs are generally made from three types of material:

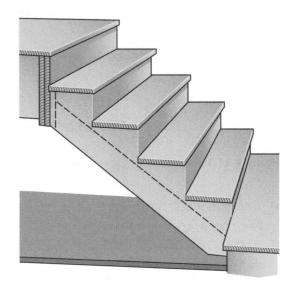

- timber – the most common type of stair, used widely in almost all buildings

- in-situ cast concrete – a wooden frame is constructed around the stairwell and concrete is poured into the frame, forming the staircase

- pre-cast concrete – concrete cast in large moulds to form the staircase, usually found in flat stairwells and other areas of heavy use

Figure 4.23 A simple staircase

- steel – usually found on the exterior of buildings in the form of fire escapes, etc.

Secondary elements

The secondary elements are not essential to the building's strength or structure, but provide a particular function, such as completing openings in walls, etc.

The main secondary elements are:

- frames and linings
- doors

- windows
- architrave and skirting.

Frames and linings

Frames and linings are fitted around openings, and are used to allow components such as windows and doors to be fitted. The frame or lining is fitted to the wall and usually finished flush with the walls; the joint between the frame or lining and the wall is covered by the architrave.

Doors

The main purpose of a door is to provide access from one room to another, and to allow a space to be closed off for security/thermal/sound reasons.

Doors come in many varieties, shapes and sizes; the type you need will be determined by where the door is being fitted and what for. Exterior doors are generally thicker and are fitted with more ironmongery such as letter plates and locks. Some interior doors will have locks fitted as well, such as bathrooms or doors that need to be secure.

As well as solid timber, doors can also have glass in them and may be graded for fire resistance.

Windows

Windows are fitted to allow natural light to enter the building with minimal loss of heat. Again, windows come in a variety of shapes and styles. There is also a choice of glass that is fitted in the window, which can be decorative and heat-loss resistant.

Architraves and skirting

Architraves are decorative mouldings used to hide the gap between frames and the wall finish. Skirting is moulding that covers the gap between the floor and base of a wall. These mouldings come in a variety of **profiles** such as torus and ogee.

As well as architrave and skirting, other mouldings can be used, such as picture and dado rails.

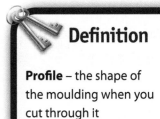

Definition

Profile – the shape of the moulding when you cut through it

Finishing elements

Finishing elements are the final surfaces of an element, which can be functional or decorative.

The main finishing elements are:

- plaster
- render
- paint
- wallpaper.

Plaster

Plaster can be used on a variety of wall surfaces to give a smooth and even finish. The plaster comes in powder form, usually bagged, and is mixed with water until it reaches a consistency that allows it to be applied to the surface and trowelled smooth. Ready-mix plaster is also available, but is more expensive, especially when a lot of surfaces have to be plastered.

These are the main surfaces to which plaster is applied.

- Brick/block work – prior to application, a bonding agent must first be applied to the wall (usually a coat of watered down PVA), to help the plaster adhere to the surface. Usually a first coat of bonding plaster is applied to the wall to give it a level and flat surface; when this is dry, a second, finish coat is applied. As the finish coat is drying, the plasterer will work on the wall, smoothing it out until it is as smooth as glass.

- Plasterboard – as plasterboard is a flat surface to begin with, a bonding coat is rarely used. Generally, the plasterboard is fixed with the back face (the face with the writing) exposed to give better adhesion. Whether it is a wall or a ceiling, the plasterer will again work the finish coat to a very smooth surface.

- Lath and plaster – this is usually found in old properties. The laths are thin strips of wood, which are fixed to the wall with small gaps between to give the plaster a **key**. Once the laths are fixed the plasterer will apply bonding and finish coats the same as before.

Plasterboard with a tapered edge can also be fixed to the walls. In this case, instead of plastering the entire wall, the plasterer will simply fill the nail/screw holes, fit tape where the plasterboard joins are, and fill only the joints. Pre-mixed plaster is usually used for this; when it is dry, a light sanding is required to give a smooth finish. This method is preferred in newer buildings, especially timber kit houses.

Lath and plaster

Not all walls are plastered smooth, as some clients may require a rough or patterned finish. Although not technically a plaster, Artex™ is often used to give decorative finishes, especially on ceilings.

Render

Render is similar to plaster in that it is trowelled on to brick or block work to give a finish. Applied to external walls, the render must be waterproof to prevent damage to the walls. Different finishes are available, from stippling to patterned.

Plaster being applied and trowelled

Paint

Paint is applied to various surfaces and is available in many different types to suit the job they are required for. Paint is applied for a variety of reasons, the most common being to:

- protect – steel can be prevented from corroding due to rust, and wood can be prevented from rotting due to moisture and insect attack

- decorate – the appearance of a surface can be improved or given a special effect (for example marbling, wood graining)

- sanitise – a surface can be made more hygienic with the application of a surface coating, preventing penetration and accumulation of germs and dirt, and allowing easier cleaning.

Paint is either water-based or solvent-based. When a paint is water-based, it means that the main liquid part of the paint is water; with a solvent-based paint, a chemical has been used instead of water to dissolve the other components of the paint.

Water-based paint is generally used on walls and ceilings, while solvent-based paint is used on timber mouldings, doors, metals, etc.

There are other surface finishes besides paint such as varnish (used on wood), masonry paint (used on exterior walls) and preservatives, which are used to protect wood from weather and insect attack.

Wallpaper

Wallpapers are used to decorate walls; thicker wallpapers can also hide minor defects.

Basic wallpapers are made from either wood pulp or vinyl.

Wood-pulp papers can be used as preparatory papers or finish papers. Preparatory papers are usually painted with emulsion to provide a finish, or they can be used as a base underneath finish papers. Types of wood-pulp paper include plain, coloured and reinforced lining paper as well as wood chip.

Vinyl wallpaper is a hard-wearing wallpaper made from a PVC layer attached to a pulp backing paper. Types of vinyl paper include patterned, sculptured or blown vinyl.

Wallpaper is hung on a wall using a paste. Not all pastes have the same strength, so make sure you choose the correct paste for the type of paper you are using.

Services

The services are specialist components within a building ranging from running water to electricity.

The main services in a standard house are:

- Electrical – covers all electrical components within the building from lights to sockets. Electrical installation and maintenance work must be undertaken by a fully trained specialist as electricity can kill.

- Mechanical – covers things such as lifts. As with electrical services, work on mechanical services should only be undertaken by a specialist.

- Plumbing – can cover running water as well as gas, but only if the plumber has been recognised and qualified as a gas installation expert.

Remember

All service work must be carried out by a fully trained and competent person

FAQ

How do I know if the materials I am using are strong enough to carry the load?

On the specification you will find details of the sizes and type of materials to be used.

Do I have to fix battens to a wall before I plasterboard it?

No – the method called dot and dab can be used where plaster is dabbed onto the back of the plasterboard and then pushed onto the wall.

On the job: Identifying load-bearing walls

Jay and Ella are out pricing up a job to place a doorway into a solid wall. Jay says that it will only take a few hours to knock through the brickwork and put a frame in. Ella is not so sure: she thinks the wall may be load bearing. How can they check the wall is load bearing? And what should be done if it is?

Knowledge check

1. State the four main principles of building.

2. List the three main types of stress.

3. What is the main purpose of the substructure?

4. List three different types of foundation.

5. What are the four main primary elements?

6. Give a brief description of external walling.

7. What is the difference between a truss roof and a cut roof?

8. What are the four main secondary elements? Why are they secondary?

9. List four main finishing elements.

10. Give a brief description of the process involved with lath and plaster.

11. What is vinyl wallpaper made from?

12. Give three reasons why paint is used.

13. What are the three main services?

chapter 3

Handling and storage of materials

OVERVIEW

Work in any building trade involves handling and storing materials, tools and equipment, sometimes under difficult conditions. The cost of injuries from poor or careless handling practice is enormous and careless storage risks damage, loss and theft of materials and equipment. This can cause delays and unnecessary cost to contractors. These risks can be minimised by following a few simple guidelines and applying a level of common sense when moving and storing materials and equipment.

This chapter will cover the following topics:

- Safe handling
- Paints and decorating equipment
- Wood and sheet materials
- Joinery components
- Ironmongery
- Adhesives
- Bricks, blocks and other bricklaying materials
- Aggregates and bagged materials
- Chemicals
- Highly flammable liquids
- Glass.

These topics can be found in the following modules:

CC 1001K	CC 1001S

Safe handling

Chapter 2 *Health and safety* explains safe **manual handling** methods in more detail – see page 43–45. When handling any materials or equipment, always think about the health and safety issues involved and remember manual handling practices explained to you during your induction.

You are not expected to remember everything but basic common sense will help you to work safely.

- Always wear your safety helmet and boots at work.
- Wear gloves and ear defenders when necessary.
- Keep your work areas free from debris and materials, tools and equipment not being used.
- Wash your hands before eating.
- Use barrier cream before starting work.
- Always use correct lifting techniques.

Ensure you follow instructions given to you at all times when moving any materials or equipment. The main points to remember are:

- always try to avoid manual handling (or use mechanical means to aid the process)
- always assess the situation first to establish the best method of handling the load
- always reduce any risks as much as possible (for example split a very heavy load, move obstacles from your path before lifting)
- tell others around you what you are doing
- if you need help with a load, get it. Do not try to lift something beyond what you can manage.

Paint and decorating equipment

Liquid material

Oil-based products

Oil-based products such as gloss and varnish should be stored on clearly marked shelves and with their labels turned to the front. They should always be used in date order, which means that new stock should be stored at the back with old stock at the front. Varied colours can also be arranged by BS4800 number, with similar colours or shades grouped together.

Oil-based products should be **inverted** at regular intervals to stop settlement and separation of the ingredients. They must also be kept in tightly sealed containers to stop the product **skinning**. Storage at a constant temperature will ensure the product retains its desired consistency.

Correct storage of paints

Water-based products

Water-based products, such as emulsions and acrylics, should also be stored on shelves with labels to the front and in date order.

Some water-based products have a very limited shelf life and must be used before their use-by date. As with oil-based products, water-based products keep best if stored at a constant temperature. It is also important to protect them from frost to prevent the water component of the product from freezing.

Powdered materials

Powdered materials a decorator might use include textured coatings such as Artex®, fillers, paste and sugar soap.

Large items such as heavy bags should be stored at ground or platform level. Smaller items can be stored on shelves while sealed containers, such as a bin, are ideal for loose materials.

Powdered materials can have a limited shelf life and can set in high humidity conditions. They must also be protected from frost and exposure to any moisture, including condensation. These types of materials must not be stored in the open air.

Definition

Inverted – tipped and turned upside down

Skinning – the formation of a skin which occurs when the top layer dries out

Did you know?

Storage instructions can usually be found on the product label or in a manufacturer's information leaflet

Remember

Heavy materials should be stored at low levels to aid manual handling and should never be stacked more than two levels high

Note

Due to frost attack, it is not a good idea to leave emulsions in a garage or shed over the winter

Definition

Volatile – quick to evaporate (turn to a gas)

Safety tip

Some larger bags of powdered materials are heavier than they first appear. Make sure you use the correct manual handling techniques (see Chapter 2)

Substances hazardous to health

Some substances the decorator will work with are potentially hazardous to health, with **volatile** and highly flammable characteristics. The Control of Substances Hazardous to Health (COSHH) Regulations apply to such materials and detail how they must be stored and handled (see Chapter 2 *Health and safety*, page 36–37, for general information about COSHH).

Decorating materials that might be hazardous to health include spirits (i.e. methylated and white), turpentine (turps), paint thinners and varnish removers. These should be stored out of the way on shelves, preferably in a suitable locker or similar room that meets the requirements of COSHH. The temperatures must be kept below 15°C as a warmer environment may cause storage containers to expand and blow up.

The storage of liquefied petroleum gas and other highly flammable liquids is covered later in this chapter on pages 108–109.

Paper material

Correct storage of wallpaper

Wallpaper

Wallpaper rolls must be stored in racks with their ends protected from damage. They should also be stored in batches with their identifying number clearly marked. Rolls should be kept wrapped and protected from dust and they should never be in direct sunlight, which can result in fading of colours.

Some special wall coverings such as **lincrusta** have a shelf life that should be taken into consideration, ensuring that the oldest stock is used first.

Abrasive papers

Abrasive papers should be stored in packets that clearly identify them with respect to grade (most abrasive papers are labelled on the back with the grade of grit and thickness of paper). They should be stored on shelves ensuring that sheets are kept flat and rolls are stored upright or on reels.

Abrasive papers must be kept away from excessive heat as this makes them brittle. Dampness and condensation must also be avoided as its weakens glass papers and some garnet papers by softening the glue that binds the grit to the paper.

Decorating tools and equipment

Dust sheets

Dust sheets should be folded neatly and stored on shelving. It is best to store clean sheets and dirty sheets separately in order to avoid contamination. Sheets must always be stored dry in order to prevent **mildew** attack and fabric fatigue (when fabric disintegrates in the hand like damp paper).

Brushes

Used brushes should be cleaned thoroughly and either hung up to dry or laid flat on well-ventilated shelving. New brushes should be kept wrapped until they are needed. Mildew can grow on wet brushes that are not left to dry thoroughly, which can destroy the filling. Brushes that are stored for long periods without use should be treated with some form of insecticide to protect them from moth attack. Moth balls are ideal for this protection.

Correct storage of a variety of tools and equipment

Rollers

After cleaning to remove all traces of paint and cleaner, roller sleeves should be hung up to dry in well-ventilated areas. Mohair and lambswool sleeves will need extra consideration and you should always refer to the manufacturer's instructions.

Steel tools

Before storing, steel tools must be thoroughly cleaned and lightly oiled. A rustproof, oiled paper wrapping may be appropriate for long-term storage.

Did you know?

When applying paints, wallpaper and decorative materials, the temperature is important as being too hot or cold will affect the finish

Definition

Lincrusta – a wall-hanging with a relief pattern used to imitate surface such as wood panelling

Definition

Mildew – a fungus that grows in damp conditions

Wood and sheet materials

There are various types of wood and sheet materials available, but the most common are as follows.

Carcassing timber

Carcassing timber is wood used for non-load-bearing jobs such as ceiling and floorboard supports, stud wall partitions and other types of framework. It should normally be stored outside under a covered framework. It should be placed on timber bearers clear of the ground. The ground should be free of vegetation and ideally covered over with concrete. This reduces the risk of absorption of ground moisture, which can damage the timber and cause wet rot. Piling sticks or cross-bearers should be placed between each layer of timber, about 600 mm apart, to provide support and allow air circulation. Tarpaulins or plastic covers can be used to protect the timber from the elements, however care must be taken to allow air to flow freely through the stack. See Figure 5.1.

Remember

The storage racks used to store wood must take account of the weight of the load. Access to the materials being stored is another important consideration

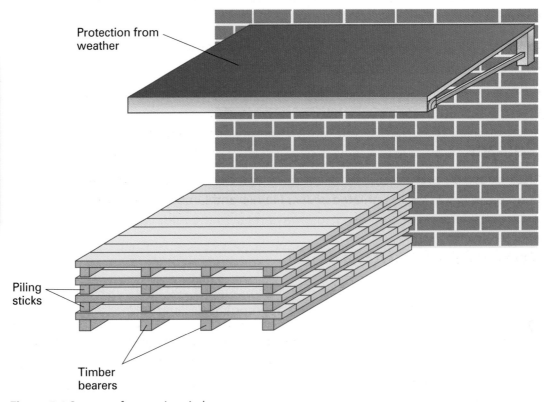

Figure 5.1 Storage of carcassing timber

Joinery grade and hardwoods

These timbers should be stored under full cover wherever possible, preferably in a storage shed. Good ventilation is needed to avoid build-up of moisture through absorption. This type of timber should also be stored on bearers on a well-prepared base.

Plywood and other sheet materials

All sheet materials should be stored in a dry, well-ventilated environment. Specialised covers are readily available to give added protection for most sheet materials, helping to prevent condensation caused when non-specialised types of sheeting are used.

Sheet materials should be stacked flat on timber cross-bearers, spaced close enough together to prevent sagging. Alternatively, where space is limited, sheet materials can be stored on edge in purpose-made racks which allow the sheets to rest against the backboard. There should be sufficient space around the plywood for easy loading and removal. The rack should be designed to allow sheets to be removed from either the front or the ends.

Leaning sheets against walls is not recommended, as this makes them bow, which is difficult to correct.

For sheet materials with faces or decorative sides, the face sides should be placed against each other to minimise the risk of damage due to friction of the sheets when they are moved. Different sizes, grades and qualities of sheet materials should be kept separate with off-cuts stacked separately from the main stack.

Sheet materials are awkward, heavy and prone to damage so extra care is essential when transporting them. Always ensure that the correct PPE is worn.

Joinery components

Joinery components, such as doors or kitchen units, must be stored safely and securely to prevent damage. Doors, windows, frames, etc. should ideally be stored flat on timber bearers under cover, to protect them from exposure to the weather. Where space is limited, they can be stored upright using a rack system (similar to the way sheet materials are stored); however, they must never be leant against a wall, as this will bow the door/frame and make it very hard to fit.

Wall and floor units – whether they be kitchen, bedroom or bathroom units – must be stacked on a flat surface, and no more than two units high. As units can be made from porous materials such as chipboard, it is vital they are stored inside, preferably in the room where they are to be fitted to avoid double handling.

Find out

What are the PPE requirements when moving sheet materials?

Storage of sheet materials

Safety tip

Due to the size, shape and weight of sheet materials, always get help to lift and carry them. If possible, use a purpose-made plywood trolley which will transport the load for you

Protective sheeting should be used to cover units to prevent damage or staining from paints, etc.

Ideally all components and timber products such as architrave should be stored in the room where they are to be fitted: this will allow them to acclimatise to the room and prevent shrinkage or distortion after being fitted. This process is known as 'second seasoning'.

Figure 5.2 Doors should be stacked on a flat surface

Ironmongery

Ironmongery includes not just fittings and fixtures made of iron, but also hardware made from other materials including brass, chrome, porcelain and glass. Items you might come across include door handles, hooks, locks, hinges, window fittings, screws and bolts.

Examples of door furniture

Door furniture

Door furniture such as locks, bolts, letter boxes, knockers and handles etc. are 'desirable' items, which means that they are very likely to be stolen unless stored securely. A store person is usually responsible for the storage and distribution of such items and keeps a check on how many are given out and to whom.

In addition to being stored securely, door furniture should also be kept in separate compartments of a racking storage system or at least on shelving. Where possible all door furniture should be retained in the manufacturer's packaging until needed. This prevents damage and loss of components such as screws and keys. Large heavy items should be stored on lower shelves to avoid unnecessary lifting.

Fixings

Each type of fixing is designed for a specific purpose and includes items such as nails, screws, pins, bolts, washers, rivets and plugs. As with door furniture, fixings tend to disappear if their storage is not supervised and controlled by a store person.

Fixings must be stored appropriately to keep them in good condition and to make them easy to find. Where possible, they should be kept in bags or boxes clearly marked with their size and type. Storing them in separate compartments is the most convenient method of storage. This enables easy and fast selection when required and prevents the wrong fixing being used. Time taken to sort out different types and sizes of fixings that have become mixed up is a waste of your time and your employer's time.

Different types of fixings should be stored separately

Safety tip

Carelessly discarded fixings, such as nails, can be costly, but can also create health and safety hazards

Remember

Broken fixings should be disposed of carefully

Adhesives

Adhesives are substances used to bond (stick) surfaces together. Because of their chemical nature, there are a number of potentially serious risks connected with adhesives if they are not stored, used and handled correctly.

All adhesives should be stored and used in line with the manufacturer's instructions. This usually involves storing them on shelving, with labels facing outward, in a safe, secure area (preferably a lockable store room). It is important to keep the labels facing outwards so that the correct adhesive can be selected.

The level of risk associated with adhesive use is dependent on the type of adhesive. Some of the risks include:

- explosion
- poisoning
- skin irritation
- disease.

Adhesives should be stored according to the manufacturer's instructions

As explained in Chapter 2 *Health and safety*, these types of material are closely controlled by COSHH, which aims to minimise the risks involved with their storage and use.

All adhesives have a recommended **shelf life**. This must be taken into account when storing to ensure the oldest stock is stored at the front and used first. Remember to refer to the manufacturer's guidelines as to how long the adhesive will remain fit for purpose once opened. Adhesives can be negatively affected by poor storage, including loss in adhesive strength and extended setting time.

Definition

Shelf life – how long something will remain fit for its purpose while being stored

Bricks, blocks and other bricklaying materials

Bricks

Storage of bricks

Most bricks delivered to sites are now prepacked and banded using either plastic or metal bands to stop the bricks from separating until ready for use. The edges are also protected by plastic strips to help stop damage during moving, usually by forklift or crane. They are then usually covered in shrink-wrapped plastic to protect them from the elements.

Safety tip

Take care and stand well clear of a crane used for offloading bricks on delivery

On arrival to site they should be stored on level ground and stacked no more than two packs high, to prevent overreaching or collapse, which could result in injury to workers. They should be stored close to where they are required so further movement is kept to a minimum. On large sites they may be stored further away and moved by telescopic lifting vehicles to the position required for use.

Great care should be taken when using the bricks from the packs as, once the packaging is cut, the bricks can collapse causing injury and damage to the bricks, especially on uneven ground. Bricks should be taken from a minimum of three packs and mixed to stop changes in colour, as the position of the bricks during the kiln process can cause slight colour differences: the nearer the centre of the kiln, the lighter the colour; the nearer the edge of the kiln, the darker the colour as the heat is stronger. If the bricks are not mixed, you could get sections of brickwork in slightly different shades; this is called banding and in most cases is visible to the most inexperienced eye.

Did you know?

Efflorescence caused by soluble salts within the bricks can leave a stain. Brushing off the stain and coating with a suitable sealer can resolve the problem

If bricks are unloaded by hand they should be stacked on edge in rows, on firm, level and well-drained ground. The ends of the stacks should be bonded and no higher than 1.8 m. To protect the bricks from rain and frost, all stacks should be covered with a tarpaulin or polythene sheets.

Blocks

Blocks are made from concrete, which may be dense or lightweight. Lightweight blocks could be made from a fine aggregate that contains lots of air bubbles. The storage of blocks is the same as for bricks.

Paving slabs

Paving slabs are made from concrete or stone and are available in a variety of sizes, shapes and colours. They are used for pavements and patios, with some slabs given a textured top to improve appearance.

Storage of paving slabs

Paving slabs are normally delivered to sites by lorry and crane offloaded, some in wooden crates covered with shrink-wrapped plastic, or banded and covered on pallets. They should not be stacked more than two packs high for safety reasons and to prevent damage to the slabs due to weight pressure.

Paving slabs unloaded by hand are stored outside and stacked on edge to prevent the lower ones, if stored flat, from being damaged by the weight of the stack. The stack is started by laying about 10 to 12 slabs flat with the others leaning against these. If only a small number of slabs are to be stored, they can be stored flat (since the weight will be less).

Slabs should be stored on firm, level ground with timber bearers below to prevent the edges from getting damaged if placed on a solid surface. To provide protection from rain and frost, it is advisable to keep the slabs under cover, by placing a tarpaulin or polythene sheet over the top.

Paving slabs stacked flat

Paving slabs on pallet

Did you know?

The temperature must be taken into account when laying bricks and blocks as, if it is too cold, this will prevent the cement going off properly

Safety tip

When working with blocks, make sure you always wear appropriate PPE (personal protective equipment), that is boots, safety hat, gloves, goggles and face mask

Safety tip

It is good practice to put an intermediate flat stack in long rows to prevent rows from toppling

Kerbs

Kerbs are concrete units laid at the edges of roads and footpaths to give straight lines or curves and retain the finished surfaces. The size of a common kerb is 100 mm wide, 300 mm high and 600 mm long. Path edgings are 50 mm wide, 150 mm high and 600 mm long.

Kerbs should be stacked on timber bearers or with overhanging ends, which provides a space for hands or lifting slings if machine lifting is to be used. When they are stacked on top of each other, the stack must not be more than three kerbs high. To protect the kerbs from rain and frost it is advisable to cover them with a tarpaulin or sheet.

Stacked kerbs

Stacked lintels

Pre-cast concrete lintels

Lintels are components placed above openings in brick and block walls to bridge the opening and support the brick or block work above. Lintels made from concrete have a steel reinforcement placed near the bottom for strength, which is why pre-cast concrete lintels will have a 'T' or 'Top' etched into the top surface. Pre-cast concrete lintels come in a variety of sizes to suit the opening size. The stacking and storage methods are the same as for kerbs.

Drainage pipes

Drainage pipes are made from **vitrified** clay or plastic. Pipes made from clay may have a socket and spigot end or be plain and joined by plastic couplings. Plastic pipes are plain ended and joined by couplings, using a lubricant to help jointing.

Definition

Vitrified – a material that has been converted into a glass-like substance via exposure to high temperatures

Storage of drainage pipes and fittings

Pipes should be stored on a firm, level base, and prevented from rolling by placing wedges or stakes on either side of the stack. Do not stack pipes any higher than 1.5 m, and taper the stack towards the top.

Clay pipes with socket and spigot ends should be stored by alternating the ends on each row. They should also be stacked on shaped timber cross-bearers to prevent them from rolling.

Fittings and special shaped pipes, like bends, should be stored separately and, if possible, in a wooden crate until needed.

Remember

Clay pipes are easily broken if misused, so care must be taken when handling these items

Stacked drainage pipes

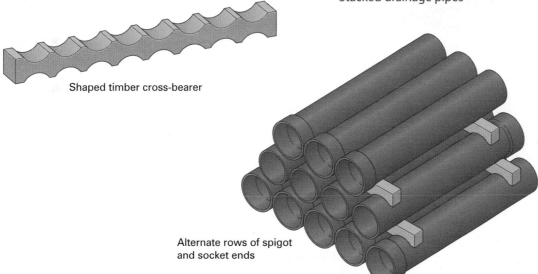

Shaped timber cross-bearer

Alternate rows of spigot and socket ends

Figure 5.3 Timber cross-bearer and pipes stacked on cross-bearer

Roofing tiles

Roofing tiles are made from either clay or concrete. They may be machine-made or handmade, and are available in a variety of shapes and colours. Many roofing tiles are able to interlock to prevent rain from entering the building. Ridge tiles are usually half round but sometimes they may be angled.

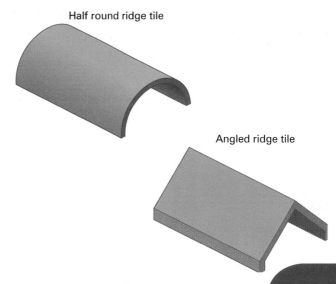

Half round ridge tile

Angled ridge tile

Figure 5.4 Roofing tiles

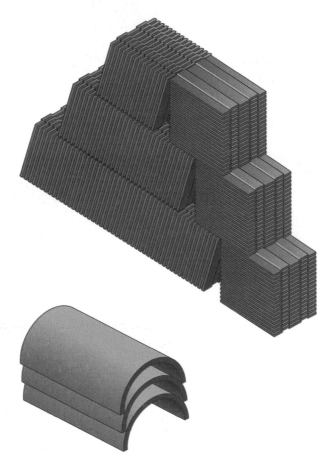

Figure 5.5 Stacks of roofing tiles

Storage of roofing tiles

Roofing tiles are stacked on edge to protect their 'nibs', and in rows on level, firm, well-drained ground. See Figure 5.3. They should not be stacked any higher than six rows high. The stack should be tapered to prevent them from toppling. The tiles at the end of the rows should be stacked flat to provide support for the rows.

Ridge tiles may be stacked on top of each other, but not any higher than ten tiles.

To protect roofing tiles from rain and frost before use, they should be covered with a tarpaulin or plastic sheeting.

Damp proof course (DPC)

A damp proof course (or DPC) and damp proof membranes are used to prevent damp from penetrating into a building. Flexible DPC may be made from polythene, bitumen or lead and is supplied in rolls of various widths for different uses.

Slate can also be used as a damp proof course – older houses often have slate but modern houses normally have polythene.

Damp proof membrane is used as a waterproof barrier over larger areas, such as under the concrete on floors etc. It is normally made of 1000-gauge polythene, and comes in large rolls, normally black or blue in colour.

Damp proof course (DPC)

Storage of rolled materials

Rolled materials, for example damp proof course or roofing felt, should be stored in a shed on a level, dry surface. Narrower rolls may be best stored on shelves but in all cases they should be stacked on end to prevent them from rolling and to reduce the possibility of them being damaged by compression.
See Figure 5.5. In the case of bitumen, the layers can melt together under pressure.

Figure 5.6 Rolled materials stored on end

Aggregates and bagged materials (sand, cement, plaster)

Aggregates

Aggregates are granules or particles that are mixed with cement and water to make mortar and concrete. Aggregates should be hard, durable and should not contain any form of plant life, or anything that can be dissolved in water.

Aggregates are classed in two groups:

1. Fine aggregates are granules that pass through a 5 mm sieve.

2. Coarse aggregates are particles that are retained by a 5 mm sieve.

The most commonly used fine aggregate is sand. Sand may be dug from pits and riverbeds, or dredged from the sea.

Good mortar should be mixed using 'soft' or 'building' sand. It should be well graded, which means having an equal quantity of fine, medium and large grains.

Did you know?

Sea sand contains salts, which may affect the quality of a mix. It should not be used unless it has been washed and supplied by a reputable company

Remember

Poorly graded sands, with single size particles, contain a greater volume of air and require cement to fill the spaces

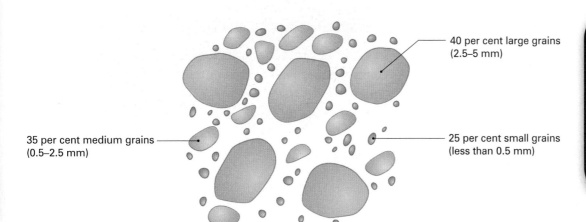

40 per cent large grains (2.5–5 mm)

35 per cent medium grains (0.5–2.5 mm)

25 per cent small grains (less than 0.5 mm)

Figure 5.7 Sand particles

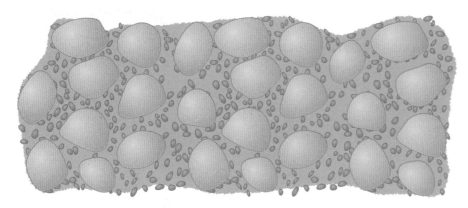

Figure 5.8 Mortar particles

Concrete should be made using 'sharp' sand, which is more angular and has a coarser feel than soft sand, which has more rounded grains.

When concreting, we also need 'coarse aggregate'. The most common coarse aggregate is usually limestone chippings, which are quarried and crushed to graded sizes, 10 mm, 20 mm or even larger.

Storage of aggregates

Aggregates are normally delivered in tipper lorries, although nowadays one-

Remember

The different sizes of aggregates should be stored separately to prevent the different aggregates getting mixed together

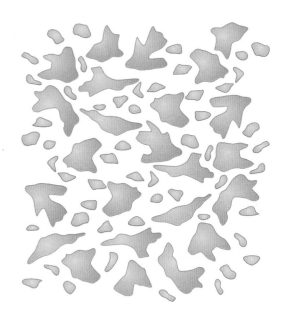

Figure 5.9 Concrete particles

tonne bags are available and may be crane handled. The aggregates should be stored on a concrete base, with a fall to allow for any water to drain away.

In order to protect aggregates from becoming contaminated with leaves and litter it is a good idea to situate stores away from trees and cover aggregates with tarpaulin or plastic sheets.

SAND

10mm

20mm

Base laid to a fall for drainage of the aggregates

Figure 5.10 Bays for aggregates

Bagged materials

Aggregates can be supplied as bagged materials, as can cement and plaster.

Plaster

Plaster is made from gypsum, water and cement or lime. Aggregates can also be added depending on the finish desired. Plaster provides a jointless, smooth, easily decorated surface for internal walls and ceilings.

Gypsum plaster

This is for internal use and contains different grades of gypsum. Plasters are available depending on the background finish. Browning is usually used as an undercoat on brickwork but in most cases, a one-coat plaster is used, and on plasterboard, board finish is used.

Cement-sand plaster

This is used for external rendering, internal undercoats and waterproofing finishing coats.

Lime-sand plaster

This is mostly used as an undercoat, but may sometimes be used as a finishing coat.

Storage of cement and plaster

Both cement and plaster are usually available in 25 kg bags. The bags are made from multi-wall layers of paper with a polythene liner. Care must be taken not to puncture the bags before use. Each bag, if offloaded manually, should be stored in a ventilated, waterproof shed, on a dry floor on pallets. If offloaded by crane they should be transferred to the shed and the same storage method used.

The bags should be kept clear of the walls, and piled no higher than five bags. It is most important that the bags are used in the same order as they were delivered. This minimises the length of time that the bags are in storage, preventing the contents from setting in the bags, which would require extra materials and cause added cost to the company.

Did you know?

On larger sites some companies use a machine spray system to cover large areas with plaster quickly, using many plasterers to complete the work

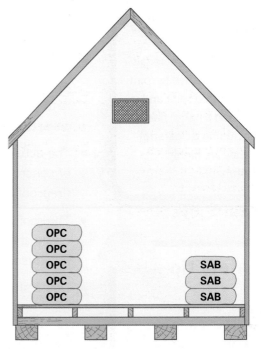

- Dry, ventilated shed

- Stock must be rotated so that old stock is used before new

- Not more than five bags high

- Clear of walls

- Off floor

Figure 5.11 Storage of cement and plaster bags in a shed

Chemicals

Chemicals such as brick cleaner or certain types of adhesive can be classified as dangerous chemicals. All chemicals should be stored in a locked area to prevent abuse or cross-contamination. You should refer to COSHH and/or the manufacturer to check storage details for any chemicals that you come across.

Highly flammable liquids

Liquefied Petroleum Gas (**LPG**), petrol, cellulose thinners, methylated spirits, chlorinated rubber paint and white spirit are all highly flammable liquids. These materials require special storage in order to ensure they do not risk injury to workers.

- Containers should only be kept in a special storeroom which has a floor made of concrete that slopes away from the storage area. This is to prevent leaked materials from collecting under the containers.

- The actual storeroom should be built of concrete, brick or some other fireproof material.

- The roof should be made from an easily shattered material in order to minimise the effect of any explosion.

- Doors should be at least 50 mm thick and open outwards.

- Any glass used in the structure should be wired and not less than 6 mm thick.

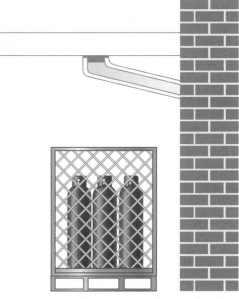

Figure 5.12 Storage of highly flammable liquids

- The standing area should have a sill surrounding it that it is deep enough to contain the contents of the largest container stored.

- Containers should always be stored upright.

- The area should not be heated.

- Electric lights should be intrinsically safe.

- Light switches should be flameproof and should be on the outside of the store.

- The building should be ventilated at high and low levels and have at least two exits.

- Naked flames and spark producing materials should be clearly prohibited, including smoking.

- The storeroom should be clearly marked with red and white squares and 'Highly Flammable' signage.

There are additional storage regulations for liquefied petroleum gas (**LPG**). LPG must be stored in the open and usually in a locked cage. It should be stored off the floor and protected from direct sunlight and frost or snow. The storage of LPG is governed by the Highly Flammable Liquids and Liquefied Petroleum Gases Regulations. Note that these regulations apply when 50 or more litres are stored, and permission must be obtained from the District Inspector of Factories.

Glass

Glass should be stored vertically in racks. The conditions for glass storage should be:

- clean – storing glass in dirty or dusty conditions can cause discoloration

- dry – if moisture is allowed between the sheets of glass it can make them stick together, which may make them difficult to handle and more likely to break.

If only a small number of sheets of glass are to be stored, they can be leant against a stable surface, as shown in the photo.

Storage of glass

Remember

Always wear appropriate PPE when handling glass

FAQ

How do I clean cotton dustsheets?

You will first need to shake the dustsheet to remove any loose dust, paint, wallpaper, etc. You should then try and remove anything that is stuck to the dustsheet, such as pieces of wallpaper. Most cotton dustsheets can be washed in a washing machine at a low temperature, but always check the manufacturer's instructions. You can also take dustsheets to a laundry, although this is only worth doing if they are expensive heavy-duty dustsheets. After washing, dustsheets should be allowed to dry thoroughly before being folded and stored in a dry place.

On the job: Storing materials and equipment

Christy is a first year apprentice and has been asked to look after the storage room of a local decorator as part of her training. Lydia has just completed her apprenticeship with the local decorator and has come over to Christy for a chat about looking after the store room. Lydia has told Christy not to worry too much about keeping the store room in order as most of the materials are constantly being used. Lydia has said that it is easier just to place items such as burning off equipment, drums of floor paint, dust sheets, powdered fillers and tubes of caulk in an easy to reach area, as it will save time when handing out items, and will save her the bother of repeatedly putting items into their correct storage place.

Do you think that Lydia is right? Would this save Christy time in the long run? Does it make sense to keep materials close at hand so Christy can hand items out more quickly, therefore making a good impression in regards to looking after the storeroom? Is Lydia thinking about safety or stock rotation when giving advice to Christy? How should the storeroom be looked after and where should these materials be kept?

Knowledge check

1. List some of the basic common sense things you can do to stay safe when loading and handling materials.

2. What might occur if dust sheets or brushes are stored in damp conditions?

3. How should wallpapers be stored?

4. What does the term 'shelf life' mean?

5. Name the four risks associated with adhesives.

6. What is the maximum height allowed for brick packs?

7. Describe how slabs should be stored.

8. Why should pipes be stacked on timber cross-bearers?

9. What is the most common fine aggregate?

10. How can you prevent aggregates from being contaminated?

11. How should bags of plaster and cement be stored?

12. What is LPG?

13. What do the labels on abrasive papers tell you?

14. Describe the characteristics of a special storeroom for highly flammable liquids.

15. What are the ideal conditions for glass storage and why?

chapter 6

Drawings

OVERVIEW

Drawings are the best way of communicating detailed and often complex information from the designer to all those concerned with a job or project. Drawings are part of the legal contract between client and contractor and mistakes, either in design or interpretation of the design, can be costly. Details relating to drawings must follow guidelines by the British Standards Institute: *BS 1192 Construction Drawing Practice*.

This chapter will help you to understand the basic principles involved in producing, using and reading drawings correctly.

This chapter will cover the following topics:

- Types of drawing
- Drawing equipment
- Scales, symbols and abbreviations
- Datum points
- Types of projection
- Contract documents.

These topics can be found in the following modules:

CC 2002K	CC 2003K
CC 2002S	CC 2003S

Types of drawing

Working drawings

Working drawings are scale drawings showing plans, elevations, sections, details and location of a proposed construction. They can be classified as:

- location drawings
- component range drawings
- assembly or detail drawings.

Location drawings

Location drawings include block plans and site plans.

Block plans identify the proposed site by giving a bird's eye view of the site in relation to the surrounding area. An example is shown in Figure 6.1.

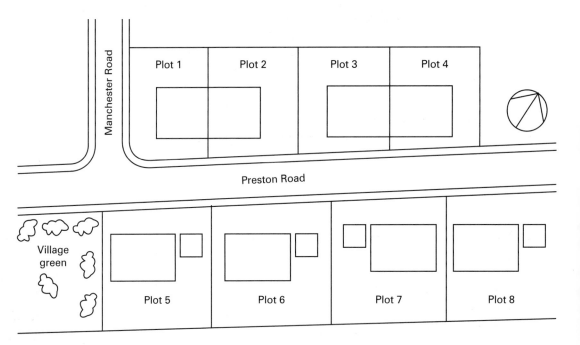

Figure 6.1 Block plan showing location

Site plans give the position of the proposed building and the general layout of the roads, services, drainage etc. on site. An example is shown in Figure 6.2.

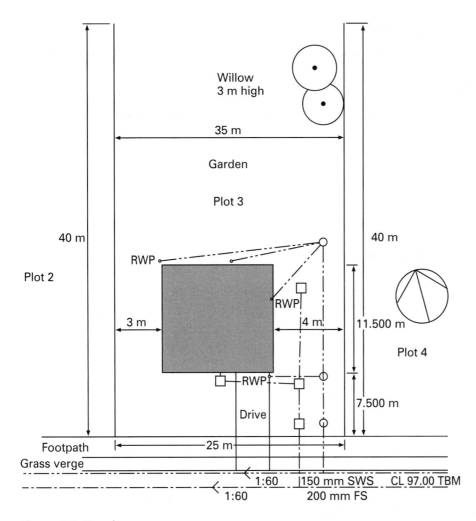

Figure 6.2 Site plan

Component range drawings

Component range drawings show the basic sizes and reference system of a standard range of components produced by a manufacturer. This helps in selecting components suitable for a task and available off-the-shelf. An example is shown in Figure 6.3.

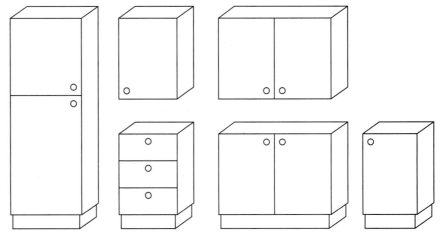

Figure 6.3 Component range drawing

Assembly or detail drawings

Assembly or detail drawings give all the information required to manufacture a given component. They show how things are put together and what the finished item will look like. An example is shown in Figure 6.4.

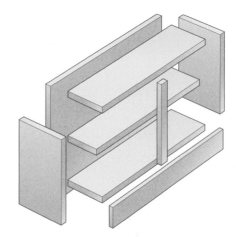

Figure 6.4 Assembly drawing

Title panels

Every drawing must have a title panel, which is normally located in the bottom right-hand corner of each drawing sheet. See Figure 6.5 for an example. The information contained in the panel is relevant to that drawing only and contains such information as:

- drawing title
- scale used
- draughtsman's name
- drawing number/ project number
- company name
- job/project title
- date of drawing
- revision notes
- projection type.

Remember

It is important to check the date of a drawing to make sure the most up-to-date version is being used, as revisions to drawings can be frequent

ARCHITECTS Peterson, Thompson Associates 237 Cumberland Way Ipswich IP3 7FT Tel: 01234 567891 Fax: 09876 543210 Email: enquiries@pta.co.uk	CLIENT Carillion Development
	JOB TITLE Appleford Drive Felixstowe 4 bed detached
DRAWING TITLE Plan – garage	SCALE: 1:50
	DRAWING NO: 2205-06
DATE: 27.08.2008	DRAWN BY: RW

Figure 6.5 Typical title panel

Drawing equipment

A good quality set of drawing equipment is required when producing drawings. It should include:

- set squares
- protractor
- compass
- dividers
- scale rule
- pencils
- eraser
- drawing board
- T-square.

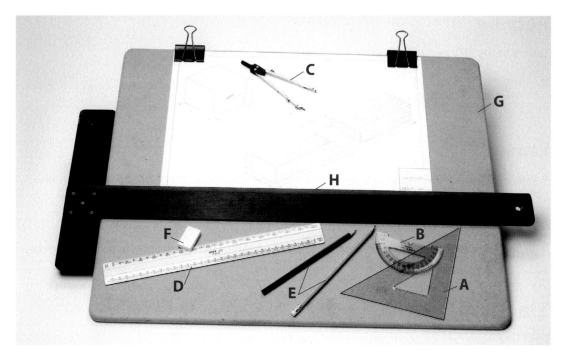

Drawing equipment

Set squares

Two set squares are required, one a 45° set square and the other a 60°/30° set square. These are used to draw vertical and inclined lines. A 45° set square (A) is shown in the photograph.

Protractor

A protractor (B) is used for setting out and measuring angles.

Compass and dividers

A compass (C) is used to draw circles and arcs. Dividers (not shown) are used for transferring measurements and dividing lines.

Scale rule

A scale rule that contains the following scales is to be recommended:

1:5/1:50   1:10/1:100   1:20/1:200   1:250/1:2500

An example (D) is shown in the photo.

Did you know?

Set squares, protractors and rules should be occasionally washed in warm soapy water

Pencils

Two pencils (E) are required:

- HB for printing and sketching
- 2H or 3H for drawing.

Eraser

A vinyl or rubber eraser (F) is required for alterations or corrections to pencil lines.

Drawing board

A drawing board (G) is made from a smooth flat surface material, with edges truly square and parallel.

T-square

The T-square (H) is used mainly for drawing horizontal lines.

Scales, symbols and abbreviations

Scales in common use

In order to draw a building on a drawing sheet, the building must be reduced in size. This is called a scale drawing.

The preferred scales for use in building drawings are shown in Table 6.1.

Type of drawing	Scales
Block plans	1:2500, 1:1250
Site plans	1:500, 1:200
General location drawings	1: 200, 1:100, 1:50
Range drawings	1:100, 1:50, 1:20
Detail drawings	1:10, 1:5, 1:1
Assembly drawings	1:20, 1:10, 1:5

Table 6.1 Preferred scales for building drawings

These scales mean that, for example, on a block plan drawn to 1:2500, one millimetre on the plan would represent 2500 mm (or 2.5 m) on the actual building. Some other examples are:

- On a scale of 1:50, 10 mm represents 500 mm.
- On a scale of 1:100, 10 mm represents 1000 mm (1.0 m).
- On a scale of 1:200, 30 mm represents 6000 mm (6.0 m).

Why not try these for yourself?

- On a scale of 1:50, 40 mm represents:…………
- On a scale of 1:200, 70 mm represents:…………
- On a scale of 1:500, 40 mm represents:………….

The use of scales can be easily mastered with a little practice.

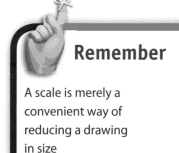

Remember

A scale is merely a convenient way of reducing a drawing in size

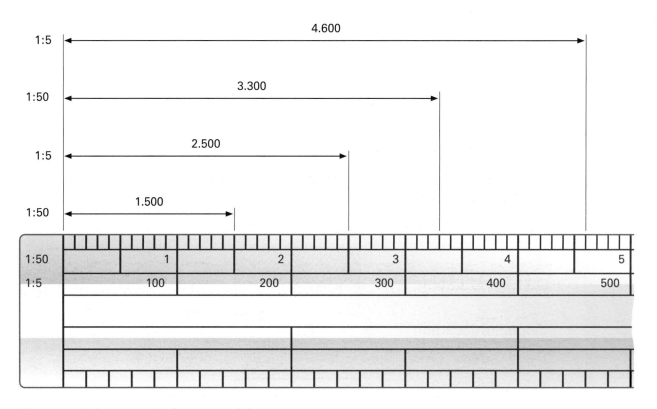

Figure 6.6 Rule with scales for maps and drawings

Variations caused through printing or copying will affect the accuracy of drawings. Hence, although measurements can be read from drawings using a rule with common scales marked, it is recommended that you work to written instructions and measurements wherever possible.

A rule marked with scales used in drawings or maps is illustrated in Figure 6.6.

Symbols and abbreviations

The use of symbols and abbreviations in the building industry enables the maximum amount of information to be included on a drawing sheet in a clear way. Figure 6.7 shows some recommended drawing symbols for a range of building materials.

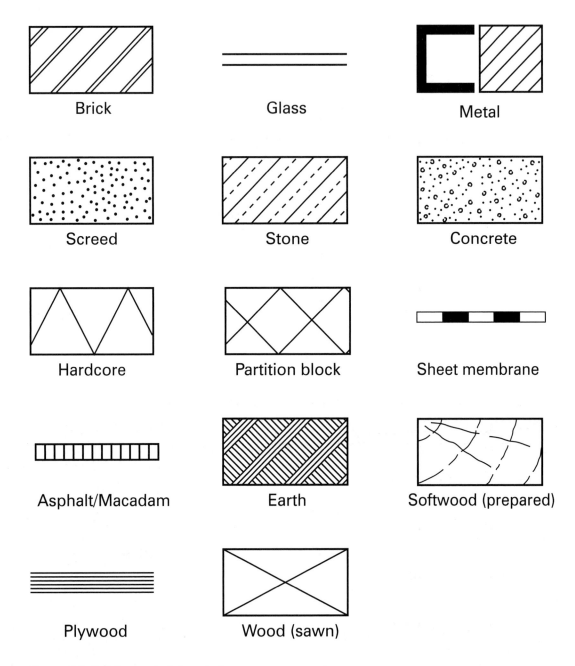

Figure 6.7 Building material symbols

Figure 6.8 illustrates the recommended methods for indicating types of doors and windows and their direction of opening.

Figure 6.9 shows some of the most frequently used graphical symbols, which are recommended in the British Standard BS 1192.

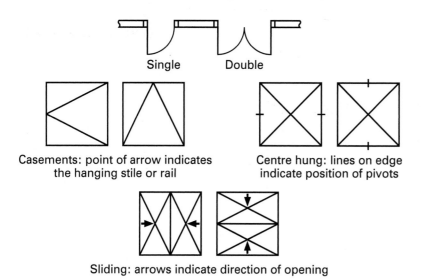

Figure 6.8 Doors and windows, type and direction of opening

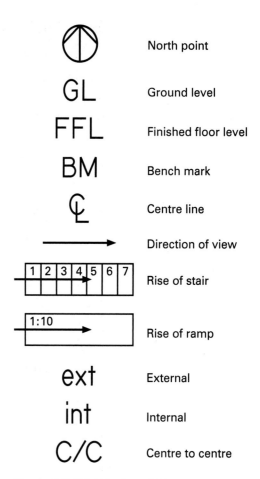

Figure 6.9 Graphical symbols

Table 6.2 lists some standard abbreviations used on drawings.

Item	Abbreviation	Item	Abbreviation
Airbrick	AB	Cement	ct
Asbestos	abs	Column	col
Bitumen	bit	Concrete	conc
Boarding	bdg	Cupboard	cpd
Brickwork	bwk	Damp proof course	DPC
Building	bldg	Damp proof membrane	DPM
Cast iron	CI	Drawing	dwg

Table 6.2 Standard abbreviations used on drawings (*continued overleaf*)

Item	Abbreviation	Item	Abbreviation
Foundation	fnd	Polyvinyl chloride	PVC
Hardboard	hdbd	Reinforced concrete	RC
Hardcore	hc	Satin anodised aluminium	SAA
Hardwood	hwd	Satin chrome	SC
Insulation	insul	Softwood	swd
Joist	jst	Stainless steel	SS
Mild steel	MS	Tongue and groove	T&G
Plasterboard	pbd	Wrought iron	WI
Polyvinyl acetate	PVA		

Table 6.2 Standard abbreviations used on drawings (continued)

FAQ

Why not just write the full words on a drawing?

This would take up too much space and clutter the drawing, making it difficult to read.

Datum points

The need to apply levels is required at the beginning of the construction process and continues right up to the completion of the building. The whole country is mapped in detail and the Ordnance Survey place datum points (bench marks) at suitable locations from which all other levels can be taken.

Ordnance bench mark (OBM)

OBMs are found cut into locations such as walls of churches or public buildings. The height of the OBM can be found on the relevant Ordnance Survey map or by contacting the local authority planning office. Figure 6.10 shows the normal symbol used, though it can appear as shown in Figure 6.11.

Site datum

It is necessary to have a reference point on site to which all levels can be related. This is known as the site datum. The site datum is usually positioned at a convenient height, such as finished floor level (FFL).

The site datum itself must be set in relation to some known point, preferably an OBM and must be positioned where it cannot be moved.

Figure 6.11 shows a site datum and OBM, illustrating the height relationship between them.

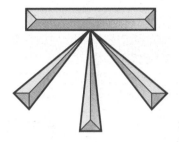

Figure 6.10 Ordnance bench mark

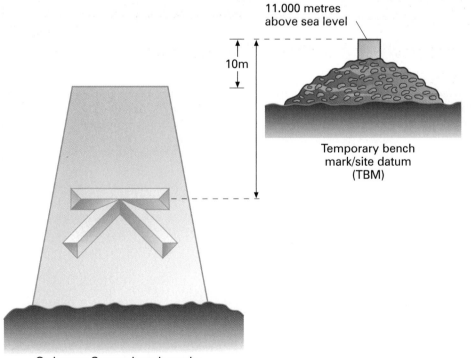

11.000 metres above sea level

10m

Temporary bench mark/site datum (TBM)

Ordnance Survey bench mark (O.S.B.M.) 10.000 metres above sea level

Figure 6.11 Site datum and OBM

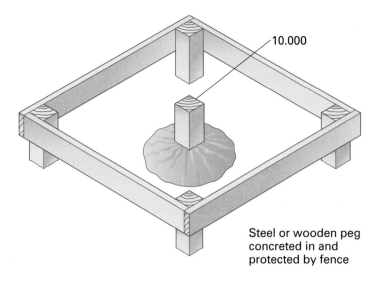

10.000

Steel or wooden peg
concreted in and
protected by fence

Figure 6.12 Datum peg suitably protected

If no suitable position can be found a datum peg may be used, its accurate height transferred by surveyors from an OBM, as with the site datum. It is normally a piece of timber or steel rod positioned accurately to the required level and then set in concrete. However, it must be adequately protected and is generally surrounded by a small fence for protection, as shown in Figure 6.12.

Temporary bench mark (TBM)

When an OBM cannot be conveniently found near a site it is usual for a temporary bench mark (TBM) to be set up at a height suitable for the site. Its accurate height is transferred by surveyors from the nearest convenient OBM.

All other site datum points can now be set up from this TBM using datum points, which are shown on the site drawings. Figure 6.13 shows datum points on drawings.

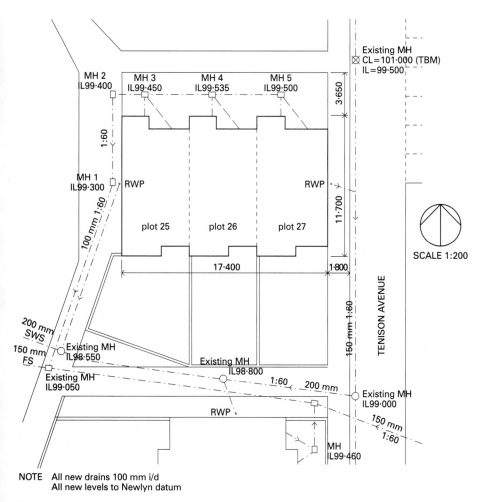

NOTE   All new drains 100 mm i/d
All new levels to Newlyn datum

Figure 6.13 Datum points shown on a drawing

Types of projection

Building, engineering and similar drawings aim to give as much information as possible in a way that is easy to understand. They frequently combine several views on a single drawing.

These may be elevations (the view we would see if we stood in front or to the side of the finished building) or plan (the view we would have if we were looking down on it). The view we see depends on where we are looking from. There are then different ways of 'projecting' what we would see onto the drawings.

The two main methods of projection, used on standard building drawings, are orthographic and isometric.

Orthographic projection

Orthographic projection works as if parallel lines were drawn from every point on a model of the building on to a sheet of paper held up behind it (an elevation view), or laid out underneath it (plan view).

There are then different ways that we can display the views on a drawing. The method most commonly used in the building industry, for detailed construction drawings, is called 'third angle projection'. In this the front elevation is roughly central. The plan view is drawn directly below the front elevation and all other elevations are drawn in line with the front elevation. An example is shown in Figure 6.14.

Front Elevation

Side Elevation

Figure 6.14 Orthographic projection

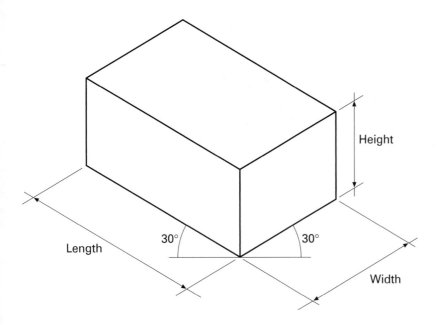

Figure 6.15 Isometric projection of rectangular box

Isometric projection

In isometric views, the object is drawn at an angle where one corner of the object is closest to the viewer. Vertical lines remain vertical but horizontal lines are drawn at an angle of 30° to the horizontal. This can be seen in Figure 6.15, which shows a simple rectangular box.

Figures 6.16 and 6.17 show the method of drawing these using a T–square and set square.

Figure 6.16 Drawing vertical lines

Figure 6.17 Drawing horizontal lines

Contract documents

Contract documents are also vital to a construction project. They are created by a team of specialists – the architect, structural engineer, services engineer and quantity surveyor – who first look at the draft of drawings from the architect and client. Just which contract documents this team goes on to produce will vary depending on the size and type of work being done, but will usually include:

- plans and drawings
- specification
- schedules
- bill of quantities
- conditions of contract.

Plans and drawings have already been covered, so here we will start with the specification.

Specification

The specification or 'spec' is a document produced alongside the plans and drawings and is used to show information that cannot be shown on the drawings. Specifications are almost always used, except in the case of very small contracts. A specification should contain:

- **site description** – a brief description of the site including the address
- **restrictions** – what restrictions apply such as working hours or limited access
- **services** – what services are available, what services need to be connected and what type of connection should be used
- **materials description** – including type, sizes, quality, moisture content etc.
- **workmanship** – including methods of fixing, quality of work and finish.

A good 'spec' helps avoid confusion when dealing with subcontractors or suppliers

The specification may also name subcontractors or suppliers, or give details such as how the site should be cleared, and so on.

Schedules

A schedule is used to record repeated design information that applies to a range of components or fittings. Schedules are mainly used on bigger sites where there are multiples of several types of house (4-bedroom, 3-bedroom, 3-bedroom with dormers, etc.), each type having different components and fittings. The schedule avoids the wrong component or fitting being put in the wrong house. Schedules can also be used on smaller jobs such as a block of flats with 200 windows, where there are six different types of window.

The need for a specification depends on the complexity of the job and the number of repeated designs that there are. Schedules are mainly used to record repeated design information for:

- doors
- windows
- ironmongery
- joinery fitments
- sanitary components
- heating components and radiators
- kitchens.

A schedule is usually used in conjunction with a range drawing and a floor plan.

The following are basic examples of these documents, using a window as an example:

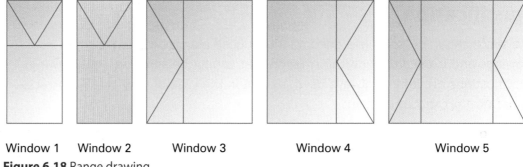

Window 1   Window 2   Window 3   Window 4   Window 5

Figure 6.18 Range drawing

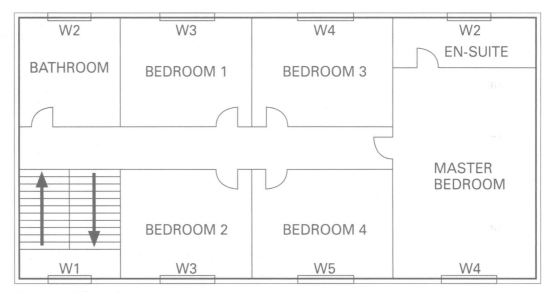

Figure 6.19 Floor plan

WINDOW SCHEDULE		
WINDOW	LOCATIONS	NOTES
Window 1	Stairwell	
Window 2	Bathroom En-suite	Obscure glass
Window 3	Bedroom 1 Bedroom 2	
Window 4	Bedroom 3 Master bedroom	
Window 5	Bedroom 4	

Figure 6.20 Schedule for a window

The schedule shows that there are five types of window, each differing in size and appearance; the range drawing shows what each type of window looks like; and the floor plan shows which window goes where. For example, the bathroom window is a type two window, which is 1200 × 600 × 50 cm with a top-opening sash and obscure glass.

Bill of quantities

The bill of quantities is produced by the quantity surveyor. It gives a complete description of everything that is required to do the job, including labour, materials and any items or components, drawing on information from the drawings, specification and schedule. The same single bill of quantities is sent out to all prospective contractors so they can submit a tender based on the same information – this helps the client select the best contractor for the job.

Every item needed should be listed on the bill of quantities

All bills of quantities contain the following information:

- **preliminaries** – general information such as the names of the client and architect, details of the work and descriptions of the site

- **preambles** – similar to the specification, outlining the quality and description of materials and workmanship, etc.

- **measured quantities** – a description of how each task or material is measured with measurements in metres (linear and square), hours, litres, kilograms or simply the number of components required

- **provisional quantities** – approximate amounts where items or components cannot be measured accurately

- **cost** – the amount of money that will be charged per unit of quantity.

The bill of quantities may also contain:

- any costs that may result from using subcontractors or specialists

- a sum of money for work that has not been finally detailed

- a sum of money to cover contingencies for unforeseen work.

This is an extract from a bill of quantities that might be sent to prospective contractors, who would then complete the cost section and return it as their tender.

Item ref No	Description	Quantity	Unit	Rate £	Cost £
A1	Treated 50 × 225 mm sawn carcass	200	M		
A2	Treated 75 × 225 mm sawn carcass	50	M		
B1	50 mm galvanised steel joist hangers	20	N/A		
B2	75 mm galvanised steel joist hangers	7	N/A		
C1	Supply and fit the above floor joists as described in the preambles				

Figure 6.21 Extract from a bill of quantities

To ensure that all contractors interpret and understand the bill of quantities consistently, the Royal Institution of Chartered Surveyors and the Building Employers' Confederation produce a document called the *Standard Method of Measurement of Building Works* (SMM). This provides a uniform basis for measuring building work, for example stating that carcassing timber is measured by the metre whereas plasterboard is measured in square metres.

Conditions of contract

Almost all building work is carried out under a contract. A small job with a single client (e.g. a loft conversion) will have a basic contract stating that the contractor will do the work to the client's satisfaction, and that the client will pay the contractor the agreed sum of money once the work is finished. Larger contracts with clients such as the Government will have additional clauses, terms or stipulations, which may include any of the following.

Variations

A variation is a modification of the original drawing or specification. The architect or client must give the contractor written confirmation of the variation, then the contractor submits a price for the variation to the quantity surveyor (or client, on a small job). Once the price is accepted, the variation work can be completed.

Interim payment

An **interim** payment schedule may be written into the contract, meaning that the client pays for the work in instalments. The client may pay an amount each month, linked to how far the job has progressed, or may make regular payments regardless of how far the job has progressed.

Final payment

Here the client makes a one-off full payment once the job has been completed to the specification. A final payment scheme may also have additional clauses included, such as:

Did you know?

On a poorly run contract, a penalty clause can be very costly and could incur a substantial payment. In an extreme case, the contractor may end up making a loss instead of a profit on the project

- **Retention** – This is when the client holds a small percentage of the full payment back for a specified period (usually six months). It may take some time for any defects to show, such as cracks in plaster. If the contractor fixes the defects, they will receive the retention payment; if they don't fix them, the retention payment can be used to hire another contractor to do so.
- **Penalty clause** – This is usually introduced in contracts with a tight deadline, where the building must be finished and ready to operate on time. If the project overruns, the client will be unable to trade in the premises and will lose money, so the contractor will have to compensate the client for lost revenue.

On the job: Drawing plans

James is about to draw a kitchen plan. What should James consider when creating the drawing in terms of openings like doors and windows, and services such as water, electricity and gas supplies? Once James has created an outline of the kitchen, where should he start drawing? What sort of things should James have already discussed with the client (think about things like appliances, an extractor, electrical points, the client's budget etc.)?

Knowledge check

1. Briefly explain why drawings are used in the construction industry.

2. What do the following abbreviations stand for: DPC; hwd; fnd; DPM?

3. Sketch the graphical symbols which represent the following: brickwork; metal; sawn timber; hardcore.

4. Can you name the main types of projection that are used in building drawings?

5. What does a block plan show?

6. What are dividers used for?

7. What type of information could be found in a drawing's title panel?

8. Name two ways in which you can find out the height of a OBM?

9. In isometric projection, at what angle are horizontal lines drawn?

10. What type of information can be found in specifications?

chapter 7

Numeracy skills

OVERVIEW

Throughout your career in the construction industry you will have to make use of numbers and calculations in order to plan and carry out work. You will therefore need to make sure you are confident dealing with numbers, which may mean that you have to develop and improve your maths and numeracy skills.

Although you may often use a calculator to do calculations, you may find that a calculator is not always available and you may have to work something out on paper or in your head. This chapter will help you refresh and practise your skills.

This chapter will cover the following topics:

- Numbers
- Calculations
- Measures.

These topics can be found in the following modules:

CC 1002K	CC 2002K
CC 1002S	CC 2002S

Numbers

Place value

0, 1, 2, 3, 4, 5, 6, 7, 8 and 9 are the ten digits we can work with. We can write any number you can think of, however huge, using any combination of these ten digits. In a number, the value of each digit depends upon its place value. Table 7.1 is a place value table and shows how the digit 2 has a different value, depending on its position.

Millions	Hundred thousands	Ten thousands	Thousands	Hundreds	Tens	Units	Value
2	9	4	1	3	7	8	2 million
	2	5	3	1	0	7	2 hundred thousand
	7	**2**	5	6	6	4	2 × ten thousand = 20 thousand
		6	**2**	4	9	2	2 thousands
		5	6	**2**	9	1	2 hundreds
			8	4	**2**	7	2 tens = 20
				1	6	**2**	2 units

Table 7.1 A place value table for the digit 2

Positive numbers

A positive number is a number that is greater than zero. If we make a number line, positive numbers are all the numbers to the right of zero.

0 1 2 3 4 5 6 7 8 9 10 11 12 13 ...

Positive numbers

Negative numbers

A negative number is a number that is less than zero. If we make another number line, negative numbers are all the numbers to the left of zero.

$$\dots \quad -13 \ -12 \ -11 \ -10 \ -9 \ -8 \ -7 \ -6 \ -5 \ -4 \ -3 \ -2 \ -1 \ 0$$

Negative numbers

Zero is neither positive nor negative.

Decimal numbers

Most of the time, the numbers we use are whole numbers. For example, we might buy six apples, or two loaves of bread or one car. However, sometimes we need to use numbers that are less than whole numbers, for example, we might eat one and a quarter sandwiches, two and a half cakes and drink three-quarters of a cup of tea. You can use decimals to show fractions or parts of quantities. Table 7.2 shows the value of the digits to the right of a decimal point.

Did you know?

Knowing about place value helps you to read numbers and to put numbers and quantities in order of size

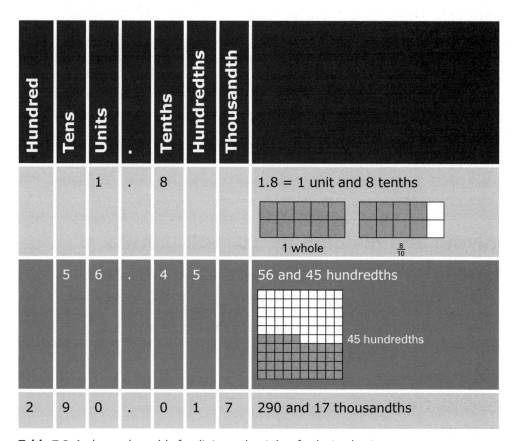

Hundred	Tens	Units	.	Tenths	Hundredths	Thousandth	
		1	.	8			1.8 = 1 unit and 8 tenths
	5	6	.	4	5		56 and 45 hundredths
2	9	0	.	0	1	7	290 and 17 thousandths

Table 7.2 A place value table for digits to the right of a decimal point

Rounding to a number of decimal places

To round a number to a given number of decimal places, look at the digit in the place value position after the one you want.

- If it is 5 or more, round up.

- If it is less than 5 round down.

For example, say we wanted to round 4.634 to two decimal places, the digit in the third decimal place is 4, so we round down. Therefore, 4.634 rounded to 2 decimal places (d.p.) is 4.63.

If we look at the number 16.127, the digit in the third decimal place is 7, so we round up. Therefore, 16.127 rounded to 2 d.p. is 16.13.

Rounding to a number of significant figures

The most significant figure in a number is the digit with the highest place value. To round a number to a given number of significant figures, look at the digit in the place value position after the one you want.

- If it is 5 or more round up.

- If it is less than 5 round down.

For example, say we wanted to write 80597 to one significant figure, the most significant figure is 8. The second significant figure is 0, so we round down. Therefore, 80597 to 1 significant figure (s.f.) is 80000.

If we wanted to write 80597 to two significant figures, the first two significant figures are 8 and 0. The third significant figure is 5, so we round up. Therefore, 80597 to 2 s.f. is 81000.

Multiplying and dividing by 10, 100, 1000...

- To multiply a number by 10, move the digits one place value to the left.

- To multiply a number by 100, move the digits two place values to the left.

- To multiply a number by 1000, move the digits three place values to the left.

For example:

	5		3.25
5 × 10 =	50	3.25 × 10 =	32.5
5 × 100 =	500	3.25 × 100 =	325
5 × 1000 =	5000	3.25 × 1000 =	3250

Remember

If a calculation results in an answer with a lot of decimal places, such as 34.568923, you can round to 1 or 2 decimal places to make it simpler

- To divide a number by 10, move the digits one place value to the right.
- To divide a number by 100, move the digits two place values to the right.
- To divide a number by 1000, move the digits three place values to the right.

For example:

80 000 ÷ 10 = 8000	473.6 ÷ 10 = 47.36
80 000 ÷ 100 = 800	473.6 ÷ 100 = 4.736
80 000 ÷ 1000 = 80	473.6 ÷ 1000 = 0.4736

Converting decimals to fractions

You can use place value to convert a decimal to a fraction. For example:

0.3 is 3 tenths which is $\frac{3}{10}$

0.25 is 25 hundredths which is $\frac{25}{100}$

$\frac{25}{100}$ simplifies to $\frac{1}{4}$ (by dividing the top and bottom numbers by 25)

Table 7.3 shows some useful fraction/decimal equivalents.

See page 137 for more on simplifying fractions.

Decimal	0.1	0.25	0.333 333	0.5	0.75	0.01
Fraction	$\frac{1}{10}$	$\frac{1}{4}$	$\frac{1}{3}$	$\frac{1}{2}$	$\frac{3}{4}$	$\frac{1}{100}$

Table 7.3 Useful fraction/decimal equivalents

Multiples

Multiples are the numbers you get when you multiply any number by other numbers. For example:

- the multiples of 3 are 3, 6, 9, 12, 15, 18, 21, 24, 27, 30 and so on
- the multiples of 4 are 4, 8, 12, 16, 20, 24, 28, 32, 36, 40 and so on
- the multiples of 5 are 5, 10, 15, 20, 25, 30, 35, 40, 45, 50 and so on.

Did you know?

Knowing how to multiply and divide by 10, 100, 1000 etc. is useful for converting metric units of measurement (see page 145) and finding percentages (see page 140)

Did you know?

Knowing how to convert between fractions and decimals helps with working out parts of quantities and calculating percentages (see page 140)

Remember

The multiples of a number are the numbers in its 'times' table (multiplication table)

Common multiples

Here are the multiples of 3 and 5:

- Multiples of 3: 3, 6, 9, 12, 15, 18, 21, 24, 27, 30, 33, 36...
- Multiples of 5: 5, 10, 15, 20, 25, 30, 35...

3 and 5 have the multiples 15 and 30 in common. 15 and 30 are common multiples of 3 and 5. The lowest common multiple of 3 and 5 is 15.

Factors

The factors of a number are the whole numbers that divide into it exactly. For example:

- The factors of 18 are 1, 2, 3, 6, 9 and 18
- The factors of 30 are 1, 2, 3, 5, 6, 10, 15 and 30
- 5 is a factor of 5, 10, 15, 20...
- 7 is a factor of 7, 14, 21, 28...

Common factors

Here are the factors of 28 and 36:

- The factors of 28 are 1, 2, 4, 7, 14, 28
- The factors of 36 are 1, 2, 3, 4, 6, 9, 12, 18, 36

From these lists you can see that 28 and 36 have the factors 1, 2 and 4 in common. 1, 2 and 4 are the common factors of 28 and 36. 4 is the highest common factor of 28 and 36.

Fractions

Fractions describe parts of a whole, for example a half of a pie, a third of a can of cola or a quarter of a cake.

In a fraction:

$$\frac{3}{4}$$ the top number is called the **numerator**

the bottom number is called the **denominator**

The denominator shows how many *equal parts* the whole is divided into. The numerator shows how many of those parts you have.

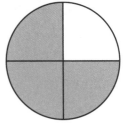

$\frac{3}{4}$

Finding a fraction of a quantity

To find a fraction of a quantity you divide by the denominator and multiply by the numerator. For example:

- to find $\frac{1}{2}$ of 500 m, divide by 2 (500 m ÷ 2 = 250 m)

- to find $\frac{2}{5}$ of £40, divide by 5 (£40 ÷ 5 = £8) and multiply by 2 (£8 × 2 = £16)

Equivalent fractions

Two fractions are equivalent if they have the same value. For example:

$$\frac{1}{2} = \frac{2}{4} = \frac{3}{6} = \frac{4}{8}$$

$$\frac{2}{3} = \frac{4}{6} = \frac{6}{9} = \frac{8}{12}$$

Simplifying fractions

To simplify a fraction, write it as an equivalent fraction with smaller numbers in the numerator and denominator.

For example, $\frac{8}{12}$ simplifies to $\frac{2}{3}$.

When a fraction cannot be simplified any more, it is in its simplest form, or its lowest terms.

For example:

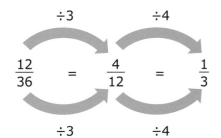

$$\frac{12}{36} = \frac{1}{3} \text{ in its simplest form.}$$

Multiplying fractions

To multiply a fraction by a whole number, multiply the numerator by the whole number.

For example:

$$\frac{2}{9} \times 4 = \frac{8}{9}$$

To multiply a fraction by another fraction, multiply the numerators and the denominators. For example:

$$\frac{2}{3} \times \frac{5}{8} = \frac{2 \times 5}{3 \times 8} = \frac{10}{24}$$

Give the answer in its simplest form:

$$\frac{10}{24} = \frac{5}{12} \qquad \text{(dividing numerator and denominator by 2)}$$

Dividing fractions

To divide one fraction by another, you invert (turn upside down) the fraction you are dividing by, and multiply.

For example:

$$\frac{3}{4} \div \frac{2}{3} = \frac{3}{4} \times \frac{3}{2} = \frac{9}{8} = 1\frac{1}{8}$$

To divide a fraction by a whole number, or to divide a whole number by a fraction, write the whole number as a fraction with denominator 1, and use the same method.

$$\frac{4}{5} \div 3 = \frac{4}{5} \div \frac{3}{1} = \frac{4}{5} \times \frac{1}{3} = \frac{4}{15}$$

$$6 \div \frac{3}{4} = \frac{6}{1} \div \frac{3}{4} = \frac{6}{1} \times \frac{4}{3} = \frac{24}{3} = 8$$

Adding fractions

To add fractions with the same denominator, add the numerators.

For example:

$$\frac{1}{3} + \frac{1}{3} = \frac{2}{3}$$

$$\frac{1}{5} + \frac{3}{5} = \frac{4}{5}$$

To add fractions with different denominators, first write the fractions as equivalent fractions with the same denominator. Use the lowest common multiple of the two denominators. You can use any common multiple as the denominator, but using the lowest common multiple keeps the numbers smaller and the calculations simpler.

For example:

$$\frac{1}{2} + \frac{1}{3}$$

The denominators are not the same. The lowest common multiple of 2 and 3 is 6.

To write $\frac{1}{2}$ as an equivalent fraction with denominator 6, multiply numerator and denominator by 3, to give $\frac{3}{6}$.

To write $\frac{1}{3}$ as an equivalent fraction with denominator 6, multiply numerator and denominator by 2, to give $\frac{2}{6}$

The calculation is now $\frac{3}{6} + \frac{2}{6} = \frac{5}{6}$

A mixed number has a whole number and a fraction part, for example $3\frac{1}{4}$.

To add mixed numbers, add together the whole number parts and then the fractions.

For example, if we wanted to add together $1\frac{1}{2}$ and $2\frac{1}{3}$:

Add the whole numbers: $1 + 2 = 3$

Now add the fractions: $\frac{1}{2} + \frac{1}{3} = \frac{3}{6} + \frac{2}{6} = \frac{5}{6}$

Combine the two answers: $1\frac{1}{2} + 2\frac{1}{3} = 3\frac{5}{6}$

Subtracting fractions

To subtract fractions with the same denominator, subtract the numerators.

For example: $\frac{7}{8} - \frac{3}{8} = \frac{4}{8} = \frac{1}{2}$ 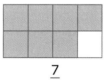 – 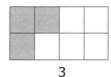 =

$$\frac{7}{8} \qquad \frac{3}{8} \qquad \frac{4}{8}$$

To subtract mixed numbers, first write them as improper (top heavy) fractions with a common denominator

For example: $2\frac{1}{3} - \frac{1}{2} = \frac{7}{3} - \frac{1}{2} = \frac{14}{6} - \frac{3}{6} = 1\frac{5}{6}$

Percentages

Percentages are another way of showing parts of a quantity. Percentage means 'number of parts per hundred'. The symbol % means per cent. For example:

- 1% means 1 out of a hundred or $\frac{1}{100}$

- 10% means 10 out of a hundred or $\frac{10}{100}$

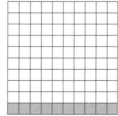

10%

- 84% means 84 out of a hundred or $\frac{84}{100}$

100% means the whole quantity.

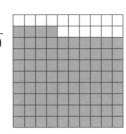

84%

Finding a percentage of a quantity

To find a percentage of a quantity, find 1% first, by dividing by 100, then multiply by the number you need. For example:

20% of £45

$$1\% \text{ of } £45 = \frac{£45}{100} = £45 \div 100 = £0.45$$

So   20% of £45 = 20 × £0.45 = £9

Percentage change

A number can be increased or decreased by a percentage. Wages are often increased by a percentage (e.g. a 4% rise in wages). Items are often reduced by a percentage in sales (e.g. 10% off, 20% reduction, etc.). For example:

A set of paintbrushes costs £12.99. In the sale there is 15% off.

(a) How much money do you save by buying the paintbrushes in the sale?

(b) What is the sale price of the paintbrushes?

(a) Work out 15% of £12.99

        1% of £12.99 = £0.1299

So   15% of £12.99 = 15 × £0.1299 = £1.9485 = £1.95 to the nearest penny

You save £1.95

(b) The sale price is

        £12.99 – £1.95 = £11.04

Ratio

A **ratio** describes a relationship between quantities. You can read a ratio as a 'for every' statement. For example:

- Green paint is made by mixing blue and yellow in the ratio 1 : 2. This means, *for every* 1 litre of blue paint you need 2 litres of yellow paint.

- A labourer and a bricklayer agree to share their bonus in the ratio 2 : 5. The bonus is £42. The ratio 2:5 means that for every 2 parts the labourer receives, the bricklayer receives 5 parts. So the bonus needs to be split into 2 + 5 = 7 parts. One part can be calculated: £42 ÷ 7 = £6. Therefore, the labourer receives two parts = 2 × £6 = £12 and the bricklayer receives five parts = 5 × £6 = £30.

Calculations

Addition

When adding numbers using a written method, write digits with the same place value in the same column. For example, to work out 26 + 896 + 1213 write the calculation:

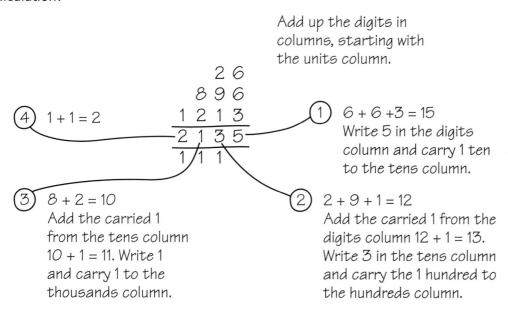

Add up the digits in columns, starting with the units column.

④ 1 + 1 = 2

① 6 + 6 + 3 = 15
Write 5 in the digits column and carry 1 ten to the tens column.

③ 8 + 2 = 10
Add the carried 1 from the tens column 10 + 1 = 11. Write 1 and carry 1 to the thousands column.

② 2 + 9 + 1 = 12
Add the carried 1 from the digits column 12 + 1 = 13. Write 3 in the tens column and carry the 1 hundred to the hundreds column.

To add decimals, write the numbers with the decimal points in line:

```
   4.56
  10.2
   0.32
 ------
  15.08
```

In a problem, these words mean you need to add:

- What is the *total* of 43 and 2457?   (43 + 2457)

- What is the *sum* of 56 and 345?   (56 + 345)

- *Increase* 3467 by 521.   (3467 + 521)

Scales for scale drawings can also be given as ratios (see page 146)

Did you know?

Subtraction

When subtracting numbers using a written method, write digits with the same place value in the same column.

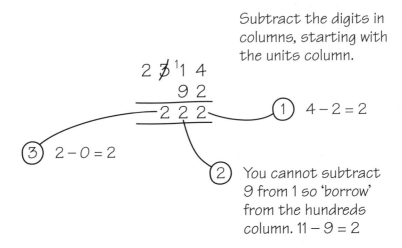

Subtract the digits in columns, starting with the units column.

$2\ \cancel{3}^{1}1\ 4$
$9\ 2$
$\overline{-2\ 2\ 2}$

(1) $4 - 2 = 2$

(3) $2 - 0 = 2$

(2) You cannot subtract 9 from 1 so 'borrow' from the hundreds column. $11 - 9 = 2$

In a problem, these words mean you need to subtract:

- *Find the difference* between 200 and 45. $(200 - 45)$

- *Decrease* 64 by 9. $(64 - 9)$

- *How much greater than* 98 is 110? $(110 - 98)$

Multiplication

Knowing the multiplication tables up to 10×10 helps with multiplying single digit numbers. You can use multiplication facts you know to work out other multiplication calculations. For example:

20×12

You know that $20 = 2 \times 10$

So $20 \times 12 = 2 \times 10 \times 12$

$= 2 \times 12 \times 10$

$= 24 \times 10 = 240$

To multiply larger numbers you can write the calculation in columns or use the grid method. Both methods work by splitting the calculation into smaller ones.

In columns

```
    2 5
 x  3 6
  1 5 0
  7 5 0
  9 0 0
```

6 x 25 } Add these to
30 x 25 } find 36 x 25

The grid method

36 x 25 =

x	20	5
30	600	150
6	120	30

30 x 20 = 600
30 x 5 = 150
 6 x 20 = 120
 6 x 5 =   30
          900

Division

Division is the opposite of multiplication. Knowing the multiplication tables up to
10 × 10 helps with division. Each multiplication fact gives two related division
facts. For example:

    4 × 6 = 24   24 ÷ 6 = 4   24 ÷ 4 = 6

To divide by a single digit number, use short division.

161 ÷ 7 =

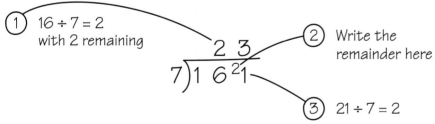

① 16 ÷ 7 = 2
   with 2 remaining

② Write the
   remainder here

③ 21 ÷ 7 = 2

$$7\overline{)1\ 6\ ^2 1}$$ 2 3

To divide by 10 or more, use long division.

$$
\begin{array}{r}
2\,4\,6 \\
12\overline{)2\,9\,5\,2} \\
2\,4 \\
\hline
5\,5 \\
4\,8 \\
\hline
7\,2 \\
7\,2 \\
\hline
0
\end{array}
$$

$2 \times 12 = 24$
$29 - 24 = \quad 5.$ Bring down the next 5
$12 \times 4 = 48$
$55 - 48 = \quad 7.$ Bring down the 2
$12 \times 6 = 72$

Estimating

Sometimes an accurate answer to a calculation is not required. You can estimate an approximate answer by rounding all the values in the calculation to 1 significant figure (see page 134). For example:

Estimate the answer to the calculation $\quad 4.9 \times 3.1$

4.9 rounds to 5 to 1 s.f.

3.1 rounds to 3 to 1 s.f.

A sensible estimate is $5 \times 3 = 15$

Did you know?

You can use values rounded to 1 s.f. to estimate approximate areas and prices

Measures

Units of measurement

The metric units of measurement are shown in Table 7.4.

Length	millimetres (mm), centimetres (cm), metres (m), kilometres (km)
Mass (weight)	grams (g), kilograms (kg), tonnes (t)
Capacity (the amount a container holds)	millilitres (ml), centilitres (cl), litres (l)

Table 7.4 Units of measurement

Metric units are all based on 10, 100, 1000 which makes it easy to convert between units.

milli means one thousandth $\qquad$ $1 \text{ mm} = \dfrac{1}{1000} \text{ m}$ $\qquad$ $1 \text{ ml} = \dfrac{1}{1000} \text{ litre}$

centi means one hundredth $\qquad$ $1 \text{ cm} = \dfrac{1}{100} \text{ m}$ $\qquad$ $1 \text{ cl} = \dfrac{1}{100} \text{ litre}$

kilo means one thousand $\qquad$ $1 \text{ kg} = 1000 \text{ g}$ $\qquad$ $1 \text{ km} = 1000 \text{ m}$

Table 7.5 shows some useful metric conversions.

Length	Mass	Capacity
1 cm = 10 mm 1 m = 100 cm = 1000 mm 1 km = 1000 m	1 kg = 1000 g 1 tonne = 1000 kg	1 l = 100 cl = 1000 ml

Table 7.5 Useful metric conversions

Remember

To convert from a smaller unit to a larger one, divide; to convert from a larger unit to a smaller one, multiply

To convert 2657 mm to metres: $\qquad$ $2657 \div 1000 = 2.657 \text{ m}$

To convert 0.75 tonnes to kg: $\qquad$ $0.75 \times 1000 = 750 \text{ kg}$

For calculations involving measurements, you need to convert all the measurements into the same unit. For example, a plasterer measures the lengths of cornice required for a room. He writes down the measurements as 175 cm, 2 metres, 225 cm, 1.5 m. In order to work out the total length of cornice needed, we first need to write all the lengths in the same units:

175 cm $\quad$ 2 metres = 2 × 100 = 200 cm $\quad$ 1.5 m = 1.5 × 100 = 150 cm $\quad$ 225 cm

So the total length is:

$\qquad$ 175 + 200 + 225 + 150 = 750 cm

Imperial units

In the UK we still use some imperial units of measurement (see Table 7.6).

Length	inches, feet, yards, miles
Mass (weight)	ounces, pounds, stones
Capacity (the amount a container holds)	pints, gallons

Table 7.6 Some imperial units of measurement

To convert from imperial to metric units, use the approximate conversions shown in Table 7.7.

Length	Mass	Capacity
1 inch = 2.5 cm 1 foot = 30 cm 5 miles = 8 km	2.2 pounds = 1 kg 1 ounce = 25 g	1.75 pints = 1 litre 1 gallon = 4.5 litres

Table 7.7 Converting imperial measurements to metric

For example, if a wall is 32 feet long, what is its approximate length in metres?

1 foot = 30 cm

So   32 feet = 32 × 30 cm = 960 cm = 9.6 m.

Scale drawings

Building plans are drawn to scale. Each length on the plan is in proportion to the real length. On a drawing to a scale of 1 cm represents 10 m:

- a length of 5 cm represents an actual length of 5 × 10 = 50 m
- a length of 12 cm represents an actual length of 12 × 10 = 120 m
- an actual length of 34 m is represented by a line 34 ÷ 10 = 3.4 cm long.

Scales are often given as ratios. For example:

- a scale of 1 : 100 means that 1 cm on the drawing represents an actual length of 100 cm (or 1 metre)
- a scale of 1 : 20 000 means that 1 cm on the drawing represents an actual length of 20 000 cm = 20 m.

Table 7.8 shows some common scales used in the construction industry.

1 : 5	1 cm represents 5 cm	5 times smaller than actual size
1 : 10	1 cm represents 10 cm	10 times smaller than actual size
1 : 20	1 cm represents 20 cm	20 times smaller than actual size
1 : 50	1 cm represents 50 cm	50 times smaller than actual size
1 : 100	1 cm represents 100 cm = 1 m	100 times smaller than actual size
1 : 1250	1 cm represents 1250 cm = 12.5 m	1250 times smaller than actual size

Table 7.8 Common scales used in the construction industry

Did you know?

A useful rhyme to help you remember the pints to litre conversion is 'a litre of water's a pint and three-quarters'

Remember

You can use a scale to:

- work out the actual measurement from a plan
- work out how long to draw a line on the plan to represent an actual measurement

Let's look at the following examples:

(a) A plan is drawn to a scale of 1 : 20. On the plan, a wall is 4.5 cm long. How long is the actual wall?

     1 cm on the plan = actual length 20 cm

So   4.5 cm on the plan = actual length 4.5 × 20 = 90 cm or 0.9 m

(b) A window is 3 m tall. How tall is it on the plan?

    3 m = 300 cm

    an actual length of 20 cm is 1 cm on the plan

    an actual length of 5 × 20 = 100 cm is 5 × 1 cm on the plan

    an actual length of 3 × 100 cm is 3 × 5 cm on the plan.

The window is 15 cm tall on the plan.

To make scale drawings, architects use a scale rule. The different scales on the ruler give the equivalent actual length measurements for different lengths in cm, for each scale.

Perimeter of shapes with straight sides

The perimeter of a shape is the distance all around the outside of the shape. To find the perimeter of a shape, measure all the sides and then add the lengths together. For example:

The perimeter of this room is

4.5 + 3.2 + 4.5 + 3.2 = 15.4 m

4.5 m

3.2 m   3.2 m

4.5 m

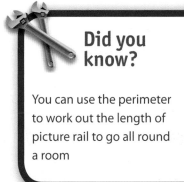

Did you know?

You can use the perimeter to work out the length of picture rail to go all round a room

Area of shapes with straight sides

The area of a 2-D (flat) shape is the amount of space it covers. Area is measured in square units, such as square centimetres (cm^2) and square metres (m^2).

This rectangle is drawn on squared paper. Each square has an area 1 cm^2.

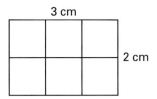

You can find the area by counting the squares. Area = 6 squares = 6 cm^2

You can also calculate the area by multiplying the number of squares in a row by the number of rows: $3 \times 2 = 6$

The area of a rectangle with length *l* and width *w* is

$$A = l \times w$$

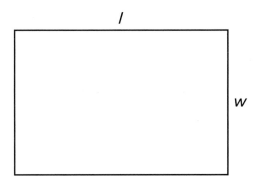

For example, if the length of a rectangular room is 3.6 metres and the width is 2.7 metres, the area is

$$A = 3.6 \times 2.7 = 9.72 \ m^2$$

Area of a triangle

The area of a triangle is given by the formula:

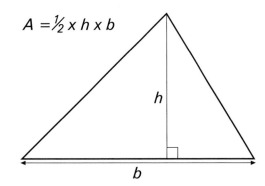

$A = \frac{1}{2} \times h \times b$

$A = \frac{1}{2} \times h \times b$ where *h* is the **perpendicular** height and *b* is the length of the base. The perpendicular height is drawn to meet the base at right angles (90°).

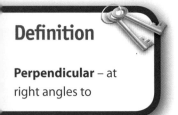

Definition

Perpendicular – at right angles to

For example, say we wanted to find (a) the area and (b) the perimeter of this triangle

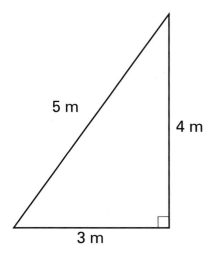

5 m

4 m

3 m

(a) Perpendicular height = 4 m, base = 3 m

$$A = \frac{1}{2} \times h \times b = \frac{1}{2} \times 4 \times 3 = 6 \text{ m}^2$$

(b) Perimeter = 5 + 4 + 3 = 12 m

Pythagoras' theorem

You can use Pythagoras' theorem to find unknown lengths in right-angled triangles. In a right-angled triangle:

- one angle is 90° (a right angle)

- the longest side is opposite the right angle and is called the **hypotenuse**.

Pythagoras' theorem says that for any right-angled triangle with sides a and b and hypotenuse c,

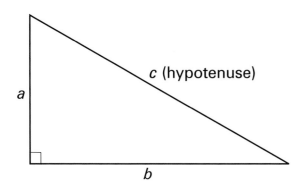

a

c (hypotenuse)

b

Definition

Hypotenuse – the longest side on a Right-angled triangle

$$c^2 = a^2 + b^2$$

For example, if we wanted to find the length of the hypotenuse of this triangle

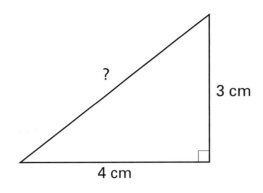

$$c^2 = a^2 + b^2$$

In the theorem, c is the hypotenuse.

$$c^2 = 3^2 + 4^2$$
$$= 9 + 16$$
$$= 25$$
$$c = \sqrt{25} = 5$$

The hypotenuse is 5 cm long.

a^2 is 'a squared' and is equal to $a \times a$. 3^2 is '3 squared' and is equal to 3×3. The opposite or inverse of squaring is finding the square root. $\sqrt{25}$ means 'the square root of 25': $5 \times 5 = 25$, so $\sqrt{25} = 5$

Learning these squares and square roots will help with Pythagoras' theorem calculations. Table 7.9 shows some square roots you will often find useful.

$1^2 = 1 \times 1 = 1$	$\sqrt{1} = 1$
$2^2 = 2 \times 2 = 4$	$\sqrt{4} = 2$
$3^2 = 3 \times 3 = 9$	$\sqrt{9} = 3$
$4^2 = 4 \times 4 = 16$	$\sqrt{16} = 4$
$5^2 = 5 \times 5 = 25$	$\sqrt{25} = 5$
$6^2 = 6 \times 6 = 36$	$\sqrt{36} = 6$
$7^2 = 7 \times 7 = 49$	$\sqrt{49} = 7$
$8^2 = 8 \times 8 = 64$	$\sqrt{64} = 8$
$9^2 = 9 \times 9 = 81$	$\sqrt{81} = 9$
$10^2 = 10 \times 10 = 100$	$\sqrt{100} = 10$

Table 7.9 Useful square roots

Using Pythagoras' theorem to find the shorter side of a triangle

You can rearrange Pythagoras' theorem like this:

$$c^2 = a^2 + b^2$$

$$a^2 = c^2 - b^2$$

For example, say we wanted to find the length of side a in this right-angled triangle

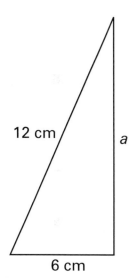

$$a^2 = c^2 - b^2$$

$$= 12^2 - 6^2$$

$$= 144 - 36 = 108$$

$$a = \sqrt{108} = 10.3923... \quad \text{Using the } \sqrt{} \text{ key on a calculator}$$

$$= 10.4 \text{ cm (to 1 decimal place)}$$

You can also use Pythagoras' theorem to find the perpendicular height of a triangle. For example, if we wanted to find the area of this triangle we would need to find the perpendicular height:

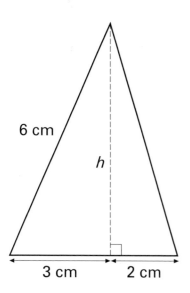

Using Pythagoras $\quad h^2 = 6^2 - 3^2$

$$= 36 - 9 = 27$$

$$h = \sqrt{27} = 5.196... = 5.2 \text{ cm (to 1 d.p.)}$$

Area $= \dfrac{1}{2} \times b \times h$

$\qquad = \dfrac{1}{2} \times 5 \times 5.2 \qquad$ Base length $= 3 + 2$ cm

$\qquad = 13 \text{ cm}^2$

Areas of composite shapes

Composite shapes are made up of simple shapes such as rectangles and squares. To find the area, divide up the shape and find the area of each part separately. For example, to work out the area of this L-shaped room:

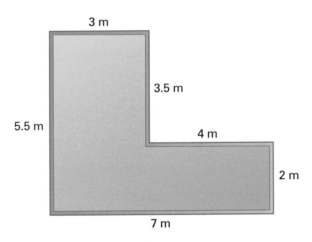

First divide it into two rectangles, A and B:

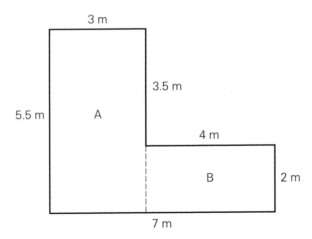

Area of rectangle A = 3 × 5.5 = 16.5 m²

Area of rectangle B = 4 × 2 = 8 m²

Total area of room = 16.5 + 8 = 24.5 m²

You could divide the rectangle in the example above into two different rectangles, C and D, like this (see page 153):

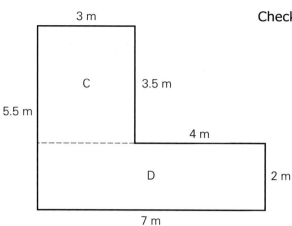

Check that you get the same total area.

Some shapes can be divided into rectangles and triangles. For example, to find the area of this wooden floor:

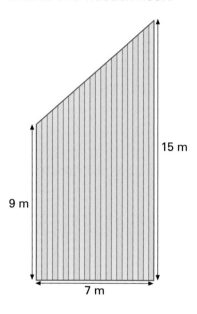

Divide the floor into a right-angled triangle A and a rectangle B

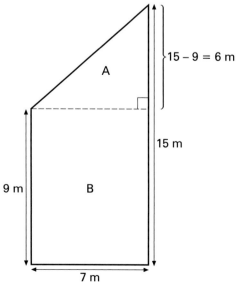

Triangle A has vertical height 6 m and base 7 m

Area triangle A $= \frac{1}{2} \times b \times h$

$= \frac{1}{2} \times 7 \times 6 = 21$ m²

Area rectangle B $= 9 \times 7 = 63$ m²

Total area $= 21 + 63 = 84$ m².

Circumference of a circle

The circumference of a circle is its perimeter – the distance all the way around the outside. The formula for the circumference of a circle of radius r is

$$C = 2\pi r$$

The radius is the distance from the centre of a circle to its outside edge. The diameter is the distance across the circle through the centre (diameter = 2 × radius).

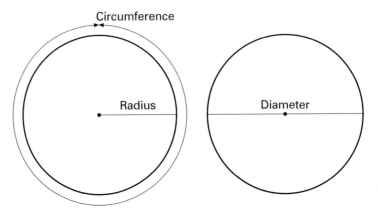

Circumference

Radius

Diameter

$\pi = 3.141\,592\,654\ldots$

To estimate the circumference of a circle, use $\pi = 3$. For more accurate calculations use $\pi = 3.14$, or the π key on a calculator.

For example, to estimate the circumference of this circular pond, with radius 2 m:

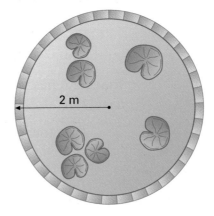

2 m

For an estimate, use $\pi = 3$

$$\text{Circumference} = 2\pi r = 2 \times \pi \times r = 2 \times 3 \times 2 = 12 \text{ m}$$

Calculate the circumference of a circular patio with radius 3.5 m.

$$\text{Circumference} = 2\pi r = 2 \times \pi \times r = 2 \times 3.14 \times 3.5$$

$$= 21.98 \text{ m}$$

$$= 22 \text{ m to the nearest metre}$$

Area of a circle

The formula for the area of a circle of radius r is

Area = πr^2

We can calculate the area of a circle with radius 3.25 m

Area = πr^2

$= \pi \times r^2 = 3.14 \times 3.25 \times 3.25 = 33.16625$

$= 33$ m^2 to the nearest metre.

Did you know?

If you are given the diameter of the circle, you halve the diameter to find the radius

Part circles and composite shapes

You can use the formulae for circumference and area of a circle to calculate perimeters and areas of parts of circles, and shapes made from parts of circles. For example, we can work out the perimeter and area of this semicircular window.

The diameter of the semicircle is 1.3 m, so the radius is 1.3 ÷ 2 = 0.65 m. The length of the curved side is half the circumference of the circle with radius 0.65 m.

Length of curved side $= \frac{1}{2} \times 2\pi r = \frac{1}{2} \times 2 \times \pi \times r$

$= \frac{1}{2} \times 2 \times 3.14 \times 0.65 = 2.041$ m

Circumference of the semicircle $=$ curved side + straight side

$= 2.041 + 1.3 = 3.341$ m

$= 3.34$ m (to the nearest cm)

Area of semicircle = half the area of the circle with radius 0.65m

$= \frac{1}{2} \times \pi r^2 = \frac{1}{2} \times \pi \times r^2$

$= \frac{1}{2} \times 3.14 \times 0.65 \times 0.65 = 0.663325$ m^2

$= 0.66$ m^2 (to 2 d.p.)

To find the area of a quarter circle, use $\frac{1}{4}\pi r^2$.

To find the perimeter of a quarter circle, work out $\frac{1}{4}$ circumference + 2 × radius.

To find the area of a composite shape including parts of circles, divide it into circles and simple shapes and find the areas separately.

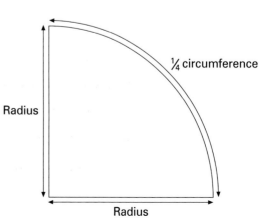

¼ circumference

Radius

Radius

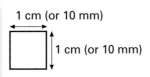

Remember

1 cm² = 100 mm²

1 m² = 10 000 cm²

Did you know?

The formula for the area of a rectangle is $A = l \times w$. For more on this, see page 148

Units of area

Area is measured in **square units** such as mm², cm², m².

1 cm (or 10 mm)

1 cm (or 10 mm)

The area of this square is 1 cm² or $10 \times 10 = 100$ mm²

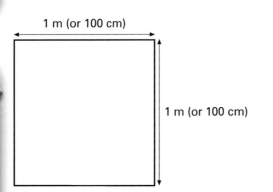

1 m (or 100 cm)

1 m (or 100 cm)

The area of this square is 1 m² or $100 \times 100 = 10\ 000$ cm²

We can work out the area of this rectangle

(a) in cm²

(b) in m²

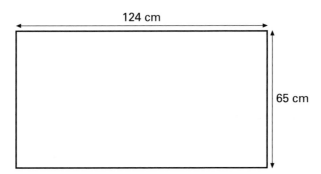

124 cm

65 cm

(a) $A = l \times w = 124 \times 65 = 8060$ cm²

(b) $8060 \div 10\ 000 = 0.806$ m²

Volume

Volume is the amount of space taken up by a 3-D or solid shape. Volume is measured in cube units, such as cubic centimetres (cm³) and cubic metres (m³).

A cuboid is a 3-D shape whose faces are all rectangles.

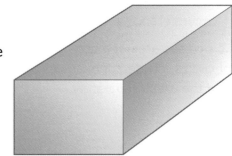

A cube is a 3-D shape whose faces are all squares.

This cuboid is made of 1 cm³ cubes.

You can find the volume by counting the cubes.
Volume = number of cubes = 36 cm³.

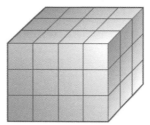

You can also calculate the volume by splitting the solid into equal rectangular layers.

Each layer has 4 × 3 cubes.

There are three layers, so the total number of cubes is 3 × 4 × 3 = 36 cm³.

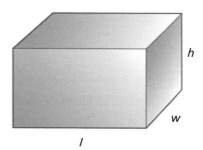

The volume of a cuboid with length *l*, width *w* and height *h* is

$$V = l \times w \times h$$

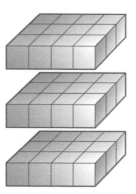

For a cube, length = width = height, so the volume of a cube with side *l* is

$$V = l^3$$

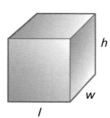

You can find the volume of concrete needed for a rectangular floor by measuring the length and width of the floor, and the depth of the concrete required and using the formula for the volume of a cuboid. For example, we can work out the volume of concrete needed for the floor of a rectangular room with length 3.7 m and width 2.9 m, if the depth of the concrete is to be 0.15 m.

Visualise the floor as a cuboid, like this

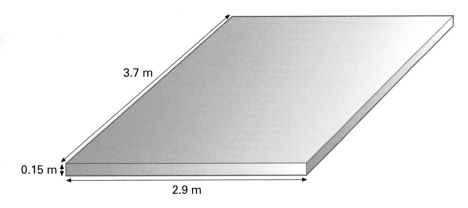

The depth of the concrete (0.15 m) is the height of the cuboid.

$$V = l \times w \times h$$
$$= 3.7 \times 2.9 \times 0.15$$
$$= 1.6095 \ m^3$$
$$= 1.61 \ m^3 \ (to \ 2 \ d.p.)$$

Units of volume

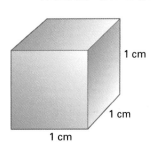

Volume is measured in **cube units** such as mm^3, cm^3, m^3. The volume of this cube is $1 \ cm^3$ or $10 \times 10 \times 10 = 1000 \ mm^3$.

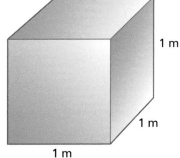

The volume of this cube is $1 \ m^3$ or $100 \times 100 \times 100 = 1 \ 000 \ 000 \ cm^3$.

Remember

$1 \ cm^3 = 1000 \ mm^3$

$1 \ m^3 = 1 \ 000 \ 000 \ cm^3$

A cuboid is a 3-D shape with rectangular faces (like a box). The formula for the volume of a cuboid is $V = l \times w \times h$. For example, we can calculate the volume of this cuboid:

(a) in cm^3

(b) in m^3

(a) $V = l \times w \times h = 56 \times 84 \times 221 = 1 \ 039 \ 584 \ cm^3$

(b) $1 \ 039 \ 584 \div 1 \ 000 \ 000 = 1.039584 \ m^2 =$
   $1.04 \ m^3 \ (to \ 2 \ d.p.)$

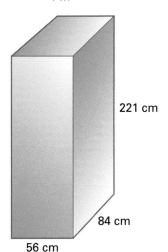

Rounding to a sensible degree of accuracy

Sometimes measurement calculations give an answer to a large number of decimal places. It is sensible to round the answer to a measurement that is practical. For example, Ahmed has a piece of wood 190 cm long. He wants to cut it into 7 equal lengths.

Remember

In some situations it is most sensible to round up

He works out $190 \div 7 = 14.28578142$ cm

You cannot measure 0.28578142 of a centimetre!

It is sensible to round to 14.3 cm (to 1 d.p.), which is 14 cm and 3 mm and can be measured.

For more on rounding to a number of decimal places, see page 134.

Let's look at another example:

A plasterer calculates the total area of walls in a room as 36 m^2.

Plasterboard sheets have area 2.88 m^2.

The number of plasterboard sheets needed is $36 \div 2.88 = 12.5$

If the plasterer buys 12 sheets he will not have enough.

If he buys 13 sheets he will have half a sheet left over.

In this case it is sensible to round up, and buy 13 sheets.

You may find there are times when you need to round down.

In some situations it is most sensible to round down. How many 2 metre lengths can be cut from 7 metres of pipe?

$7 \div 2 = 3.5$

You can cut three 2 metre lengths. The rest (0.5 of a 2 metre length) is wasted.

So in this case it is sensible to round down: you can only cut three 2 metre lengths.

chapter 8

Tools and equipment

OVERVIEW

This chapter provides a basic introduction to some of the tools and equipment used within the painting and decorating profession. The tools and equipment described are those most commonly used for both preparation and a variety of application methods. We will also look at some of the basic maintenance tasks required to ensure that the tools are kept in good condition. The equipment that you build up throughout your working life helps you make a living. You should therefore look after your tools, which will also help avoid any unnecessary and costly repairs and replacements.

This chapter will cover the following topics:

- Preparation tools and equipment
- Painting tools and equipment
- Paper hanging tools and equipment
- Specialist tools and equipment
- Glazing tools and equipment.

These topics can be found in the following modules:

CC 2002K	CC 2003K	CC 2024K
CC 2002S	CC 2003S	CC 2024S

Preparation tools and equipment

Before you start any painting or decorating task, you will need to prepare the area and surfaces you are going to work on. If you don't do this, the results will be poor and you may have to start again, which will cost time and money.

Knives and scrapers

Stripping knife/scraper

A stripping knife (or scraper) is used to remove old or flaking paint, wallpaper and other loose debris from surfaces to be decorated. When not in use, it is advisable to clean off the knife and protect the tip with a suitable cover.

Stripping knife/scraper

Filling knife

A filling knife looks very similar to a stripping knife but is used to apply fillers as part of the preparation process. The blade is made of a thinner gauge metal, which makes it more flexible allowing manipulation of the filler. A filling knife requires the same cleaning and protection as a scraping knife.

Filling knife

Filling board

The filling board is used to hold large amounts of polyfiller while you are filling any holes or cracks in surfaces. Having a filling board allows the painter to cover large areas at a time.

Filling board

Shave hooks

Shave hooks are used to scrape off loose deposits and old coatings from beadings and mouldings during burning off or basic paint removal processes. They can also be used to prepare areas which are to receive fillers. Shave hooks are available in three different shapes: triangular, pear-shaped and a combination of the two. The blade edges should be kept sharp to ensure maximum performance and avoid unnecessary damage to surfaces.

Shave hooks

Chipping hammer

Chipping hammers are used to remove heavy rust, millscale and loose rust while preparing surfaces before painting. These tools come in both hand-held and powered versions.

Chipping hammer

Filling tools and equipment

Hand-held hawk and trowel

Painters use hawks and trowels to repair small holes in plastered walls or plasterboards before painting.

Hand hawk

Pointing trowel

Pointing trowels are used by painters to repair lightly damaged brickwork while preparing before painting or protecting.

Pointing trowel

Torches and strippers

LPG torch/gun

LPG (liquefied petroleum gas) torches or guns are used to remove old paint and varnish. They do this by producing a naked flame that makes the area being treated hot, allowing the paint or varnish to be scraped off with a stripping knife or shave hook.

As an alternative to an LPG torch that runs from a large gas canister (see photo), a smaller disposable cartridge type gas torch is also available. These are light and easy to use, although they do produce less heat and have a shorter burning time.

There are a number of safety precautions that should be followed when using this type of equipment and these are dealt with in Chapter 10 *Preparation of surfaces* (see page 200).

LPG torch/gun

Remember

LPG torches or guns should never be used to remove lead-based coatings. This is because toxic fumes or dust can be released, which can cause lasting damage to the airways and lungs and possibly permanent breathing problems

Safety tip

Always follow the manufacturer's instructions regarding the correct use and maintenance of LPG torches

Hot air gun/stripper

Hot air guns or strippers are used in the same way as LPG torches, but they produce hot air via an electrical element rather than a naked flame. This reduces the risk of fire and scorching of surfaces such as timber. In addition, hot air guns/strippers are more suited to use on surfaces where there is a risk of **combustion** or where there is glass present, which could crack due to the high temperature.

Hot air gun/stripper

> **Definition**
>
> **Combustion**
> – burning or catching on fire

Fire extinguisher

You will need various types of fire extinguisher when carrying out 'burning off' tasks as part of your preparation work.

Steam stripper

Using a steam stripper is a very efficient way of removing surface coverings from both walls and ceilings. However, care must be taken when using this method because over-application of the steam process can result in damage to the covered surface, leading to blistering and/or removal of small areas of plaster finishes. Care must also be taken when using these items on ceilings because the user can be at risk from burns or scalding due to the hot water/steam produced by the stripper.

Steam stripper

Brushes

All brushes need to be cleaned thoroughly after use. Leaving traces of material on the bristles could damage them, making the brush useless. Care of brushes depends upon the material from which they are made. It is therefore best to read any manufacturer's instructions on cleaning and storage.

Dusting brush

Dusting brushes are used to remove loose dust, grit and other fine debris from surfaces before applying paint.

Dusting brush

Dustpan and brush

A dustpan and brush can be used for general cleaning before and after decorating and is an important part of the decorator's tool kit. If you fail to remove dust and debris from your work area, it may result in the contamination of surfaces and paint systems, leading to poor workmanship and a damaged reputation.

Dustpan and brush

Wire brush

Wire brush

A wire brush is used to remove loose rust and corrosion from various types of metalwork. They are available with either steel wire or bronze wire bristles. Bronze wire versions are suited to situations where there is a fire hazard as they will not cause sparks.

Rotary wire brush

Rotary wire brushes are used in the same way as ordinary wire brushes, although they are more powerful and less manually demanding to use (i.e. they do some of the work for you).

Rotary wire brush

Masking tools and equipment

Masking shield

A masking shield is a sheet of springy aluminium used while spray painting. Masking shields come in 24", 36" and 48" lengths, and each is about 10" wide. The shield is reinforced along one edge, and has an 18" handle fitted to the middle of it.

Masking gun/machine

Masking guns and masking machines are used with rolls of masking tape. They are ideal if you want to save time when masking up areas before spraying or painting.

Masking gun/machine

Abrading equipment

Abrading is an important part of preparing a surface to be decorated. You will often need to remove substances from the surface you are going to work on and abrading can also be useful after decorating, for example if paintwork has dried too quickly and wrinkled.

Abrasive paper

Sometimes known as sandpaper, abrasive paper is grit on flexible backing sheets used to wear down a surface. Abrasive paper is available with different sizes of grit, each suited to a different type of task (e.g. for coarse or fine abrasion). Wet abrasive paper can be used with water to give a very fine abrasion or, when used with mineral oil, for smoothing and polishing metals.

You should always use the correct type of abrasive paper for the job and you should never use hand abrasive paper in a power tool such as an orbital or belt sander. Abrasive papers should be stored in a cool dry place and replaced regularly.

Pole sander

Pole sander

A pole sander is used when preparing surfaces with sandpaper or abrasive paper, to help you reach high areas such as ceilings and the tops of walls.

Rubbing blocks

Rubbing blocks are used to support both wet and dry abrasive papers and make handling and working with abrasive papers easier. They are available in wood, plastic, cork or rubber versions.

Rubbing block

Sanders

There are two main types of sander used for the purpose of abrading:

1. orbital sander

2. belt sander.

The orbital sander is the slower of the two, but is lighter and easier to use. It can be used to prepare surfaces ready for painting, including timber, plastic, most metals and previously painted surfaces. This type of sander is more suited to small areas. The belt sander is much faster than the orbital sander and is more suited to larger surface areas.

Orbital sander

Belt sander

Chapter 10 *Preparation of surfaces* provides further information on the use of abrading materials (see page 197).

Other types of preparation tools and equipment

Needle gun

Needle guns are used to remove rust from around corroded nuts, bolts, rivets and welds. They can also be used in the preparation of stonework. There are various types of needles available for use with the gun depending on the surface to be prepared. Needle guns are powered by compressed air and great care must be taken to ensure safe operation.

Needle gun

Caulking tool

Made up of a flexible flat metal or plastic blade set in a wooden or plastic handle, a caulking tool is used for applying filler and jointing materials. It is also sometimes used to smooth out decorative coverings applied to plasterboard surfaces. A caulking tool should be maintained in the same way as a filling knife.

Caulking tool

Nail punch

A nail punch enables you to countersink any nail heads that are protruding on timber surfaces while preparing for painting.

Nail punch

Screwdrivers

A selection of screwdrivers for removing fixtures and fittings such as switches, sockets and radiators should be kept in your toolkit.

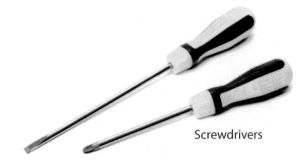

Screwdrivers

Pincers and pliers

Pincers and pliers are used to remove nails, wire clips and picture hooks while decorating.

Pliers

Pincers

Painting tools and equipment

Paint is used to give protection and colour to walls, ceilings and other surfaces. Made up of pigment (the colour) and an oil- or water-based binder, paint can be applied very easily and quickly to give a basic addition of colour or, with the aid of special tools and techniques, paint can also give very creative and striking effects and finishes. For more information on paint application techniques, see Chapter 13 *Applying paint and creating special effects* (page 259) and Chapter 14 *Applying surface coverings* (page 285).

Paintbrushes

A brush's bristles, also known as the **filling**, can be either pure bristle (animal hair), man-made fibres, natural fibres or a combination of these. The filling is attached to the handle of the brush via the stock and secured with the use of an adhesive.

After use, a brush must be thoroughly cleaned. This means that all traces of paint should be removed with a suitable solvent. The solvent should then be washed out of the filling with warm soapy water. Brushes should be hung up to dry and should never be put away while still wet or damp.

Always store brushes flat and *never* stand the brush upright on the filling because this will permanently change the shape of the filling and leave the brush useless.

Find out

What are the pros and cons (advantages/disadvantages) of the different fillings available?

Always read the paint manufacturer's instructions regarding their recommended cleaning process.

Flat brush

A flat brush is the type of brush used for the majority of paint and varnish work and is available in a wide variety of sizes and filling types. The 1" flat brush is also known as a sash brush as it is normally used for painting sashes and frames. Larger flat brushes, including the 4" size, are used mainly for painting walls and ceilings. The handle is usually made from beech or birch, although cheaper varieties with plastic handles are available.

Flat brushes

Radiator brush

Radiator brush

A radiator brush is used to apply paint behind radiators and pipes. It has a long flexible handle and is ideal for painting awkward and hard-to-reach areas.

Crevice brush

Crevice brushes are much the same as radiator brushes but are angled to allow access to the most awkward of areas.

Crevice brush

Lining brush

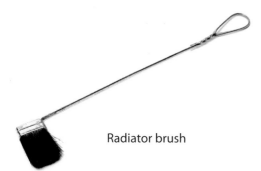

Lining brush

Lining brushes are used together with a straight edge to produce straight lines. This type of brush is very flat and thin.

Stencil brush

A stencil brush is a short, stumpy brush used for applying paint to stencils or around templates.

Stencil brush

Masonry brush

Masonry brushes are used to apply paint to surfaces such as stonework, brick, concrete and **rendering**. They are cheap to buy and very **durable**.

Masonry brush

Fitch

A **fitch** is ideal for painting areas difficult to reach with a standard paintbrush and also for more detailed work. They are available in either a flat or round style.

Fitch

Rollers

A roller can quickly and effectively coat large flat surface areas with paint. Specially shaped rollers are also available for painting corners and other unusually shaped surfaces, although sometimes it can be easier to simply use a brush.

The part of the roller that holds the paint is the roller sleeve and it is a plastic tube covered with fabric. The type of sleeve, and thus the type of fabric, chosen depends upon the kind of coating to be applied and the structure of the surface. The sleeve slides onto the frame of the roller. The frame will be either a cage type or a stick type.

Roller sleeves

Rollers are available in many sizes and can have single or double arms. A double arm roller is available for roller sleeves of 300 mm and above.

All rollers must be cleaned thoroughly after use. Always hang them up to dry because if left resting wet on a surface, damage will be caused to the fabric which will seriously affect the finish of future paint applications.

Roller frame (single arm cage type)

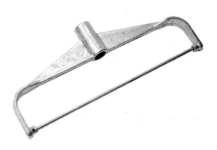

Double arm roller

Radiator roller

Radiator rollers are also known as mini rollers and are available in sizes of up to 150 mm. As the name suggests, they are ideal for use on radiators and other small surface areas where the use of a standard roller would be impractical.

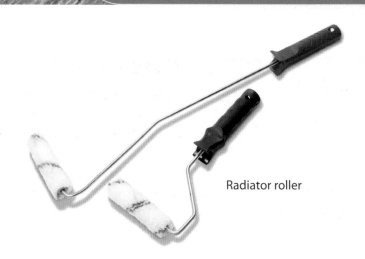

Radiator roller

Specialised rollers

There are a number of types of roller designed for specific tasks such as painting pipe work or producing decorative and textured effects. One such roller is the Duet® roller, which is made from uneven pieces of chamois leather attached to a spindle.

Duet® roller

Find out

What types of roller fabric are available? What type of decorative or textured effects does each type produce?

Other types of painting tools and equipment

Paint stirrer

Quite simply, this is used to stir paint, as well as other decorating materials such as varnish and paste. Available in various lengths, they consist of a blade with a series of holes, through which the paint passes as it is stirred. Stirring in this way enables the paint or other liquid to be mixed more thoroughly than if mixed with a stirrer without holes (i.e. with a stick).

Paint stirrer

Paint kettle (work pot)

Made from either plastic or metal, a paint kettle (often known as a work pot) is a convenient way of holding manageable amounts of paint while working from stepladders or other platforms. Always ensure that your paint kettle is thoroughly cleaned out after use in order to avoid contamination of paints and to prolong the life of the kettle.

Paint kettle (work pot)

Brush keep

A brush keep is used to store brushes in a wet state. It works by way of a solvent being placed in a bottle with an evaporating wick. The fumes from the evaporating solvent replace the air in the brush keep, preventing the brushes from drying out.

Brush keep

Extension pole

Extension poles are attached to roller handles in order to give additional reach, thus reducing the need for working on stepladders when painting areas such as ceilings or high walls.

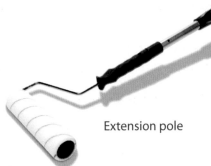

Extension pole

Roller tray

Roller trays are used to hold paint when using a roller. They are made from either plastic or metal and are designed to ensure even coverage of the roller sleeve with paint.

Roller tray

Scuttle

A **scuttle** is used to hold paint when using a roller from a ladder. Some have attachments that allow them to be hung on the ladder's rungs

Scuttle

Paper hanging tools and equipment

Paper hanging is the technique of applying wallpaper to areas such as walls, ceilings etc. The term also includes the hanging of **relief materials**, fabrics and vinyl papers.

Brushes

Paste brush

Apart from being used to apply paste to wallpaper, a paste brush can also be used for washing down and sizing. They are available in a range of sizes between 100 mm and 175 mm.

Paste brush

> **Definition**
>
> **Relief materials** – a material that has a pattern that stands out from the background

Paper hanging brush

The paper hanging brush is also known as a sweep. It is used to remove all air bubbles between the wall covering and the surface to which it is being applied. After use, the brush should be cleaned in soapy water and hung up to dry.

Paper hanging brush

Measuring and levelling tools

Straight edge

Bevel-edged lengths of steel or wood provide straight edges and can also be used for several other activities such as, when used with a trimming knife (see below), producing butt joints and mitres when hanging wall coverings.

Straight edge

Spirit level

Spirit level

A spirit level can be used as a straight edge. It can also be useful when marking horizontal and vertical lines and can aid cutting of coverings before pasting.

Plumb bob and line

A **plumb bob** is a weight to which string or twine is attached in order to produce a completely vertical line. These are still sometimes used instead of straight edges and spirit levels.

Plumb bob and line

Cutting equipment

Scissors or shears

Scissors or shears usually have polished stainless blades and are used for cutting or trimming wall coverings. Make sure they are kept clean and dry to prevent rusting. Scissors and shears must also be kept sharp or damage to wall coverings will result.

Scissors

Trimming knife

A trimming knife can be used as an alternative to scissors or shears but is most effective when used with a straight edge of some kind, for example a caulking blade or spirit level.

Trimming knife

Casing wheel

Casing wheels can have a serrated or plain blade and are used for trimming surplus paper around angles and obstacles such as light fittings and brackets.

Casing wheel

Other types of paper hanging tools and equipment

Pasteboard

A pasteboard is a long sturdy table made from wood that can be folded down for easier transportation, either in the same location or between locations. It is used to support coverings during preparation, cutting and pasting. The pasteboard surface should be kept clean both during and after the work.

Pasteboard

Wallpaper trough

A wallpaper trough is a container that is filled with water, in which pre-pasted wallpaper is submerged before hanging.

Wallpaper trough

Caulking blade

Caulking blades can be used as alternatives to paper hanging brushes when hanging fabrics or vinyl papers, but only on flat surfaces.

Caulking blade

Seam and angle roller

A seam and angle roller is used to roll down joints in wall coverings during hanging.

Seam and angle roller

Tape measure

A retractable metal tape measure is an important element of any decorator's toolkit. Available in a variety of lengths, most have both metric (centimetres and metres) and imperial (inches and feet) measurements. It is important to keep a tape measure clean as a dirty tape measure is likely to eventually clog up, making retraction of the tape back into the casing difficult.

Tape

Felt roller

Felt rollers are either a felt covered one-piece roller or several felt cylinders in line on a roller cage. They act as another alternative to the paper hanging brush.

Felt roller

Rubber roller

Rubber roller

Rubber rollers are used to hang very heavy materials, generally when a felt roller or paper hanging brush would not be heavy enough.

Pasting machine

Available as either table-top machines or as free-standing heavy duty pieces of equipment, a pasting machine makes applying paste to wall coverings easy. Paper is drawn through a paste trough which coats the backing of the wall covering evenly. Care must be taken when using these machines and you need to be aware that some delicate, decorative and other specialist coverings may be damaged if passed through a pasting machine. Always check the manufacturer's instructions.

Specialist tools and equipment

With the use of some special tools and some remarkably everyday items, it is possible to create some amazing decorative paint finishes, such as:

*   graining – the imitation of wood

*   marbling – the imitation of natural marbles, granite and stone

*   broken colour – a multi-coloured effect

*   stencil work – a cut-out pattern or design.

Creating paint finishes such as those listed above is now a separate and specialised division of the painting and decorating trade. Used mostly in the **restoration** of historic buildings, creating specialist paint finishes takes a lot of time to master but, if done well, can be extremely satisfying and rewarding.

For more information on the creation of specialist paint techniques and the use of some of the tools detailed below, see Chapter 13 *Applying paint and creating special effects* (page 259).

Definition

Restoration – returning a building to its original condition

Graining combs

Graining combs can be made from steel or rubber and are available with various teeth sizes and different shapes to enable different types of grain effects.

Graining combs

Stippling brush

Stippling brushes are also available in various sizes and they are used to remove brush marks from **scumble** to give a stippled finish.

Stippling brush

Flogger

Flogging recreates the fine pore marks associated with wood by drumming on the surface with a long bristled brush – a flogger. The bristles of these brushes can be made from horse or hog hair.

Flogger

Mottler

A mottler is used to produce highlights and various other patterns in graining work.

Mottler

Overgrainer

An overgrainer is used in much the same way as a mottler and produces finer highlights in the graining work.

Overgrainer

Pencil overgrainer

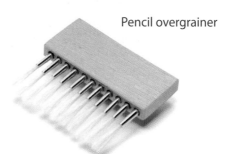

Pencil overgrainer

A pencil overgrainer can be made from hog or sable and is used for figure work that creates depth. This brush creates an intricate secondary grain effect and is especially useful in the imitation of American walnut.

Drag brush

A drag brush is a coarse bristled brush made from horsehair, fibre or nylon. It is used to produce straight grained patterns.

Drag brush

Softener

A softener is used to soften and blend harsh edges of patterns. It is made from badger or hog hair and available in flat or round versions.

Softener

Sea sponge

Sea sponge

Sea sponges can be used to produce some of the best broken colour effects and softer patterned effects.

Veining horn

Veining horns are made from plastic and have one round end and one square end. They are used for reproducing the veins seen in many marbles and can also be used to produce oak grain patterns.

Veining horn

Heart grain simulator

A heart grain simulator is a moulded rubber tool with a heartwood pattern imprinted on the face. It is used to produce the repeating heartwood patterns seen in various timbers.

Heart grain simulator

Check roller

A check roller is used to reproduce the broken pore markings of various timbers. This tool is a combination of a mottler-type brush fitted to a series of serrated metal discs. The mottler provides the paint supply and the discs provide the pattern.

Check roller

Mahl stick

A mahl stick is a stiff rod made from timber or metal and is designed to support and steady the hand during signwriting and other work that requires a steady hand.

Mahl stick

Gilder's cushion, knife and tip

Gilding is the art of covering a surface with a very thin layer of gold. A gilder's cushion is a padded felt board covered in leather that is used when preparing and applying gold leaf. A shield is formed at one end using parchment which protects the gold and stops it from moving or being blown away. The knife and tip are used to cut and prepare the gold leaf (and sometimes other leaf).

The filling of a gilder's tip is made from squirrel or badger hair which is secured between two pieces of card. Before use, the filling has to be rubbed vigorously together in order to charge it with static electricity. The static then attracts the gold leaf to the tip, ready for application to the surface.

Gilder's cushion, knife and tip

Stencil knife

A stencil knife is a tool used for cutting stencils out of stencil card or plastic.

Stencil knife

Spray painting tools and equipment
Transformer

A transformer can be used on site to allow power tools to operate (110 volts), even when the main voltage is a domestic voltage (230 volts).

Extension cable

Used in conjunction with a transformer, an extension cable allows you to use power tools without having to be right near the power source.

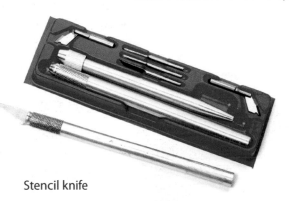

Transformer

Compressor

Compressors come in petrol, diesel and electric models. They are used to power spray equipment and other items used in the trade.

Pressure feed tanks and pots

Pressure feed tanks and pots are used when large quantities of paint or coatings are to be sprayed. Having a large tank or pot saves time, as cup-guns, etc. need filling up frequently.

Compressor

Glazing tools and equipment

Painters and decorators will sometimes have to replace small panes of glass and re-putty windows due to accidental breakages when decorating. The following tools and equipment are required for the replacement of glass.

Glasscutter

Glasscutters have wooden or plastic handles and can have up to six small cutting wheels that can be rotated. Tips can be made from tungsten or diamond.

Glasscutter

Putty or glazing knife

This tool is used to apply putty or stopper to small cracks and holes when repairing surfaces or applying putty during the glazing process. It can also be used while forming the bevel finishes to putty used in glass replacement. The blade should be cleaned thoroughly after every task and checked regularly for any damage, which could result in imperfections in the surface of the finished putty.

Putty (or glazing) knife

Hacking knife

This is used for the removal of old putty. It can also be used with a hammer if required. It is advisable to retain the blade's sharpness with regular maintenance.

Hacking knife

Straight edge and T-square

These items are used together to get straight edges and right angles when cutting glass.

T-square

Did you know?

An old wood chisel can be used instead of a hacking knife

Glazing pliers

Glazing pliers grip onto glass when cutting it into thin strips and are useful when removing pieces of broken glass.

Suction pads

Suction pads enable holding and carrying of panes of glass.

Glazing pliers

Suction pads

Tenon saw and mitre block

A mitre block has 45° cutting slots that help with the cutting of precise angles for beads on windows where putty is not used as the finish.

Tenon saw and mitre block

Definition

Sprig – a very fine nail used in glazing

Pin hammer

Pin hammers are used to lightly tap in glazing **sprigs**.

Pin hammer

Claw hammer

Claw hammers are used to remove sprigs from hardened putty and, with the aid of a hacking knife, can also be used to remove putty.

Claw hammer

FAQ

Will I need my own tool kit? If I do, how can I buy all the tools I need if I don't have much money?

While you are training, all the tools you need will be supplied by your training provider. When you have successfully completed your training, you may need your own tool kit, depending on who you work for. If you work for a large company, all tools and equipment are usually provided. If you work for a small company, they may not provide you with a tool kit. If you start your own business, you will definitely need to provide your own tool kit and equipment. It is a good idea to start a small collection of tools as soon as possible while you are training. You don't need to buy everything, but the essentials will always be useful. It is usually best to buy quality tools, which do cost a little more, but you will notice the difference.

On the job: Replacing glass

Stuart is a self-employed decorator and is currently working on a client's bungalow. He is removing the old and flaking paint from the bungalow's windows, making repairs and applying a new coat of paint. While Stuart is burning off the old paintwork with a LPG torch, a pane of glass cracks.

What PPE will Stuart need to replace the pane of glass? What specialist tools do you think he will need? Describe in a few words the procedure you would follow when replacing the glass.

Knowledge check

1. Name two pieces of equipment that can be used for removing surface coatings.

2. What different kinds of abrasive paper are available?

3. Draw a picture of a putty knife.

4. Why should you check electrical equipment before use?

5. What are the three parts of a paintbrush?

6. Name two types of roller.

7. What container can be used to hold paint when using a roller?

8. What is a pure bristle brush?

9. What could you use to paste wallpaper with instead of a paste brush?

10. What is the difference between a seam roller and a felt roller?

11. What is a sweep another name for and what is its use?

12. Why might a painter and decorator need a screwdriver?

13. What brush would you use to soften grain effects?

14. Name two tools that create highlights in graining work.

15. What is a veining horn used for?

16. What are chipping hammers used for?

17. Why would a painter and decorator need to use a hand-held hawk and trowel?

18. Draw a masking shield with appropriate measurements marked on it.

19. When removing picture hooks, clips and nails from a surface, what is the best tool to use to avoid damage to the surface?

20. When would a painter need to use a compressor?

chapter 9

Site preparation

OVERVIEW

Site preparation is what the decorator does before starting any work. Many items need to be protected before decorating is started, for example carpets, curtains and pictures and garden furniture and plant pots. Some items can simply be removed from the work area, however this is not always possible and clearly when something is a permanent fitting (e.g. a banister or a radiator) it is impractical to move it.

This chapter will cover the following topics:

- Materials used to provide protection
- Common items requiring protection and methods used
- Protection of external items
- Site preparation when spray painting.

These topics can be found in the following modules:

CC 2002K	CC 2024K
CC 2002S	CC 2024S

Materials used to provide protection

Before any decoration is done, the most important task for the decorator is the protection of any areas, items, fixtures and fittings that are not being worked on that could be damaged.

Common items that need protecting include:

- carpets, rugs and other types of flooring
- sofas, curtains, chairs, tables, electrical equipment
- pictures, shelving, wall lights and sockets
- ceiling light fittings, shades and fire alarms/smoke detectors
- door furniture (handles, hinges, locks etc.)
- plant pots, garden seats and patio areas.

It is very important that, before you start any work, you look around and make sure that all items are protected by removing them or covering them with the appropriate material. Damage caused during decorating could be very costly, both to the decorator's pocket and reputation.

Dustsheets, tarpaulin and corrugated sheeting

Sheet materials such as dustsheets, tarpaulin and corrugated sheeting are the most commonly used and useful of protective materials. Sheeting can protect against paint and paste splashes and spillages and also small particles that are created when sanding or scraping.

Dustsheets

Dustsheets of the highest quality should be used wherever possible as cheap alternatives do not always provide adequate protection. There are two basic types of dustsheet available, each with very different characteristics: cotton twill and polythene sheets.

Dustsheets

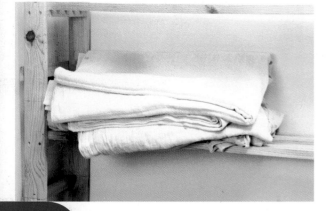

Cotton twill dustsheets

The best quality dustsheets are cotton twill sheets, which should be double folded to increase thickness. Cotton twill dustsheets are generally used to protect flooring and furniture and can be purchased in a variety of sizes, the most common being 4 m x 6 m. Other sizes are available and there are also special width and length dustsheets for use when working on staircases.

Advantages:

- present a professional image (when clean)
- when laid they remain in place well and are not easily disturbed when walked on
- available in different weights and sizes.

Disadvantages:

- expensive to purchase and clean
- heavy paint spillage can soak through the sheet
- can absorb chemicals such as paint stripper
- possible fire risk.

If laid well, a cotton dustsheet provides good protection

Polythene dustsheets

Polythene dustsheets can be used in the same way as cotton twill sheets, but they are waterproof and can be thrown away after use.

Advantages:

- inexpensive to purchase
- heavy paint spills do not soak through the sheet
- do not absorb chemicals such as paint strippers.

Disadvantages:

- do not present such a professional image as cotton dustsheets
- when laid they do not remain in place well and are easily disturbed.

Tarpaulin

Tarpaulin sheets are made of different types of material including:

- rubber-coated cotton
- heavy cotton canvas (usually very expensive)
- **PVC**-coated nylon
- nylon scrim (coated with a polyester resin).

The most common size of tarpaulin sheets is 6 m x 4 m although larger sizes can be made to order. Because tarpaulin is protective against moisture, it is best to use it when washing down surfaces or when steam stripping wallpaper.

Remember

It is important to select the type of sheet that is most suitable for the task at hand

Definition

PVC – polyvinyl chloride (a tough plastic)

Tarpaulin sheeting is also used on and around scaffolding in order to give workers and the work area protection from bad weather conditions. It also offers protection to equipment and surfaces if there is a lot of movement around them.

Corrugated sheeting

Some work is aggressive and/or extensive (e.g. paint stripping to restore ceiling plaster), in which case the sheeting materials already discussed would not provide enough protection.

Corrugated PVC and cardboard can be purchased in sheet form and laid over the floor and jointed with 50 mm masking tape, offering more appropriate protection. Although this type of protection may be expensive to install, it helps avoid corrective work and undamaged sheets can be reused.

Other materials used for protection

As well as specially designed protective equipment, a decorator can use all manner of ordinary items in site preparation. Plastic bags, such as carrier bags or bin liners, are excellent for protecting light fittings, wall lights and chandeliers etc. The item is simply inserted into the bag, which can then be tied up and secured with masking tape – cheap and simple but very effective.

Masking paper and tapes are also used in the protection of items. Masking paper is a smooth brown paper and is used to protect floors, furniture and also windows. It comes on a roll in various width sizes from 150 mm to 450 mm. Masking paper can be held in place with masking tape but it is quite often self-adhesive.

Masking tape is often used to block off areas when painting, such as light switches, door handles and woodwork.

Cardboard boxes can be used to store smaller items such as pictures and ornaments. A small container, such as a box or a bag, can also be used to hold screws and nails that are collected when removing items and preparing the area (e.g. picture hooks, shelves, ventilation grilles etc.). This will ensure that nothing is lost or damaged.

Remember

Take care when handling items during site preparation – you will be responsible for any breakages you cause! It may be prudent to ask the client to remove valuables prior to beginning work.

Common items requiring protection and methods used

As previously stated, you should always assess a work area for items that need to be protected before starting any work.

Figure 9.1 What do you think may need protecting in this room? See below image for answers

Mirror, TV, TV stand, pelmet, curtains, glass (doors), rug, light switch, wall light, plug socket, ventilation grille, fireplace, mantelpiece, clock, candlesticks, carpet, skirting

Some common examples of door furniture

Door furniture

Any items on an internal or external door, such as handles, finger plates, letter boxes, numbers, knockers, hinges, kick plates, push plates, door bell buttons, spy holes etc., are known as door furniture.

The easiest way to protect door furniture from paint, varnish or scratches is to remove it. To avoid the loss or accidental damage of any door furniture and screws, pack straight into a box or crate, covering individual items with newspaper, bubble wrap or something similar. Store the container in a safe and dry place.

If the removal of door furniture is impossible or inappropriate, covering it with masking tape is an acceptable alternative.

Safety tip

Site preparation can result in injury. Always be aware of hazards involved with the work you do such as slips, trips, falls and manual handling injuries

Curtains and pelmets

Curtains should ideally always be removed before carrying out any work since cleaning, repair or replacement is usually very costly.

Remove curtains by first pulling them apart and then taking them off their track or pole. Next, carefully and neatly place the curtains into a plastic bag and remove them from the room, storing them safely in a dry place.

A pelmet is a piece of cloth or other material that covers the curtain pole or track. After it has been removed, cover it with a protective sheet or place it in a bag and again store in a safe dry place.

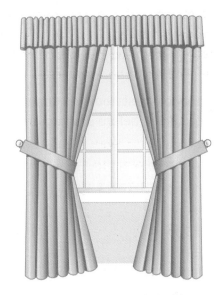

Figure 9.2 Curtains and a pelmet should ideally be removed

Curtain poles and tracks

Again, the best protection is to remove the item from the work area. Alternatively, the pole or track should be securely covered with a suitable material.

Figure 9.3 A wooden curtain pole

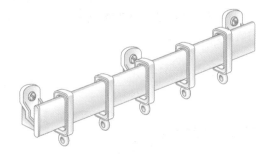

Figure 9.4 A curtain track

Remove the pole or track from its brackets, then unscrew the brackets from the wall. Place any small parts into a container to prevent them from being lost. All items should then be taken from the room and stored in a safe place.

Blinds

There are various types of blind, such as:

- roller blind
- vertical blind
- Venetian blind.

Remember

When removing items such as curtains, blinds and shelving where there is more than one of each, it is a good idea to keep them separate and find a method of remembering what item went where. This will prevent mix-ups and save time when the job is finished

Roller blind

Before removal, the blind should be in a retracted or rolled-up position (where the window is visible). Next, remove the blind from its bracket and then unscrew the brackets from the wall. Place any small parts in a container and remove all parts of the blind from the work area.

Shelves

It is possible to work around shelving, but it is much easier to remove it. Removal also helps protect the shelving.

Wooden shelves can be easily removed, placed in a box or wrapped in protective material and moved out of the way. Glass shelving should be wrapped in newspaper, bubble wrap or other similar material to avoid breakage. Shelves are attached to walls with brackets, which are screwed on to walls with the aid of Rawlplugs™. Brackets and fixing screws should also be removed and put in a safe place.

FAQ

After a shelving bracket has been removed, how do I find the screw hole after wallpapering?

It is a good idea to place something in the hole as soon as you have finished sweeping over the paper. This could be a match or a screw.

Light fittings

These can be anything from wall lights to ceiling lights but may also include larger and heavier items such as chandeliers.

Only a qualified electrician should remove light fittings, although a decorator can remove light shades once the electricity has been turned off at the mains. The fuse must be removed from the mains fuse box or a warning notice put in place to prevent the power from being accidentally reconnected.

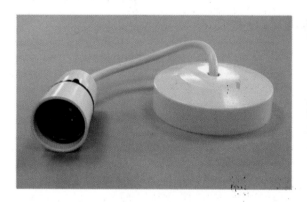

A typical light fitting

Fittings, once removed, should be wrapped and stored in a box or crate and kept in a safe location. Shades should be bagged and secured with tape. If chandeliers cannot be removed, they should be covered with light polythene sheeting and securely taped.

Covers and grilles

You may come across various types of covers and grilles used in ventilation, heating and air conditioning systems.

Made from plastic, metal and, in some instances, fibrous plaster, they can be found in various positions on walls throughout a building, providing cover for inlets and outlets.

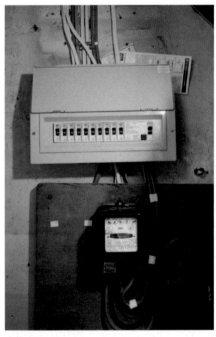
Mains fuse box

A typical ventilation grille

Remove by unscrewing. The cover or grille can then be stored in a safe place. If removal is inappropriate or impossible, a cover or grille can be covered with masking tape.

Furniture

This can be anything from a small coffee table to a dining table or a three-piece suite. Furniture also includes electrical equipment such as televisions, DVD players and stereos.

If possible, furniture should be removed from the work area to another room or a suitable temporary storage location. Where removal is not possible, furniture should be stored in a way that maximises the work space (e.g. moved to the middle of the room) and covered with suitable sheeting material depending on the type of work being carried out.

Furniture should be protected or removed

Carpets

Decorators are not usually qualified to remove or refit carpets. If necessary, removal and refitting should be arranged by the client.

Where carpets have not been removed a combination of dustsheets, polythene sheeting and masking tape should be used to protect them.

Ornaments, pictures and small valuable items

Wrapped in newspaper, bubble wrap or another suitable material, ornaments, pictures and valuables should be packed into containers such as crates or boxes. These should then be stored within the premises in a safe and dry place in order to protect them from damage, loss or theft.

Radiators

When working on new buildings, a decorator is able to carry out decorating tasks before radiators are fitted. Other situations may require the removal of radiators in order for certain work to be completed. If properly instructed in how to do so, a decorator may remove a radiator from a wall themselves. The following sequence should be followed:

1. Protect the area from leaks and damage.

2. Turn off the water supply.

3. Undo the radiator connections and drain (bleed) the radiator.

4. Remove the radiator from its brackets and store safely.

5. After decoration is complete, place and attach the radiator on to its brackets.

6. Reconnect the pipe work to the radiator.

7. Open the bleed valve.

8. Turn the water supply back on.

9. Close the bleed valve.

10. Check for leaks and leave the area clean and tidy.

There are three main types of radiator: panel, column and radiant panel.

Panel radiator

Protection of external items

When carrying out decorating tasks outside, it can be easy to forget about site preparation, but external items need protecting for the same reasons as internal items. External items that require protection include paths and patio areas, garden furniture, plant pots and alarm boxes. As with internal items, removal is the best form of protection, but where this is not possible, covering with an appropriate material is acceptable.

When you have finished decorating, always place items back in their original position. This will leave the client with a good impression of your workmanship so you will develop good relationships and benefit from customer recommendation.

Site preparation when spray painting

Site preparation is important to any decent painter and decorator, but it is particularly so when applying coatings to surfaces by spray painting.

It is important to make sure that any surface that is not to be sprayed is masked up correctly.

Spraying interiors

If you were to spray the interior of a commercial building (such as an office), you would need to mask any windows to avoid paint damaging them. To do this, you would cover the glass with a masking paper and masking tape, making sure that the paper was overlapped correctly and sealed with tape.

If you were spraying the interior of a house, and only the walls and ceiling were to be sprayed, you would have to make sure that all removable items were taken out, then mask up any items that could not be removed (carpets, skirting boards, etc.). Carpets would need to be protected with dust sheets, covered with polythene sheeting and then taped up correctly around the room; skirting boards and architrave around doors would need taping up with a low-tack masking tape, applied correctly with no gaps.

Buildings such as factories also need the correct masking, as there could be expensive items such as machinery inside, or tiled floors that need protecting. You would need to mask correctly any pipes, electric cables and tubing which were not being sprayed, using polythene sheets and masking tape, ensuring there were no gaps or spaces. To protect the flooring, you would use sheets of hardboard, corrugated plastic or heavy cardboard, sealed around the floor edges with a heavy, well-applied masking tape. As the sprayer would be walking around the area, the masking would need to be sturdy enough not to lift, letting overspray hit the floor.

Spraying exteriors

When spraying any premises or building externally, you need to 'tent in' the area. The 'tent' comprises of a scaffold structure covered with polythene sheeting, which must be taped up correctly. A tent prevents overspray coating any other buildings and avoids damage to any vehicles nearby. Tenting in also prevents hazards to the public and reduces pollution, as the tented in area will have extraction and ventilation systems added to it.

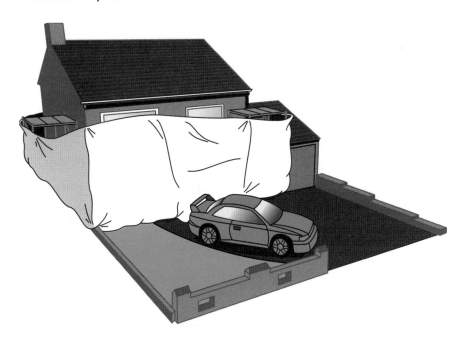

Figure 9.5 Tent used to protect surroundings when spraying externally

On the job: Preparation

Arthur has been asked to strip the paint from and repaint the cast iron guttering and pipework at the rear of a client's property. Before Arthur begins the work, he looks around the part of the garden nearest the house. He can see a set of patio furniture, a bicycle lent against the house and clothes on a washing line attached to one of the external walls. There is also a variety of pot plants and shrubs on the patio near the house.

Before Arthur begins the paint job, what items and areas do you think he will need to protect? What is the best way to protect each of these items/areas? What safety precautions will Arthur have to consider? Think about things like the equipment and tools Arthur will use and the fact he will be working at height.

Knowledge check

1. What are good quality dustsheets made from?

2. Name an everyday object (i.e. one that doesn't have to be specially bought) that could be used for protection.

3. What is the voltage usually used on site?

4. Name three different types of radiators.

5. Name three different types of blinds.

6. What is the best way to protect flooring from damage?

7. Name four different pieces of door furniture.

8. Can you name the correct sequence of events for removing a radiator?

9. What assessment should you do before starting any work?

10. What special consideration should be taken account of when removing and storing electrical equipment?

11. How would you protect windows when spraying inside a factory, commercial building or a home?

12. Describe how you would protect any pipes, electric cables or tubing prior to spraying.

13. How would you 'tent in' an area prior to spraying?

14. Name the different sizes/names of masking tapes used in site preparation.

15. Name five different types of masking materials.

16. What can you use to make 'masking up' with tape easier?

17. What is 7-day masking tape?

chapter 10

Preparation of surfaces

OVERVIEW

Most surfaces that the decorator works with require some kind of preparation before work can begin. The correct preparation of a surface is essential if you are going to produce work that looks good and lasts well.

It is important that all surface contaminants such as dirt, oil, rust and loose or flaking existing coatings are removed. If contaminants are not removed, the ability of paint or paper to adhere (stick) to the surface will be affected.

This chapter will cover the following topics:

- Defects
- Corrosion or rust
- Painted surfaces in poor condition
- Cleaning surfaces
- Abrading surfaces
- Special types of surface preparation
- Typical surfaces and their preparation
- Environmental considerations.

These topics can be found in the following modules:

CC 2002K	CC 2019K	CC 2024K
CC 2002S	CC 2019S	CC 2024S

Defects

Before working on a surface, you will need to inspect the area for any defects. Surface defects include holes, cracks, dents and pitting and, if left, will affect the finished result. Correcting a defect is sometimes called 'making good' and just means the repair of a surface defect.

There is a wide range of substances that can be used to repair a surface defect and they generally fall into one of two categories:

- Filler – a smooth paste that is used to fill minor defects such as shrinkage cracks and nail or screw holes.

- Stopper – a similar material to filler but better for use on large holes and cracks.

Fillers and stoppers are both often referred to as 'filling agents' and this is how we will refer to them throughout this book.

Corrosion or rust

During your inspection of the work surface, you may notice areas where the surface has **corroded**, usually due to **rust**. This will have to be cleaned and removed before work can be carried out.

Removing rust by hand

Cleaning off rust by hand is hard work but is possible and is normally done when repainting rusty steelwork, as it is usually the cheapest method in the short-term. The problem with hand cleaning off rust is that the use of scrapers, chipping hammers, wire brushes and abrasives will not remove all traces of rust from the surface. In addition, the overuse of a wire brush can serve to only polish the rust on the surface, which can affect the ability of the primer to **adhere** to the surface.

The following procedure should be followed when cleaning by hand:

- Remove any traces of oil or grease to avoid spreading it around the surface.

- Scrape off all loose rust, **millscale** and previous coatings.

- Use a chipping hammer around rusted nails, bolts and rivets.

- Use a wire brush to remove loose rust, but avoid **burnishing**.

- Finish off by abrading with a rough aluminium oxide abrasive (P40–P60) (see page 203 for more information on abrading).

(see page 203 for more information on abrading).

Definition

Corroded – been destroyed or damaged by a chemical reaction

Rust – a red or yellowish-brown coating of iron oxide

Definition

Adhere (same as adhesion) – stick

Millscale – a scale that forms on steel

Burnishing – polishing

A paint scraper and wire brush can be used to remove loose rust

Removing rust with power tools

Power tool cleaning is generally quicker and more effective than hand cleaning and the life of the paint system will be extended by using this method.

Loose rust, millscale and the existing surface coating can be removed using power wire brushes, grinders and needle guns, although some millscale will not be removed even with power tools. Again, care should be taken not to over-polish the surface or the adhesion of the primer will be negatively affected.

The following procedure should be followed when cleaning with a power tool:

- Remove any traces of oil or grease from the surface.
- Scrape off all loose rust, millscale and previous coatings.
- Use a needle gun to remove rust around corroded nuts, bolts and rivets etc.
- Select the most effective method of removing rust to suit the nature and condition of the surface (e.g. rotary wire brush, disc sander or angle grinder).

Power tools such as needle guns and angle grinders can be used to remove rust from surfaces

Painted surfaces in poor condition

If the condition of the surface you are going to work on already has a coating of paint that is in poor condition (i.e. it has a brittle paint film or paint actually flaking off), it will be necessary to remove the entire paint coating in order to produce a good finished effect. This can be done using heat or chemical means.

Removing paint with heat

Removing paint by burning it off with heat, using either a LPG (liquefied petroleum gas) burning off torch or a hot air stripper, is the fastest method of removing coatings from timber surfaces.

LPG burning off torch

Advantages:

- a fast and efficient method of removing even thick layers of paint

- can be used when there is no mains electricity supply

- low running costs.

Disadvantages:

- many local authorities have banned the LPG burning off torch because of the fire risks involved

- there is a danger of cracking the glass in windows when working on the frames

- scorches timber easily.

LPG burning off torch

Some important safety notes when using a LPG burning off torch

- When starting up, check the hose and fittings for gas leaks with a solution of detergent and water.

- Ensure that a fire extinguisher is nearby.

- Avoid burning off any timber adjacent to the roof structure of a building. This is because there are often birds' nests present or denatured timber, which can easily be ignited by the flame of a torch.

- Remove all curtains and furnishings when burning off around window frames.

- Always cease burning off operations at least one hour before you leave site and always carry out a final check for smouldering timber just before you go.

Did you know?

Some local authorities have banned the use of LPG strippers in favour of hot air strippers. This is because there is a reduced risk of fire and damage to property

Hot air strippers

Whereas a LPG burning off torch uses a naked flame, a hot air stripper, as the name suggests, uses hot air to heat the paint, which can then be scraped off.

Removing paint with chemicals

There are two types of chemical paint remover: water-based (which comes in gel form) and solvent-based (which comes in paste form). Both types use chemicals to soften the paint coating, which can then be removed using hand tools such as shave hooks and scrapers.

Hot air stripper

Water-based paint remover

Water-based paint remover is the one most commonly used in the trade.

Advantages:

- can be used as an alternative to burning off with heat (so suited to areas where risk of fire or heat damage is high)
- doesn't scorch or damage the surface
- can be used on most types of paint.

Disadvantages:

- water-based paint removers raise the grain of timber
- slow and messy
- expensive
- can soften some plastic surfaces
- all traces of the paint remover must be cleaned from the surface after scraping off the paint. If any remains, future coatings may be damaged
- the chemicals in the paint remover and the fumes produced can be harmful to health.

Safety tip

Paint fumes give off toxic gases when burnt so make sure you are wearing the correct PPE

Safety tip

Always wear the appropriate PPE when using chemical paint remover (gloves and goggles)

Solvent-based paint remover

This type of paint remover is very good at removing thick layers of paint (up to 3 mm thick) from many different types of surface such as fibrous plaster, timber, stone, marble, brick and cast iron. The paste should be applied thickly to the surface (between 3 and 6 mm thick) with a trowel or filling knife.

The paint remover can then be covered with cling film or greaseproof paper to prevent the solvents from evaporating and improve their action (sometimes referred to as a poultice after a type of medical dressing). The paint remover can be left to act on the surface for periods ranging from two hours to five days, depending on the type and thickness of the coating being removed:

- thin layers of paint – two to three hours
- thick layers of paint – overnight
- very thick layers of paint – two or more days
- ornamental mouldings such as plaster cornices or ceiling roses may have to be left for up to five days.

Advantages:

- same as for water-based paint remover
- if left for the correct period of time, no scraping is necessary and the paint remover can just be washed off, making it ideal for delicate surfaces that cannot be scraped.

Disadvantages:

- expensive
- the process can take a long time
- all traces of the paste must be removed from the surface after the paint has been taken off. The surface will also have to be neutralised with water or white spirits to stop the chemicals from continuing to work.

Cleaning surfaces

Definition

Spot primed – the application of primer (base coat) to small areas

After a surface has been sufficiently repaired, it has to be cleaned in preparation for decorating. You may find that the surface you are to work on is in good condition (also known as sound), and will not need any repair, but even sound surfaces can have patchy areas where the existing coating has peeled off or is flaking. In these situations, before you can clean the surface, the flaking paint has to be removed to form a solid edge. The bare areas then need to be **spot primed**. When the primer has dried, the edges of the repaired area can be surface-filled with a suitable filling agent.

Did you know?

Tar from tobacco smoking affects the adhesion of paint to a surface and can bleed through emulsion paint

Cleaning the work area is the next stage in surface preparation. Various substances such as dirt, grease and everyday grime can contaminate a surface without it looking like the area is dirty. You may also find that substances such as tar from cigarette smoking will need to be removed from ceilings and other surfaces.

When washing a surface down, it is very important that the correct washing agent is used. Dirt can be removed with sugar soap or a mild detergent and elbow grease (i.e. scrubbing with a brush!). Oily and greasy marks will probably only come off with the use of white spirit or turps, applied to the surface with a cloth or brush. Make sure that the area is thoroughly rinsed after cleaning and allowed to completely dry.

When working on some types of building, such as hospitals, a special cleaning contractor may be brought in to wash surfaces down due to possible health risks.

Abrading surfaces

Abrading a surface means wearing away the top layer by rubbing (i.e. creating friction). This is a very important part of surface preparation and provides a **key** for the coating or covering to be applied and smooths the surface in order to give a good quality finish.

It is important that the correct type of abrading material is used:

- An abrasive that is too rough can leave scratches on surfaces that show through to the finish.
- An abrasive that is too fine can result in preparation time taking longer than necessary and may be ineffective at removing or levelling rough surface imperfections.
- Cheap, inadequate abrasives such as glass paper can greatly extend the preparation time of any job because they tend to get blunt and clog very quickly.

Abrading materials and equipment

Abrasive materials fall into two broad categories:

- wet and dry abrasives
- dry abrasives.

Wet and dry abrasives

Wet and dry abrasives can, as the name suggests, be used in both wet and dry conditions. A waterproof adhesive fixes the abrasive particles to the backing, which means that the paper doesn't lose the particles when it gets wet – in fact, if wet and dry paper is used dry, it tends to clog up and so is more suited to wet use.

Safety tip

Always wear appropriate PPE when cleaning a surface and make sure you read the product safety information. Most cleaning agents can remove natural oils from the skin, which can cause skin conditions such as dermatitis

Did you know?

When washing a surface, you should always start at the bottom and work upwards. This avoids streaking of painted surfaces, which can damage the finish

Definition

Key – roughness on a surface provided to aid adhesion

The aggregates (abrasive particles) used in wet and dry abrasive paper have traditionally been silicon carbide, but aluminium oxide is now becoming increasingly popular. The particles of aggregate are closely grouped together and are referred to as being 'closed coated'. Water, or sometimes mineral oil, can be used as a lubricant, which prevents the paper from becoming clogged. Wet and dry abrasive paper is available in grades from P80 (coarse) through to P1200 (very fine).

Advantages:

- extremely good for high-quality work
- wide range of grades available
- cleans the surface as it abrades
- low dust levels.

Disadvantages:

- more expensive than dry abrasives
- unsuitable for bare timber
- clogs up easily if used dry
- the surface has to dry before it can be decorated.

Dry abrasives

This is an abrasive that uses a non-waterproof adhesive to fix the particles of abrasive to the backing paper. The aggregates used in this type of paper have traditionally been glass and garnet, but they are very poor when compared with aluminium oxide grit, which is now used extensively on dry abrasives.

Aluminium oxide abrasive, sometimes referred to as production paper, is usually available 'open coated', where the particles of aggregate are spaced apart on the backing paper. This reduces the risk of clogging as the gaps between the aggregate particles allow waste to escape. A dry powder lubricant can be used on some types of dry abrasives, which breaks away when heat is generated by the abrading process, preventing clogging of the abrasive.

Advantages:

- aluminium oxide papers are available in grades ranging from P20 (coarse) through to P320 (very fine)
- when aluminium oxide wears down, particle edges shear off revealing another smaller but sharper edge (see Figure 10.1)
- available in sheet, roll, disc and belt form

- also available in self-adhesive rolls so that the abrasive can be torn off and then fixed to a purpose-made rubbing block.

Disadvantages:

- aluminium oxide abrasive paper can be expensive, but when compared with other abrasives it is more economical in the long-term
- high dust levels.

New abrasive

Aluminium oxide particles wear down and break away

Remaining particles are smaller and sharper

Figure 10.1 How aluminium oxide breaks down

Grades of abrasives

We have already briefly touched on the range of grades available but it is important you know what a grade is. A grade that gives a coarse abrading effect will have large particles and therefore less of them. Figure 10.2 shows aggregate on a P20 grade dry abrading paper where only 20 particles of aggregate will fit on to a 25 x 25 mm area.

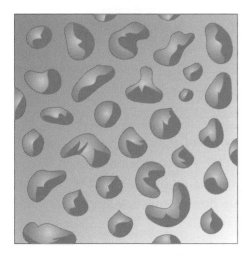

Figure 10.2 A small number of large aggregates will give a coarse abrading effect

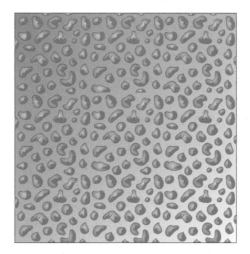

Figure 10.3 A large number of small aggregates will give a fine abrading effect

A grade that gives a fine abrading affect will have lots of small particles. Figure 10.3 shows aggregate on a P80 grade dry abrading paper where 80 particles of aggregate will fit on to a 25 x 25 mm area.

It is important to select the correct grade of abrasive for each job. The incorrect use of abrasive can either affect the finished appearance of the work or increase the time spent on preparations. The grade can be found printed on the back of an abrasive paper and relates to the particles of aggregate to every square 25 mm.

Mechanical sanding

Abrading material attached to an electrical tool can greatly reduce the time spent preparing surfaces and increase the surface area covered. Electrical sanders work by moving an abrasive pad or belt at a fast speed and some models are equipped with a convenient dust collection bag.

Belt, drum and orbital sanders

The heavy duty sanders most commonly used by a decorator are belt, drum and orbital sanders.

Belt sander

Drum sander

Orbital sander

Belt and orbital sanders are hand-held power tools best used for sanding large, flat items of joinery. A drum sander on the other hand is self-propelled and used for stripping floors. A rough grade of abrading material should be used first to remove the surface coating. The rough surface can then be brought up to a smooth finish by progressively using finer and finer abrading material.

Advantages:

- effective at abrading large areas
- mechanical sanders have a faster rate of abrasion than abrading by hand.

Disadvantages:

- more expensive than abrasive papers
- only suitable for work on large, flat areas
- can create large amounts of dust.

Small electric sanders are also available with triangular heads for use when sanding corners.

Disc or rotary sanders

Rotary sanding involves the use of rotating discs of abrasive material and can be used to prepare small or contoured surfaces.

Different types of abrasive disc are available:

- flat discs that require a backing pad
- flap discs made up from flaps of abrasive, which are more expensive but also more effective
- grinding discs that can be used for removing very heavy, small areas of rust.

Advantages:

- do not burnish the surface
- relatively low initial cost of equipment
- effective at removing isolated patches of rust.

Disadvantages:

- only suited to small areas
- not suited to complex surfaces (discs cannot reach into awkward corners).

Did you know?

Abrasive discs can be fitted to electric drills and angle grinders

Disc (or rotary) sander – in this instance, an electric drill fitted with an abrasive disc attachment

If the electrical sander you are using is equipped with a dust collection bag, make sure it is working and empty before using the tool. After you have finished sanding, the wood dust collected should be disposed of appropriately. Sanding dust should not be left in bags indoors as there is a danger of spontaneous combustion (sudden bursting into flames).

See Chapter 8 *Tools and equipment* (page 161) for additional information on abrading equipment.

Special types of surface preparation

Some surfaces may need special preparation in addition to the methods already discussed in this chapter.

Timber knots

It is useful for any decorator to know the various types of timber used in the construction industry: it will help you to prepare and decorate surfaces correctly. Timber is divided into two main categories: softwoods and hardwoods.

Softwoods

- Douglas Fir
- Larch
- Pitch Pine
- Redwood (Pine)
- Whitewood (Spruce)
- Western Red Cedar

Hardwoods

- Ash
- Oak
- Beech
- Mahogany
- Maple
- Teak
- Walnut

During the preparation of timber surfaces, you may notice knots in the wood. A knot is a place in the timber where a branch was joined to the tree. If you were to paint bare timber without preparing the knots first, you may find that sap bleeds from the knot staining the paint finish. A material called knotting solution is available that can be applied to areas where the wood is knotted in order to seal it.

Knotting solution can also be applied to areas of timber that have been stained with resin, tar splashes, felt pen and biro marks – again, the knotting solution will stop the stains bleeding through the paint. The main ingredient in most knotting solutions is shellac which is produced by an insect and melted into thin flakes.

A knotting bottle will prevent knotting solution from evaporating and drying out. Make sure the surface is clean and dry before applying the knotting solution with a brush. It should dry quite quickly, after which time the surface coating can be applied.

Knotting bottle

Stain sealing

Shellac is also available coloured (known as pigmented shellac). Aluminium provides a silver pigment while titanium provides a white pigment, and these are very effective stain sealers especially on:

- stains made by fire and smoke
- water stains
- previously creosoted timber.

Pigmented shellac can even seal pet, smoke and fire odours (smells).

Alkaline surfaces

The chemical nature of surfaces such as concrete, cement rendering, asbestos sheeting and some plasters is **alkaline**. This can cause problems if a solvent-based paint system is to be applied because the alkalinity in the surface can attack the paint rather like a paint stripper, causing a paint defect known as **saponification**.

To prevent saponification, it is necessary to apply an alkali-resistant primer, which forms a barrier between the surface and the paint. Acrylic surface coatings are resistant to alkalis, so you would think an alkali-resistant primer wouldn't be needed, however their **permeable** nature allows any alkalinity through if the surface becomes damp.

Definition

Alkaline – having a pH greater than 7 (an acid has a pH of less than 7)

Saponification – a chemical reaction that makes soap and so foams up as a result

Permeable – allowing things to pass through

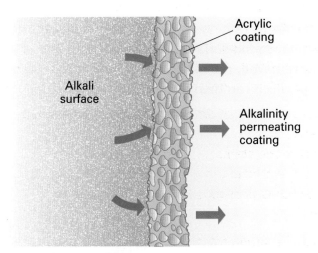

Figure 10.4 Alkalinity permeating through an acrylic coating

Friable surfaces

A friable surface is one which crumbles away easily when you rub your hand over it. Examples of this kind of surface include weathered cement rendering or old, weathered brickwork (known as spalled). If paint is applied to a friable surface, it won't last very long as it will come off with the crumbly parts of the surface.

In order to get around this problem, a stabilising solution can be applied before the paint. The surface should be brushed down first with a stiff brush, which will remove any loose particles. The stabilising solution can then be applied, which soaks deep into the surface acting like a glue, binding it down. A good paint finish can now be achieved.

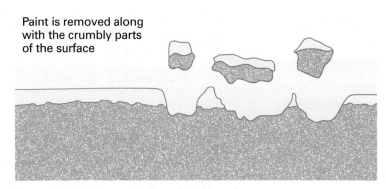

Paint is removed along with the crumbly parts of the surface

Figure 10.5 Paint applied to a friable surface

Figure 10.6 Silicone water repellent used on porous brickwork

Porous surfaces

A porous surface is one that contains tiny holes through which liquids or gases can pass. In order to prevent porous surfaces, such as brickwork, from being penetrated by water or damaged by frost, a silicone water-repellent layer can be applied, which waterproofs the surface and protects it. It dries clear and unless you compared it with an untreated surface during wet weather, you wouldn't know it was there.

Surfaces affected by mould growth

Mould is a furry growth of micro-organisms (a fungus), which often grows in moist and warm conditions. If mould is found during surface preparation, all traces of it must be removed. If it is not totally removed, the mould can quickly re-establish itself underneath an applied coating, which can then lead to the premature failure of that coating.

The following procedure should be followed to remove mould growth:

Mould growth

- Wet the mould to avoid the spread of spores to other areas.

- Remove heavy patches of the mould with a scraper or wire brush.

- Apply a fungicidal wash to the affected area and allow it to dry.

- If possible, the affected area should be left for a week or so and re-treated if the mould reappears.

In most cases only one application will be necessary. This is because fungicidal wash has a residual effect on the surface, which means that traces of it remain, continually removing mould growth from the surface, sometimes for many years.

Surfaces affected by wet rot

Wet rot is a growth of brown fungus that can occur in damp timber, such as that in window frames. As the fungus grows, it destroys the wood and the only long-term treatment of wet rot is the removal of moisture from the timber. Before you can work on an area affected by wet rot, you must treat it using the following procedure:

- Rake out any defective timber using a scraper, shave hook or chisel. Allow the surface to dry out if possible and flood the exposed timber with a clear wood preservative. Allow it to dry and spot prime the affected areas with wood primer.

- Fix wood screws (non-ferrous, i.e. non-iron) into the timber.

- Apply a coat of two-pack polyester filler to the surface and allow to dry. The screws will help the filler adhere to the surface.

- Apply a second coat of filler and allow to dry. Use abrading paper to rub down the filler so it is **flush**. It may be necessary to use an acrylic spot filler (a soft putty) to fill any minor imperfections.

Defective putty

During the removal of old paint from window frames, some of the putty is likely to break away. After other surface preparations have been completed, the bare timber can be primed and any defective putty replaced with linseed oil putty.

Any old putty that has not broken away, will be firmly adhered to the window frame and will not need to be replaced. You may, however, notice a gap between the old putty and the glass. This gap must be completely sealed by forcing in linseed oil putty using a putty knife. See Figure 10.7.

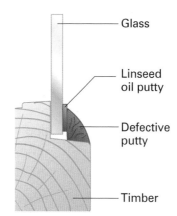

Glass

Linseed oil putty

Defective putty

Timber

Figure 10.7 Defective putty

Bonded asbestos

Asbestos is a fibrous mineral that was used as a form of insulating material, especially from the 1950s to the mid-1980s. We now know that asbestos particles, when they are breathed into the lungs, can cause lung cancer and a disease called asbestosis. These diseases can kill, which is why since 1999 it has been illegal to use asbestos in construction, except for some very exceptional reasons.

Bonded asbestos is where the asbestos is bonded in cement and it usually comes in corrugated sheet form and was commonly used for garage and shed roofs as well as pipes and guttering. Although bonded asbestos is not thought to present significant risks to health, it should still be handled with care. Never use any dry abrading methods – instead, if you have to abrade the surface to remove mould or dirt, always use a wet abrasion method. This will avoid the release of potentially harmful dust particles.

Before work starts on a site, it must be inspected for asbestos. However, if you think you have discovered the fibrous form of asbestos, stop work *immediately* and tell your supervisor. If tests reveal that the material is asbestos, specially trained teams will then be brought in to deal with its removal or stabilisation. No one can work with asbestos unless they hold a special licence issued by the Health and Safety Executive. Remember, be alert – your actions now could make you seriously ill in years to come.

Plasterboard

Another surface you will come across while on a new build or refurbishment project is plasterwork, including dry lining. Many new buildings now have dry lining carried out rather than having full plastering done. Dry lining is where dividing walls within a building are made from plasterboards (square- and feather-edged), which are attached to timber structures (stud walls) and taped up. The joints of the two boards are sealed with joint tape (an adhesive tape used in plastering) then the joint is plastered over to give an even finish. The same technique is applied to corners of the walls, which are taped up with reinforced jointing tape, then plastered over at the taped point.

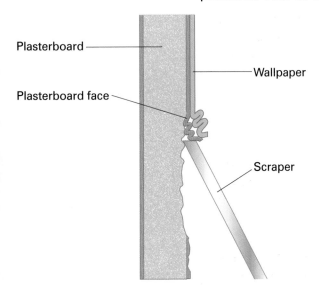

Plasterboard

Plasterboard face

Wallpaper

Scraper

Figure 10.8 Plasterboard damaged during wallpaper removal

Plasterboard is plaster sandwiched between two boards and is used for interior partition walls and ceilings. The two boards are actually only a stiff lining paper and so will soak up moisture. By applying a hard waterproof coating to the plasterboard before applying surface coverings such as wallpaper, the wallpaper will not bond with the plasterboard surface and the plasterboard will not be damaged when the wallpaper is removed.

Figure 10.8 shows plasterboard being damaged by the removal of wallpaper which has been applied without first applying a waterproof coating.

To complete the finish, you would apply a coating system – emulsion or eggshell – to this surface, but sometimes the taped joint comes apart or has not been completely sealed. To rectify this defect, you would have to re-apply the tape and then re-plaster the small area affected (larger defects may have to be re-done by a plasterer).

Another defect with regards to plasterboards is 'popping' – when the plaster breaks away from the plaster nail heads because of movement. Here you would first need to dry scrape and dust off. Then you would spot prime the nail head, and apply the correct filling agent so that it is 'proud' – this means overfilling the hole so that, when the filler dries out, it still keeps the hole filled. When the filler is dry, you need to rub it down to leave an even surface before applying a coating. If a hole or crack on a surface is not filled 'proud', it can shrink with the drying process, and will need filling all over again.

Surfaces affected by efflorescence

Efflorescence is the appearance of white patches on cement-based surfaces and can occur on brickwork, rendering and internal plaster. Because cement is porous, (look back at page 210 to remind yourself about porous surfaces) moisture such as rain can penetrate the cement, dissolving some of the lime and creating calcium hydroxide. The calcium hydroxide rises to the surface when the cement dries out and, once all the moisture has disappeared, calcium carbonate is left on the surface as the white patch we can see.

Although efflorescence will eventually disappear on its own, if a surface is to be decorated, any efflorescence will have to be removed during preparation. The treatment for surfaces affected by efflorescence is removal by scrubbing with a stiff fibre brush or a wire brush. Never try and remove efflorescence by washing the surface as the calcium carbonate will simply dissolve in the water and sink back into the cement.

Efflorescence

Defective rendering

Rendering is a coating of plaster applied to stonework and during your assessment of this type of surface, you may notice cracks in the rendering. There are several different methods of filling in these cracks and the most commonly used methods are as follows.

For small cracks:

- Scrape away any loose coatings and particles of masonry.

- Apply filling agent – exterior grade filler (polyfiller type) could be used but this would probably re-crack after a short period of time, whereas exterior acrylic caulking will provide more permanent flexible repair.

For large cracks:

- Rake out and undercut the crack using a 25 mm scraper or pointing trowel (see Figures 10.9 and 10.10). Fill the crack with a sand and cement mortar to a ratio of one part cement to three parts soft sand (see Figure 10.11). This action

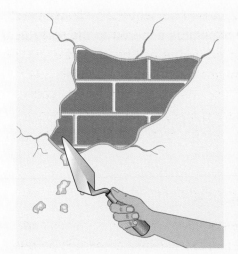

Figure 10.9 Step 1 Rake out any loose coatings and rendering

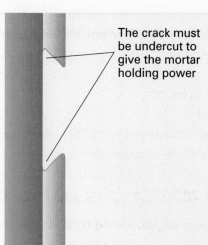

The crack must be undercut to give the mortar holding power

Figure 10.10 Step 2 Undercut the crack

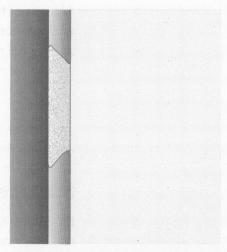

Figure 10.11 Step 3 Point up the crack with mortar

is known as 'pointing up' and when dry it can be painted over, but this repair would probably re-crack after a short period of time.

- Alternatively, rake out, undercut and fill as above and then allow to dry. Apply a bituminous caulking compound over the crack and bed a nylon type bandage over the length of the crack. Further applications of the caulking compound can then be made over the bandage to provide an invisible reinforced repair, which will last longer than the first method described.

Caulking

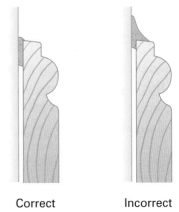

Caulk is a waterproof filler and sealant and is used in cracks and gaps. Mastic is an acrylic type of caulk and is applied using a mastic gun, which is a frame that holds and helps dispense mastic from its tube. When dry, mastic feels a bit like rubber.

A mastic gun is easy to use, but the process of filling a crack is often done incorrectly. In order to caulk correctly, the bead of applied caulk must be wiped off with a wet finger, after which surplus caulk can be removed with a filling knife. Any remaining material can then be sponged off.

Correct   Incorrect

Figure 10.12 Correct and incorrect caulking

Caulking with a mastic gun

Figure 10.12 shows two examples of how caulking can be applied to the tops of skirting boards. The illustration on the left shows the caulk applied correctly. The illustration on the right shows incorrect application.

Painting an already painted surface

Before painting over an already painted surface, it is important that you carry out a simple test to find out how well the old layer of paint is adhered to the surface. If

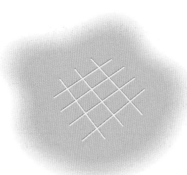

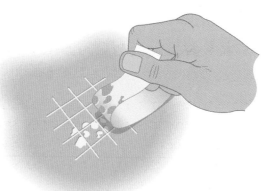

Figure 10.13 The scratch test

Use a sharp trimming knife to make a few cuts in one direction and a few cuts in the opposite direction

Cover the scratches with a piece of masking tape, pressing down firmly. Quickly rip the tape from the surface. The adhesion of the paint is poor if it comes off on the masking tape

it is not strongly adhered to the surface, there is little point painting over it as your finish will not last very long. Figure 10.13 illustrates how to perform the 'scratch test', which can be performed on most surfaces as part of the preparation process.

Typical surfaces and their preparation

By now, you have learnt that surface preparation is a very important task and that if you prepare a surface thoroughly, you will end up with a high-quality finish and a good reputation. You have also read about a number of different preparation processes. Over the next few pages we will look at some typical surfaces you may find yourself working on during your career, along with appropriate preparation tasks for each.

New softwoods/hardwoods

Abrading a new softwood or hardwood may result in damage due to scratching or furring (the lifting of wood fibres). For this reason, it is best to simply dust off the surface prior to painting. If you notice any raised nail heads, they will need to be punched down below the surface and filled with a suitable filling agent prior to painting.

Rough sawn timber

Rough sawn timber should be dry brushed thoroughly to remove soil, vegetation and dust.

New plaster and plasterboard

New plaster and plasterboard should be dry scraped with a scraper to remove any bits and nibs and then dusted down. Never abrade the surface as this would scratch it.

Brickwork, stonework, rendering, pebbledash and concrete finishes

These types of surface can be thoroughly cleaned with scrapers and dry brushing in order to remove dirt and powdery residue. The surface may need to be scrubbed if efflorescence is present or washed if mould is present, but it should be allowed to dry thoroughly before being worked on. Dusting off should be carried out prior to painting.

Remember

Take care when scrubbing with a wire brush so as not to damage surfaces with scratches

Ferrous metalwork

Ferrous metals contain iron and include cast iron, wrought iron, mild steel and stainless steel. These surfaces are prone to rusting and will need to be cleared of all rust prior to painting. Depending upon the extent of the rust, it can be removed with the use of a wire brush, mechanical wire brush, abrasive papers and/or scrapers.

New metalwork needs to be cleaned down with white spirit or an emulsifying agent to remove grease and oily residues.

Non-ferrous metalwork

Non-ferrous metals do not contain iron and include aluminium, zinc, copper and brass. These should be dry and free from grease prior to painting. Previously painted non-ferrous metals need to be abraded and any corrosion deposits found should be scraped back to a firm edge where any flaking paint is evident.

Painted wood

Painted wood should be washed down using sugar soap and warm water, then rinsed with clean water. The surface should then be abraded to provide a key and then dusted down to remove surface dust.

Painted plaster

Wash the surface down with sugar soap and warm water, then rinse off with clean water and abrade the surface. Repair any indentations, cracks, holes etc. with a filling agent. Areas filled should be sanded down once dry and dusted off ready for painting.

Plastic

Plastic surfaces might include guttering and down pipes. Although, normally, plastic guttering and down pipes are used because they are virtually maintenance-free, there may be occasions when a client wants a colour change. Special primers are required for preparing plastic surfaces to receive paint finishes, as good adhesion is hard to achieve. Plastic surfaces should be degreased and abraded using wire wool and a suitable degreaser to provide a key before application of the primer.

Glazed tiles

These should be washed down using a detergent, for example sugar soap.

Polystyrene tiles

Polystyrene tiles should be dusted off and filled with a plaster-based filler where any damage is evident. Oil-based fillers should not be used because they will dissolve the polystyrene.

New wallpaper

Wallpapered surfaces, including those covered with embossed and blown vinyl paper, should be dusted off and any paste marks washed off before painting.

Old wallpaper

Old wallpaper is best stripped off using either water and a scraper or a steam stripper and a scraper. Some papers, such as vinyl, can be peeled off, leaving the backing paper on the surface.

Environmental considerations

It is pointless preparing and painting a surface if it is damp or weather conditions are wet or very cold as this will affect the paint finish or its ability to dry. These are environmental considerations and must be taken into account during surface preparation.

Damp surfaces

We have already looked at how a dirty and greasy surface can affect decorating, but a damp surface can also cause problems. Wet, unseasoned timber or wet, newly plastered or washed walls must be given an adequate drying out period. Applying any kind of surface coating or covering before the surface is totally dry will result in any of the following:

- blistering
- peeling (due to lack of adhesion)
- discoloration
- staining.

Cold or wet weather conditions

Decorating in cold conditions (below 5°C) or wet weather can result in the following:

- failure of water-based paints to dry (due to lack of adhesion)
- washing off of water-based paints
- blooming of alkyd finishes (i.e. loss of gloss and a cloudy surface)
- rain pitting of alkyd finishes
- peeling.

FAQ

What is lead paint and why is it dangerous?

Some older houses and buildings, usually built before 1960, may have surfaces that are decorated with paint containing lead. Lead is a soft, heavy metal that can be hazardous to health if breathed in or swallowed. Years ago, even though the health risks were well known, lead was sometimes added to paint to speed the drying and give the paint protective properties. During your training, you will learn about the precautions to take when dealing with lead paint, but as some general advice, remember: always wear PPE, including a face mask and goggles; never burn off lead paint with a LPG torch or gun; don't rub down the surface with dry abrasive paper. Finally, you will not be able to tell from looking whether or not paint contains lead. As a general rule, on older properties, treat all paint as if it is lead-containing paint.

Knowledge check

1. What is a disadvantage of removing rust by hand?

2. What surface preparation process can result in burnishing and why should this be avoided?

3. Name two different methods of removing paint.

4. Suggest a substance you could use to remove oily and greasy marks from a surface.

5. Explain what a key is.

6. What tends to happen if wet and dry abrasive paper is used dry?

7. When would you use knotting solution?

8. What could you apply to a surface to seal a stain or an odour?

9. How could you prevent saponification on an alkaline surface?

10. What might happen if you don't get rid of all mould growth on a surface before you decorate it?

11. What is wet rot and what does it do?

12. What should you do if you think you have discovered asbestos?

13. What happens if you try to remove efflorescence by washing it away?

14. How could you prepare a rendered surface that had both small and large cracks?

15. What might happen if you decorate in wet weather or cold conditions below 5°C?

16. Name three hardwoods and three softwoods a painter may come across.

17. If you are about to paint a dry-lined wall area and part of the tape is peeling off, how would you prepare this?

18. What's the difference between 'proud' filling and 'flush' filling?

19. What is 'popping', with regards to plasterboards?

chapter 11

Colour

OVERVIEW

What would the world be like without colour? Colour brings vitality to everything it touches, be it the clothes we wear or the homes we live in – and as a painter and decorator, you need to understand colour, as it is a major part of your profession.

As a painter and decorator, you need to have a knowledge of colour, understanding what it is and how and where it can be used. When you become a painter and decorator, you may decide to start your own business where you will be asked to offer advice to customers. If you have a knowledge of colour, the advice you give will allow your customers to arrange their own colour schemes, and enable you to offer a more rounded service than just doing the work.

This chapter will cover the following topics:

- Colour terminology
- The colour spectrum
- The colour wheel
- Organisation of colour.

These topics can be found in the following modules:

CC 2002K	CC 2020K	CC 2022K	CC 2024K
CC 2002S	CC 2020S	CC 2022S	CC 2024S

Colour terminology

Here are some of the key of terms relating to colour that you may come across as you become a painter and decorator.

- **Achromatic colours** These are not technically classed as colours as they are without a hue. These range from black through to white, and are sometimes known as sensations.

- **Advancing colours** Warm colours such as orange, red and yellow, which create the sensation of coming towards the eye.

- **Analogous colours** Adjacent colours on the colour wheel (see page 225) which share strong undertones, creating a pleasing **harmony**. They are rich in colour and are easy to work with.

- **Accent colours** A colour used in small quantities to lift or to add punch to a colour scheme.

- **Complementary colours** Colours directly opposite each other on the colour wheel. They are contrasting and convey energy, vigour and excitement (also see **split complementary**).

- **Contrasting colours** Colours that are opposite each other on the colour wheel, but not necessarily directly: for example, strong colours against greyed colours, and dark colours against light colours, such as purple opposite yellow.

- **Contrasting harmony** This is where you take various colours from the colour wheel to produce a pleasing effect.

- **Cool colours** Colours found on the right-hand side of the colour wheel, which give the appearance of coolness.

- **Discordant colour** Reversal of the natural order of colour, producing an unpleasant sight to the eye: for example, using a pale yellow and a deep green.

- **Harmonious colours** Colours that appear pleasant when used together (see **contrasting harmony**).

- **Juxtaposition** When you place one colour next to another. Sometimes a distortion occurs, giving the appearance of other colours being present. For example, when you place red and yellow together, the red will have a purplish tinge, while the yellow will have a greenish appearance.

- **Monochromatic colour** When adding tints (white) and shades (black) to one colour you can create a tonal scale of that particular colour.

- **Natural order of colour** The spectrum's lightest colour is yellow, which is on the outside of the colour wheel, and its darkest is deep purple, which is in the centre of the colour wheel. In this order, the colours are pleasing to the eye, but if the darkest colours such as purple became the lightest, they would then become unpleasing to the eye or **discordant**.

- **Neutrals** Non-colours – black, grey, white – and sometimes brown and beige. These all go together and can be layered and mixed or matched without one dominating another.

- **Pastel colours** Colours that have tints or shades added. This usually refers to pale colours with a lot of white (tint) added to them.

- **Primary colours** The three key colours – red, blue and yellow. They cannot be made from any other colour.

- **Receding colours** Opposite to **advancing colours**, these are cool colours such as blue/light blue, which are used to create the appearance of receding from the eye.

- **Saturation** The intensity of a colour.

- **Secondary colours** If you mix equal amounts of the primary colours, you get the secondary colours – purple, green and orange.

- **Split complementary** Colours one step either side of the complement's own **analogous colour** (see above). In a colour scheme, you could use one hue, contrasted with two hues either side of the complementary colour.

- **Shades** Colours produced when you add black to the main colour.

- **Tertiary colours** If you mix a primary colour with a secondary colour, in a ratio of 2:1, you get a tertiary colour – red-orange, blue-green, etc.

- **Tints** Colours produced when you add white to a main colour.

- **Tones** A colour's lightness or darkness: for example, dark brown or light brown.

- **Warm colours** Colours found on the left-hand side of the colour wheel, which give the appearance of warmness.

The colour spectrum

Without light, colour does not exist. The purest form of light is known as 'white light', which originates from the sun and contains all the other colours. When light from the sun passes through a prism, the light is split into seven colours – red, orange, yellow, green, blue, indigo, and violet – by refraction. This array of light is called a spectrum.

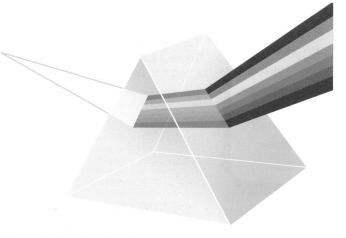

Figure 11.1 Light refracting through a prism

A rainbow is very similar to this. When sunlight shines through droplets of moisture in the earth's atmosphere, this causes a spectrum of light to appear in the sky, proving that colour simply comes from light.

Light travels from the sun to the earth in waves, which come in short wavelengths and long wavelengths. When light waves hit a surface, some are absorbed and some are reflected. It is these reflected wavelengths that are picked up by our eyes and registered by the brain as colours.

You can think of light travelling like waves in the sea. These waves have properties of wavelength and frequency. To measure a wavelength, you have to measure the distance between one wave hitting a location and the second wave hitting the same location. For example, if the sea is full of waves 15 metres apart, it could be said to have a wavelength of 15; if the waves were 25 metres apart, it would have a wavelength of 25, and so on. As for frequency, the frequency of a wave is determined by the number of complete waves, or wavelengths, that pass a given point each second.

The same ideas apply to light, and help to explain what colour is. Colour is simply light of different wavelengths and frequencies, in a form of energy that we can actually see.

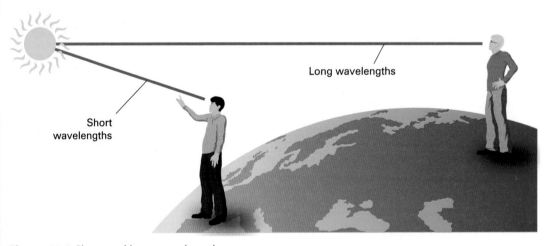

Figure 11.2 Short and long wavelengths

Short wavelengths are seen as blue because, as light travels from the sun to the earth during midday, it only travels a short distance – hence the sky is seen as blue. At dawn and dusk, the light from the sun has to travel further as it hits the earth on a tangent. These wavelengths are long wavelengths, and are seen as red.

The colour wheel

A colour wheel is a radial diagram of colours in which primary, secondary and sometimes tertiary colours are displayed. Colour is a powerful visual force, and the colour wheel is a tool for understanding how colours relate to each other. Colour wheels help many professionals such as artists and decorators with their work, by helping them to mix and think about colours.

A system had to be created to help us make sense of colour, to understand it and put it into some kind of order. This system became known as the 'natural order' of colour or, more commonly, as the colour wheel.

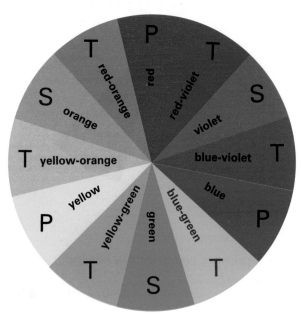

Where's there's light, there's colour and white light contains all visible colours (see page 223 for information on the spectrum). These form an infinite spectrum that appears in a sequence from red to violet, just like the rainbow. The colour wheel represents this infinite spectrum through 12 basic hues (colours). These 12 basic hues consist of 3 groups: primary, secondary and tertiary colours.

Figure 11.3 The colour wheel

Did you know?

High frequency colours are violet, indigo and blue; low frequency colours are yellow, orange and red

Did you know?

Sir Isaac Newton was the first person to understand the rainbow, creating the first colour wheel after conducting a series of experiments in 1672

Did you know?

A rainbow does not actually exist at a particular location in the sky. It is an optical illusion, whose apparent position depends on the observer's location and the position of the sun

Primary, secondary and tertiary colours

The three primary colours are red, blue and yellow. Primary colours cannot be made from other colours because they are pure colours, but by mixing these three colours, you can create all the colours of the rainbow.

The three secondary colours are green, orange and purple. These are created by mixing two primary colours together: each secondary colour is made from the two primary colours closest to it on the colour wheel. To create green, you would mix yellow and blue together; to create orange, you would mix red and yellow together; and to create purple, you would mix blue and red together.

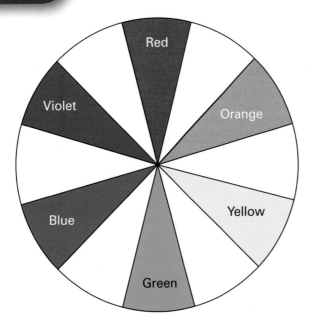

Figure 11.4 Primary and secondary colours

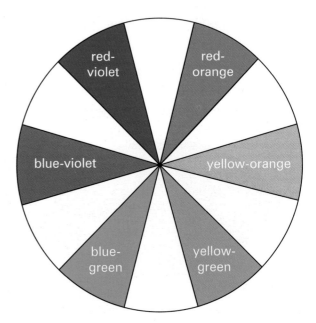

Figure 11.5 Tertiary colours

To create a tertiary colour, you have to mix a primary colour with a secondary colour in a ratio of 2:1.

Constructed in an orderly progression, the colour wheel represents the range of visible light – the twelve basic hues – formed into a circle. The twelve basic hues are red, red-orange, orange, yellow-orange, yellow, yellow-green, green, green-blue, blue, blue-violet, violet, red-violet. This circle allows the user to visualise the sequence of colour balance and harmony.

On the main part of the colour wheel, each individual hue is at a level of full saturation or brightness. There is no black (shade) or white (tint) added to it, but when a black or white is added to a hue, the colour has lightness or darkness, called 'value'. To show value, the colour wheel has more rings: two outer rings, which represent the dark shades, and two inner rings, which represent the light tints.

As you can see, no one colour stands alone on the colour wheel: a segment of colour is always seen in the context of other colours. The effect of a colour is determined by the light reflected from it, the colours that surround it and the perspective of the person looking at it. No one colour is 'good' or 'bad' – it's just one part of an arrangement that as a whole is pleasing or not.

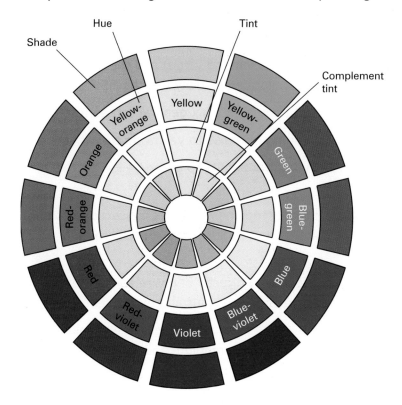

Figure 11.6 Colour wheel with outer and inner rings

Creating moods with colour

By using different colours, you can 'create a mood' within your colour scheme or make a room feel 'cosier' or 'lighter'. Knowing the colour wheel can help you if are asked by clients to design a colour scheme for their home or business.

You will see that, on the left-hand side of the colour wheel the colours, which range from red through orange to yellow, are classed as 'warm' or 'hot'. When used in a colour scheme, these warm colours tend to come towards you, or feel closer to you.

On the opposite side of the wheel you have the 'cool' or 'cold' colours of the spectrum, ranging from light blue through green to yellow. These cool colours tend to recede from you, or feel distant to you when used in painting schemes.

You can also mix in and use a small amount of a warm colour – red, for example – to 'warm up' a cool colour, or a little of a cool colour – such as blue – to 'cool down' a warm colour.

Colours have meaning and express moods and emotions in almost everything in our lives. Some colours raise or lower our feelings or expectations; other colours convey a universal meaning, such as yellow and red being used as warnings or cautions.

Six categories of colours

Colours can be interpreted through one of three systems: the RGB system (red, green and blue), the HSV system (hue, saturation and value) and the CMYK system (cyan, magenta, yellow and black). Painters usually use the HSV system.

You can combine the colours on the colour wheel into six general categories:

- **warm colours**, which are colours ranging from red to yellow on the wheel

- **cool colours**, which are colours ranging from violet to green/yellow on the wheel

- **analogous colours**, which are colours occupying any three consecutive colour segments on the wheel; i.e. they share strong undertones, which create a pleasing harmony

- **complementary colours**, which are colours directly opposite each other on the wheel. These are contrasting: they give energy, vigour and excitement

- **monochromatic colours**, which are all the hues (variations) of one colour segment on the colour wheel, showing the dark, medium and light values of that colour

- **triadic colours**, which are any three colours on the wheel that are 120° apart, If the colour wheel were a clock face, it could be one colour at 12 o'clock, one at 4 o'clock and one at the 8 o'clock position.

As you will see, black, grey, white and sometimes brown and beige, do not appear on the colour wheel as these are classed as neutrals. However, these colours or non-colours are the easiest group to work with. Neutral colours all go together and can be layered, mixed and matched, as no neutral colour will try to dominate any other.

Organisation of colour

As a painter, you will come across many different colours and colour codes within the industry. These colour coding systems have been developed to make it easier to refer exactly to particular colours, and to give some consistency in communications.

The BS 4800 series

The main system used is the *British Standards 4800 series of paint colours for building purposes.*

The BS 4800 series, as it is commonly known, is a framework made up of letters and numbers. Under the system, each colour is given a code so it is easily identified and this code consists of three parts. The three parts are called hue, greyness and weight.

The hue (colour) is the first part of the code and is an even number, such as 04. There are 12 main hues, numbered from 02 to 24 (see Table 11.1), plus the neutrals. There is an extra set of numbers, 00, which represent the neutrals black and white. These numbers run in horizontal rows within the framework.

The greyness is the second part of the code, and represents the amount of greyness in one colour compared to another. Greyness is represented by letters A to E, with A having the most and E having none at all.

The weight is the third part of the code. This was added as an afterthought, because it was found that the yellow hues looked heavy in comparison to the other colours. To overcome this, the value of the yellowish colours was raised, resulting in the weight becoming more uniform. The weight of the hue is given in pairs of numbers ranging from 01 to 56, as shown in the table.

Within each of the five greyness ranges, the groups of colour have a value to them which graduates from a high value to a low value:

    A greyness = 01 to 13
    B greyness = 15 to 29
    C greyness = 31 to 40
    D greyness = 43 to 45
    E greyness = 49 to 56

So, for example, a **lighter** yellow in the E range would read

    10 E 49

while a **deeper** pure yellow in that range would read

    10 E 53.

The BS 4800 system was developed so that the correct amount of colours would be produced for building use, in order to meet economic trends and build a relationship between colour and building materials. The system also met design and technical requirements and made it easier to identify items.

There are one hundred colours within the BS 4800 framework, counting the neutrals, black and white. Of the standard range of 100 colours, 32 are grouped under the 'basic' selection, which includes black and white. These colours should always be available from stock. There are two 'supplementary' selections: category G, which relates to all oil-based finishes, and M, which relates to emulsions.

Over time, you will become familiar with the BS 4800 system, as any paint you use will be identified by its colour code on a specification sheet or a paint schedule.

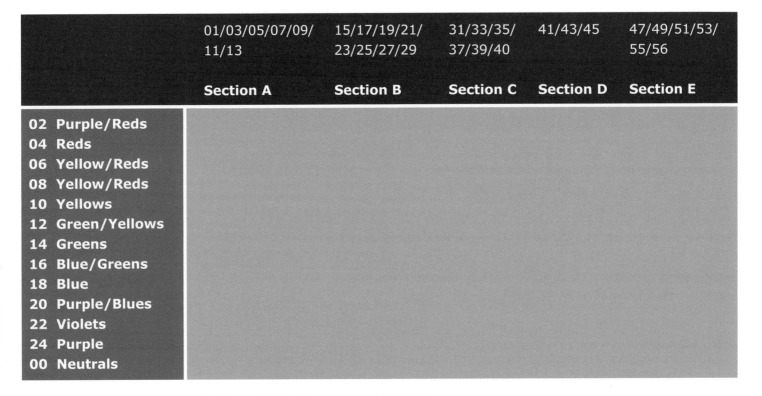

	01/03/05/07/09/ 11/13	15/17/19/21/ 23/25/27/29	31/33/35/ 37/39/40	41/43/45	47/49/51/53/ 55/56
	Section A	Section B	Section C	Section D	Section E
02 Purple/Reds					
04 Reds					
06 Yellow/Reds					
08 Yellow/Reds					
10 Yellows					
12 Green/Yellows					
14 Greens					
16 Blue/Greens					
18 Blue					
20 Purple/Blues					
22 Violets					
24 Purple					
00 Neutrals					

Table 11.1 BS 4800 paint colours for building purposes

On the job: Colour codes for paint

Lydia is a second year apprentice and has just taken delivery of a batch of paint and materials for a job she is to complete. While checking the items, Lydia notices that one of the five-litre tins of paint has a different colour code to the rest of the batch. She tells her supervisor, Christy, this, but is told not to worry, as all the tins are the same colour anyway and it will not matter as the specification states this colour is to be used.

Is Christy right to say this? Are Lydia's concerns valid? What do you think Lydia should do?

Knowledge check

1. What is colour?

2. Who created the colour wheel?

3. What are the three primary colours?

4. What is a prism?

5. If you mixed two primary colours together, what would you create?

6. Briefly describe what the 'natural order' of colour is.

7. How can you create a tertiary colour?

8. What are complementary colours, with regards to the colour wheel?

9. Which two colours would you mix to create green?

10. Explain what the letters HSV refer to with regards to the colour wheel.

11. What is a spectrum?

12. Where does white light come from?

13. What is the colour code for magnolia?

14. Identify the three parts of a colour code.

15. What is BS 4800?

chapter 12

Surface coatings

OVERVIEW

Applying a surface coating can be one of the cheapest, quickest, easiest and most effective tasks a decorator will perform. A variety of surface coatings such as varnish, wood stain and paint can preserve, protect and decorate a surface. A decorator can also put their creative skills to good use, producing interesting and attractive effects if requested.

This chapter will cover the following topics:

- What are surface coatings?
- Applying coatings to various surface types
- Surface coating defects.

These topics can be found in the following modules:

CC 2002K	CC 2020K	CC 2022K	CC 2024K
CC 2002S	CC 2020S	CC 2022S	CC 2024S

What are surface coatings?

Surface coatings are applied in order to:

- **Protect** – steel can be prevented from corroding due to rust and wood can be prevented from rotting due to moisture and insect attack.

- **Decorate** – the appearance of a surface can be improved or given a special effect (e.g. marbling, wood graining).

- **Sanitise** – a surface can be made more hygienic with the application of a surface coating, preventing penetration and accumulation of germs and dirt and also allowing easier cleaning.

- **Identify** – different colours or types of surface coating can be used to distinguish areas or components (e.g. pipework identified using the British Standards Institution's colour coding system).

Surface coatings generally fall into one of the following categories:

- Paint
- Varnish
- Wood stain
- Sealers and preparatory coatings.

Paint

Paint is either water-based or solvent-based. Water-based paint means that the main liquid part of the paint is water. Solvent-based paint means that a chemical has been used instead of water to dissolve the other components of the paint (see page 236 for more information on the components of paint). When paint is applied to a surface, the water or the solvent (depending on the type of paint) evaporates into the air leaving the other components behind on the surface.

Until recently, solvent-based paints were the number one wall coating choice for plaster, masonry and other surfaces, but changes in safety and environmental legislation have forced manufacturers to develop water-based products as safer alternatives to solvent-based paints.

Water-based paints are now widely used on both internal and external surfaces that were traditionally the strict domain of solvent paint systems.

The reasons for painting include preservation, sanitation, identification and decoration, but none of these is possible if the paint has not been produced or applied properly. Paint has to have basic qualities if it is to be used for these tasks. It should be:

- appliable – easily brushed, rolled or sprayed

- dry – in a reasonable length of time

Definition

Sanitise – to make something clean and free of germs

Safety tip

Solvents used in solvent-based paints are usually toxic and highly flammable so take proper precautions when using them

- adaptable to physical changes to the surface, such as weather conditions

- able to maintain its function – for an acceptable time.

Paint should also have the right consistency for application – this refers to the thinness or thickness of the paint. Paints such as non-drip gloss are classed as thick paints and are known as thixotropic paint. Thixotropic agents give paint gel-like properties. When stirred, the paint turns into a liquid due to friction, which makes it easy to apply. Once laid off correctly, the paint will turn back into a gel, reducing the likelihood of runs or drips.

Paint should be flexible too, as certain surfaces have a small amount of movement: for example, metal and timber naturally contract and expand throughout their life. Atmospheric conditions such as humidity and different temperatures will also affect the surfaces of different items, so paint needs to be able to stretch and shrink to the same degree (this property is called elasticity).

Opacity and adhesion are also important properties of a coating or paint. Opacity refers to the covering power of the paint. If the opacity is not correct, the coating or paint will be too transparent and will not block out the surface it is being applied to. If a coating or paint does not have the correct adhesion ('stickability'), it will not stick to the surface.

Many coatings and paints can be applied by brush and roller, but only those mentioned below can be sprayed onto a surface – again, provided you have prepared the paint and surface correctly. A sprayed application gives a much better finish to a coating or paint, but this technique cannot always be used due to different factors (see Chapter 15 for more information).

Water-based coatings that can be used in spraying

- acrylic primer/undercoat

- matt emulsion paints

- vinyl silk emulsion paints

- masonry paints (water-based)

- moisture vapour permeable coating

- low-odour eggshell finish

- emulsion varnish

- wood stain

- quick-drying acrylic metal primer

- blockfiller.

Oil-based coatings that can be used in spraying

- alkali-resisting primer
- etch primer
- zinc chromate metal primer
- zinc-rich epoxy primer
- eggshell/satin finish
- multicolour finish (fleck)
- masonry paint (oil-based)
- cellulose coating
- moisture vapour permeable/microporous coatings (spirit-based)
- anti-graffiti paint
- chlorinated rubber paint
- machinery enamel
- epoxy resin paint
- flame retardant paint
- micaceous iron oxide paint
- oil-based wood stain
- oil resin varnishes
- interior varnishes.

As you can see, there are far more oil-based coatings and paints suitable for spraying, many of which are used in the shipbuilding industry. As a painter and decorator, you may move into this type of work sometime in your working life. If this does happen, remember: health and safety and correct training will help you overcome any situations or problems you may come across when spraying.

The components of paint

Paint is a liquid material that changes into a solid material when it dries, forming a decorative and protective film on a surface. You could say that the liquid part of paint is only temporary and is a way of getting the other components on to the surface.

Paint consists of three components:

1. Thinner – this is either the water or solvent part of the paint that dissolves the other components and makes them suitable for surface application. When paint is applied to a surface, the thinner evaporates totally as it dries.

2. Binder – this is a **resin** and forms the film of the paint. The binder also determines the performance of the paint (how long it lasts) and the degree of gloss (shine).

3. Pigment – the colour. Pigment is also responsible for the paint's opaqueness (the ability to cover the underlying surface). Some pigments, in paints such as primers, also influence the performance of the paint, for example rust-inhibiting pigments prevent the formation of rust.

Watching paint dry

Not the most exciting thing to do, but the process of paint drying is quite complex and it is useful that you understand the basic principles. Paints dry in one of two ways:

1. Air-drying – the thinner (the water or solvent) evaporates (see Figure 12.1a). You may become aware of this during the paint application, for example when brush applying oil-based gloss to a large surface, you may find that the coating becomes difficult to brush, indicating that the thinner is evaporating.

Definition

Resin – this can be either natural (produced by plants and trees) or man-made (plastic)

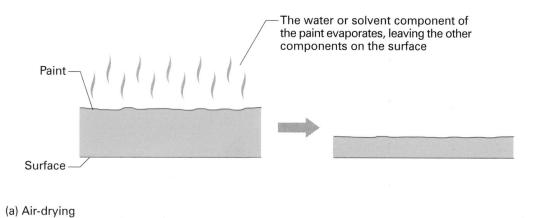

The water or solvent component of the paint evaporates, leaving the other components on the surface

Paint

Surface

(a) Air-drying

Did you know?

As paint dries, the thickness of the film shrinks (wet film thickness is greater than dry film thickness)

In oxidation, the paint reacts with oxygen molecules in the air

Oxygen

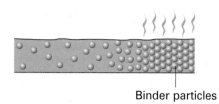

In coalescence, as the liquid part of the paint evaporates, the binder particles are drawn together, causing them to fuse and bind the pigment into a film

Binder particles

(b) Chemical reaction

Figure 12.1 The paint drying process

2. Chemical reaction – drying either happens as the paint reacts with oxygen in the air (a process known as oxidation) or as ingredients in the paint that have been kept separated in the solvent combine on the surface to create a film (a process known as coalescence). This reaction can also be heat-activated. See Figure 12.1b.

Air-drying paints are usually single-pack paints and are supplied in one container. Paints that dry using a chemical reaction (which are usually special purpose paints, such as floor paints and corrosion-resistant coatings used on structural steel) are supplied in two packs. One pack contains the base (Part A) and the other pack contains the hardener (Part B). They are kept separate so that the chemical reaction that causes the paint to start drying only happens when they are mixed together. Once two-pack paint is mixed together, it must be used within about four hours, after which the consistency becomes unworkable. The amount of time two-pack paints remain at a workable consistency is known as the **pot life**.

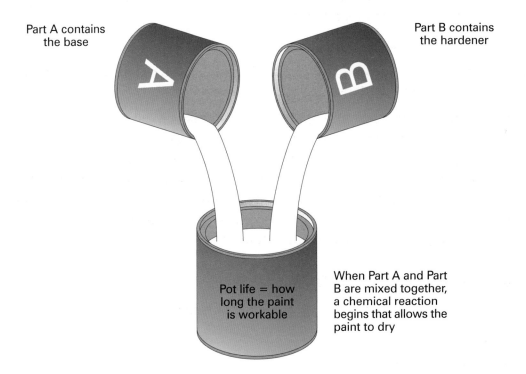

Part A contains the base

Part B contains the hardener

Pot life = how long the paint is workable

When Part A and Part B are mixed together, a chemical reaction begins that allows the paint to dry

Figure 12.2 Part A and Part B of a two-pack paint

If two-pack paint is not used up within its pot-life period, expensive mistakes can be made:

- If too much paint is made up (mixed together), it will set in the tin resulting in an expensive waste.

- If application equipment, such as brushes, rollers and spray equipment, is not cleaned in good time it could be ruined.

Manufacturers usually give a mixing ratio, for example 2 parts of base per 1 part of hardener. You can use this ratio to determine how much paint you should mix, depending on how quickly you can apply the paint to the surface.

For example, if you can use 54 litres of paint, with a mixing ratio of 2:1, before its pot life expires, then you can figure out the amount of paint you need to mix using the following method:

Ratio of base to hardener – 2:1

2 + 1 = 3

54 litres / 3 = 18 litres

To determine how much base you need, multiply your answer of 18 litres by the manufacturer's ratio proportion of 2:

$$18 \text{ litres} \times 2 = 36 \text{ litres}$$

To determine how much hardener you need, multiply your answer of 18 litres by the manufacturer's ratio proportion of 1:

$$18 \text{ litres} \times 1 = 18 \text{ litres}$$

By mixing 36 litres of base with 18 litres of hardener, you will have the 54 litres of paint that you can apply during the pot life of the paint.

Special attention should be paid to any safety information provided with paints. Some types of paint contain chemicals known as isocyanate groups. These chemicals give off vapours (gases), which irritate the airways (windpipe and lungs) and could cause conditions such as asthma. You should also avoid contact with the skin or eyes. The correct PPE should be worn when working with these materials, including air-fed masks and powered respirators. In addition, make sure the area you are working in is well ventilated and take regular breaks.

Good painting practice

Successful painting is dependent on a number of factors:

- Preparation
- Environmental conditions
- Film thickness
- Workmanship.

Preparation

The importance of proper surface preparation prior to painting cannot be over-emphasised. No surface should be painted unless it is in a sound, firm, clean, dry condition. (For more detailed information on surface preparation, see Chapter 10 page 197.)

Environmental conditions

Environmental conditions refer to the dampness or wetness of the surface and the temperature of the surface and the surrounding atmosphere. Wet timber and wet plaster are obvious examples of surfaces that cannot be painted successfully. They must be allowed to dry out thoroughly before painting can be attempted.

Weather conditions affect the drying time and finish of paint films and are especially important when working on an outdoor surface. Warm, dry conditions accelerate drying. Cold and humid conditions **retard** drying and can detrimentally affect the finish of gloss paints, causing them to dry flat or 'bloom' (develop a cloudy white film on the surface).

Paints should not, therefore, normally be applied during cold or humid conditions, or just before these conditions can be expected.

Film thickness

On new surfaces, it is necessary to apply an initial paint film build-up of adequate thickness. This can usually be achieved by the application of at least three coats of solvent-based systems, such as one coat of primer, one coat of undercoat and one coat of gloss. Alternatively, at least two coats of emulsion and acrylic water-based paints can be used, all applied at the correct spreading rate as indicated for the specific product. The use of an additional coat, sometimes of primer, undercoat or finishing paint, is often also beneficial.

Workmanship

Good workmanship is a very important factor in good painting practice. Site and surface preparation may seem like boring and time-consuming jobs, but if corners are cut, your work will be of a poor quality and your reputation as a good decorator will soon suffer.

Water-based or solvent-based paint?

These two types of paint protect surfaces in different ways. Solvent-based paint, such as alkyd gloss, protect surfaces by forming a waterproof layer. This keeps out any moisture, preventing the formation of wet rot in timber surfaces.

Water-based paints protect surfaces by providing a moisture screen that prevents most of the water from penetrating the surface. Any moisture that does penetrate is allowed to escape as water vapour through the **permeable** coating.

Most water-based paints do not have the ability to soak into the surface of timber, which means that they do not stick as well as oil-based paints. Solvent-based gloss is sometimes used over water-based acrylic undercoat, but its performance is marred by the lack of adhesion of some water-based coatings.

There are products on the market that have managed to combine the adhesion of solvent-based paints with the flexibility of water-based coatings.

Primers

A primer is the first coat of paint applied to a surface. If the surface preparation for the priming coat or the application and choice of the primer is incorrect in any way, the durability of the paint system will be reduced.

Some manufacturers market their primers as 'universal', which means that they are intended for use on a wide range of surfaces. However, these primers should not be expected to out-perform those primers specifically designed for a particular surface. For example, when painting on an aluminium surface, a two-pack etch primer designed specifically for use on aluminium would be a far better primer than a universal primer, which is listed as being suitable for use on non-ferrous metal.

The main purpose of a priming coat is to make the surface suitable to receive further coats of paint. See Table 12.1 on page 250 for further information on primers.

Undercoats

Undercoats, or intermediate coats as they are sometimes called, are designed to provide a sound base for the finish coats by providing:

• opacity (the ability to cover and hide the underlying coating)

• adequate film build for protection and finish quality.

Ordinary oil-based undercoats can become brittle with age, thus reducing the performance of the finishing paint system. Water-based undercoats are best used as part of a full water-based system and do not perform well under solvent-based paints, particularly on exteriors.

For further information on undercoats, see Table 12.1 on page 250.

Finishes

A finish is the top layer of paint – the one that will be seen. Matt and silk emulsions are the most commonly used type of finish on interior wall and ceiling surfaces. Matt emulsion is smooth, non-reflective (i.e. not glossy), quick-drying and available in countless colours. Silk emulsion is washable and gives a sheen finish when dry. It is ideal for areas such as kitchens and bathrooms. Vinyl soft sheen is a modern subtle alternative to vinyl matt and silk emulsions, drying to a soft mid-sheen and suitable for most wall and ceiling surfaces.

For more information on matt and silk vinyl emulsion finishes, see Table 12.1 on page 251.

Did you know?

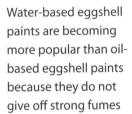

Water-based eggshell paints are becoming more popular than oil-based eggshell paints because they do not give off strong fumes

Eggshell finishes are durable paints suitable for interior use, particularly conditions of high-humidity such as in kitchens and bathrooms. It is optional whether or not eggshell paint is stirred before use. Unstirred, the paint has a semi-gel consistency that doesn't drip from the brush but liquefies on application. Alternatively, the paint can be beaten to a full-bodied fluid consistency, which is recommended for roller or spray application.

The standard finish used to protect joinery components is a gloss finish. The most common type used is alkyd gloss.

Alkyd gloss

Alkyd gloss paint is solvent-based and is usually used over a solvent-based alkyd undercoat. The advantages of alkyd gloss paint include:

- good covering power (with the exception of strong yellows, reds and oranges)
- it provides a good waterproof barrier
- it provides a durable, easy-clean, high-gloss finish
- it is available in a wide range of colours.

The disadvantages of alkyd gloss paint include:

- white alkyd gloss is prone to yellowing, or chalking, and loses its gloss on exteriors after a number of years
- it becomes brittle with age, which means that it is prone to cracking and flaking when it can't accommodate any movement in the timber surface
- the waterproof nature of the finish prevents any water trapped within the surface from escaping, which can lead to blistering of the paint system or even wet rot.

Water-based gloss

Water-based gloss is made from acrylic polymers and is fast becoming an alternative to traditional solvent-based gloss due to legislation and environmental issues. Water-based gloss is sometimes labelled 'microporous' which means it is permeable. Permeable paints are said to let the surface 'breathe', which means that the small holes in the coating allow air to reach the surface.

Advantages of water-based gloss paint:

- easier to apply than alkyd gloss
- provides a flexible, non-yellowing film
- does not give off toxic fumes when drying
- equipment can be easily washed out in water after use
- dries quickly in dry, warm conditions
- resistant to alkalis

- does not chalk upon ageing.

Disadvantages of water-based gloss paint:

- does not provide a high-gloss finish
- does not provide a seal between the glass and putties on timber window frames
- drying can be retarded by cold, damp conditions and it can freeze, both on the surface and in the can, due to its water content
- can be washed off exterior surfaces by rain while still wet
- not as resistant to abrasion as alkyd gloss.

Varnish

Varnish is a transparent finish that is applied to wood. It comes in matt, satin and gloss varieties and provides a tough water- and heat-resistant protective coating. The components of varnish are as follows:

- **Drying oil** – this is a substance such as linseed oil, tung oil or walnut oil, which dries to form a hardened solid film.
- **Resin** – yellow-brown resins such as amber, copal or rosin are used in many varnishes.
- **Thinner or solvent** – white spirit or paint thinner is commonly used as the thinner or solvent.

Table 12.2 on page 252 gives some information about some of the types of varnish available.

Remember

Because varnish is transparent (see-through), careful preparation of the wood surface is very important, as any faults or defects will be clearly visible

Wood stain

Wood stain is a type of dye, which when applied to timber soaks deep into the fibres and emphasises the grain of the wood. Available in a variety of colours and suited to either indoor or outdoor purposes, wood stain can transform bare timber surfaces into beautiful shades of natural wood. Quite often, wood stain does not offer any protection to a surface, it simply colours it. Always check the type of stain you are using and seal the wood with a varnish or polish after staining if necessary.

For more information on wood stain, see Table 12.3 on page 254.

Sealers and preparatory coatings

Sealers and preparatory coatings are substances that are applied to a surface in order to prepare it to receive subsequent surface coatings. Sealers, such as knotting solution, act by sealing in the surface material, thus preventing anything from leaking out of or into the surface. Preparatory coatings are special substances that protect and preserve the surface from things such as water, mould, rust or

alkali surface coatings. Applying a suitable and appropriate sealer or preparatory coating to your surface before decorating it, will preserve the surface and ensure a high-quality, long-lasting finish.

Table 12.4 on page 256 gives information about some common examples of sealers and preparatory coatings.

Applying coatings to various surface types

Timber
Bare untreated timber

For basic painting tasks:

- Seal any knots in timber using knotting solution.
- Prime the surface using oil-based wood primer (for external surfaces) or acrylic primer undercoat (for internal surfaces).
- Fill using polyfiller and decorator's caulk.
- Rub down and dust off.
- Apply one coat of undercoat.
- Rub down and dust off.
- Apply another coat of undercoat if necessary.
- Apply one coat of gloss.

Alternatively, for staining or varnishing tasks:

- Fill holes in timber with putty or coloured stopper.
- Apply basecoat.
- Rub down and dust off.
- Apply one coat of wood stain or varnish.
- Lightly rub down and dust off.
- Apply second coat of wood stain or varnish.

Previously painted timber

- Rub down using sandpaper.
- If necessary, fill using polyfiller or caulk.
- Apply one coat of undercoat.
- Rub down undercoat and dust off.
- Apply one coat of gloss.

Rough cut timber

- Apply one coat of timber preservative or wood stain.
- Apply second coat of timber preservative or wood stain.

Plaster

Untreated plasterboard

- Apply one coat of emulsion thinned by up to 10 per cent.
- If necessary, fill using polyfiller then lightly rub down and dust off.
- Apply one coat of emulsion as an undercoat.
- Rub down and dust off.
- Apply second coat of emulsion.

Did you know?

Newly plastered walls can be painted with emulsion because they allow the wall to 'breathe'

Bare plaster

- Dry scrape with a scraper or broad knife.
- Apply one coat of alkali-resisting primer or one coat of emulsion thinned by up to 20 per cent.
- Fill any holes or dents using polyfiller then rub down using sandpaper and dust off.
- Apply first coat (eggshell or emulsion).
- Rub down and dust off.
- Apply second coat of paint (eggshell or emulsion).

Previously painted plaster

- Wash down using sugar soap solution.
- Fill any holes or cracks using polyfiller and decorator's caulk then rub down.
- Dust off.
- Apply first coat (eggshell or emulsion).
- Rub down and dust off.
- Apply second coat of paint (eggshell or emulsion).

Artex

- Apply one coat of emulsion thinned by up to 20 per cent.
- Apply one coat of emulsion.
- Rub down and dust off.
- Apply second coat of emulsion.

Steelwork

Previously painted steelwork

- Dry abrade using emery paper or a scraper and wire brush to remove any rust.
- Dust off.
- Apply good general purpose metal primer or zinc phosphate to areas where rust has been removed.
- Apply undercoat.
- Lightly abrade and dust off.
- Apply gloss coating.

Previously unpainted steelwork

Same procedure as for previously painted, but using a full coat of primer rather than spot priming or touching up.

Other metal surfaces

Ferrous metals (iron and steel)

- Remove all corrosion and millscale via mechanical means.
- Degrease with white spirit if necessary.
- Allow the surface to dry thoroughly.
- Apply primer with a brush.
- **Bitumen**-coated surfaces will require sealing with shellac knotting or aluminium primer.
- Four coats of paint will be required to achieve adequate film thickness (as recommended by the British Iron and Steel Association).

Non-ferrous metals (aluminium, copper, zinc, brass etc.)

- Degrease surface with white spirit.
- Galvanised and zinc-sprayed surfaces should be treated with **mordant solution**.
- Etch the surface with wet and dry abrasive paper and white spirit to provide a key.
- Apply one coat of metal primer or universal primer.

Masonry

- Clean the surface with a jet wash or scrub with a suitable detergent, remove loose materials and treat any efflorescence.

Did you know?

Ferrous metals rust; non-ferrous metals do not rust

Definition

Bitumen – a heavy, semi-solid, brown-black substance created as a result of the oil refining process (also known as asphalt or tar)

Definition

Mordant solution a substance that provides a key

- Any mould, mildew, algae or lichen should be treated with a sterilisation wash before being removed with a scraper or stiff brush. The surface should then be re-treated with the sterilisation wash.

- Ensure surface is completely dry before applying any coating.

- Prime new masonry and older or weathered masonry with stabilising solution or all-purpose primer, applying with a brush. Previously painted surfaces in good condition may not need priming.

- Subsequent coatings can be applied by brush, roller or spray.

Surface coating defects

During your career as a painter and decorator, there may be occasions when the surface coating you have applied fails in some way. This may be because you did not adequately prepare the surface prior to applying the coating, because the environmental conditions (e.g. the weather) were not favourable or because your tools or materials were of poor quality.

Figure 12.3 shows some common types of surface coating defect and how they might be caused. Familiarise yourself with these defects and do everything possible to prevent them from occurring.

Did you know?

The reason the first layer of primer applied to masonry should be applied with a brush, is because the action of brushing forces the paint into the surface

Find out

Look at each surface coating defect detailed in Figure 12.3. How can each defect be prevented?

Bittiness – where a coating, once applied, appears gritty or filmy. Caused by inadequate surface preparation or dirty equipment

Discolouration – a change in pigment colour, usually resulting in a pale or faded coating. Caused by exposure to strong sunlight or a reaction with chemicals on the surface or in the atmosphere

Flashing – where painted sections of a large surface dry off and leave a mark as the next application of paint is applied next to it. Caused by painting sections of a surface at different times

Blooming – a reduction in the gloss finish of varnish and oil-based gloss. Caused by draughts, a damp surface or high humidity

Misses – simply where a coating has been applied but missed some areas of the surface. Caused by careless application, the undercoat being similar in colour to the finished colour and poor lighting

Rain spotting or cratering – a wet coating that has been damaged by rain or condensation

Common surface coating defects

Lyting – where a coating is applied before the underlying coat has properly dried. Lyting can also happen if the solvent in the coat applied softens the surface of the paint below it

Orange peel – can occur when paint is roller- or spray-applied and is so-called because the finish resembles orange peel. Caused by applying the paint too thickly, holding the gun too close to the surface and incorrect gun pressure

Fat edges – a heavy edge of paint, normally seen around door edges where a surface receives a double coating of paint and a ridge is formed. Caused by poor brush work

Grinning – where the undercoat or first coat can be seen through the top coat. Caused by over-brushing, using thin paint and using the wrong colour undercoat

Figure 12.3 Common surface coating defects

Surface coating defects can occur before the coating is even applied to the surface. Most defects that occur in the tin are normally caused by:

- incorrect storage
- incorrect mixing
- the coating going past its use-by date.

Common defects of coatings in the tin include:

- Settling – where the components of the paint (see page 236) become separated because of long-term storage.
- Skinning – where the coating forms a skin. The skin can usually be easily removed and the surface coating used as normal
- Fattening or livering – where paint has thickened to such an extent that the adding of a solvent or oil does not thin it. This defect can also occur when the wrong solvent or thinner has been used or when the paint is past its use-by date.

FAQ

Why is oil-based paint usually called 'alkyd paint'?

Oil-based paint and alkyd paint are not the same thing. Alkyd paint is a *type* of oil-based paint. Some oil-based paints are made from natural oils and resins, whereas alkyd paint is made from synthetic materials, but it is still oil-based.

What is a spreading rate?

The term 'spreading rate' refers to the amount of surface area a surface coating will cover per litre. Some surface coatings will have a high spreading rate (for example, 18 square metres per litre), while others will have a lower spreading rate (for example, 10 square metres per litre).

On the job: Knotting solution

Charlie is a final-year apprentice and is working on a new build property. He is working with Dave who is an experienced painter and decorator. They have just started work on the property and as part of his surface preparation, Charlie gets out a knotting bottle. He is just about to start treating the knots on some timber when Dave tells him 'not to bother'. Dave tells Charlie that treating the wood with knotting solution is a waste of time, and he should just prime all the timber instead.

Do you think treating timber with knotting solution is a waste of time? What do you think Charlie should do?

Knowledge check

1. Name four reasons why a surface coating might be applied.

2. What happens to the water or solvent component of paint when it is applied to a surface?

3. Name three things the pigment in paint might be responsible for.

4. Briefly describe what happens when paint dries via chemical reaction.

5. How might weather conditions affect a surface coating's drying time?

6. What is a universal primer and why might you choose to use one?

7. What two things does an undercoat provide?

8. What is the most commonly used paint finish on interior walls and ceilings?

9. What are the three components of varnish?

10. Why might you apply wood stain to a timber surface?

11. Briefly describe the procedure you would follow if applying surface coatings to a bare plaster wall.

12. How many coats of paint does the British Iron and Steel Association recommend are applied to ferrous metal surfaces?

13. Name three reasons why a surface coating might fail.

14. What is lyting?

15. How are most surface coating defects that occur in the tin caused?

Table 12.1 Paint – primer, undercoat, finishes (vinyl emulsions)

Acrylic wall primer *A water-based alkali-resisting paint made from high-quality pigments and a tough acrylic resin; air-drying and water-based*	**Uses** Primer is the first coating applied to a wall and provides better adhesion of paint to a surface, increases the durability of subsequent coatings and also serves as a protector **Special properties** Low odour, fast-drying, easily applied, good opacity and flow; can also contain ingredients that cover most stains **Colour range** Various **Pack sizes** 2.5 litres to 10 litres **Spreading rate** Between 10–12 square metres per litre on smooth, non-porous surfaces **Drying time** In normal conditions it dries in four to five hours **Equipment cleaner** Water **Storage** Replace lid firmly; protect from frost **Surface preparation** Ensure the surface is sound, clean and dry **Application** Stir well before use and apply one full coat in even strokes using a brush or roller, ensuring the primer is applied firmly to the surface
Undercoat *A dense covering made from lead-free pigments bound-in by a durable alkyd resin; air-drying and solvent-based*	**Uses** The coating applied to a surface after the primer but before the finish. Suitable for both interior and exterior surfaces **Special properties** Easy to apply, excellent opacity with good flow and levelling characteristics; provides a smooth, well-bound surface for finishes **Colour range** Various **Pack sizes** 750 ml, 2.5 litres and 5 litres **Spreading rate** Approximately 10–12 square metres per litre on smooth, prepared surfaces **Drying time** 16 to 24 hours **Equipment cleaner** White spirit or turpentine substitute **Storage** Replace lid firmly; store away from heat and flame **Surface preparation** Ensure surface is sound, clean, dry and completely free from grease. Previously painted surfaces should be rubbed down with wet abrasive paper to provide a good key. Bare surfaces should be primed with the appropriate primer. After priming, fill cracks and nail holes with filler

	Application Stir well before use. Apply one or more coats of undercoat as required with a brush or roller. Give each coat 16 to 24 hours to dry thoroughly, then rub down lightly to remove any nibs before applying gloss finish. If there is a lengthy time between undercoat and gloss application, another coat of undercoat will be required before applying gloss finish **Restrictions** None
Vinyl emulsions *Available in matt or silk varieties, easy to apply and suitable for the decoration of most interior walls and ceilings; air-drying and water-based*	**Uses** Both matt and silk emulsions are the number one choice for most domestic internal surfaces. Matt emulsion is best suited to surfaces where a shine is not desired, particularly those that are uneven or have imperfections. Silk emulsion leaves an attractive sheen when dry and is more durable and washable than matt emulsion **Special properties** Easy to apply, high opacity, resistant to yellowing and fading **Colour range** Huge **Pack sizes** 1 litre, 2.5 litres, 5 litres and 10 litres **Spreading rate** Approximately 14 square metres per litre for matt and approximately 12 square metres per litre for silk, depending on surface porosity and texture **Drying time** Under normal conditions, touch-dry in one hour; can be re-coated after two to four hours **Equipment cleaner** Water **Storage** Replace lid firmly; protect from frost **Surface preparation** Attend to all surface imperfections and cracks. Prime and undercoat as necessary. Previously gloss-painted surfaces will need to be rubbed down thoroughly to provide a good key **Application** Stir well before use and apply with a brush or roller. When the paint is to be applied to absorbent surfaces, thin the first coat with clean water. Further coatings can be applied un-thinned. Two coats are normally recommended for a good film build, although a third coat may be necessary with severely contrasting colour changes. For spray application, thin with clean water as required, up to approximately 10% by volume of water to paint. Do not apply when the air or surface temperature is below 5°C. Conditions of high humidity can prolong the drying time

Table 12.2 Varnishes

Quick-drying varnish *A fast-drying high-quality varnish made from a special acrylic resin; air-drying and water-based*	**Uses** Good for the protection and decoration of interior bare wood surfaces and previously varnished surfaces in good condition **Special properties** Fast drying time, low odour, easy application **Colour range** Clear (gloss and satin finishes) **Pack sizes** 750 ml and 2.5 litres **Spreading rate** Approximately 12 square metres per litre, depending on the porosity (number of pores absorbency) of the timber **Drying time** Under normal conditions, touch-dry in one hour; hard dry after four hours **Equipment cleaner** Water **Storage** Replace lid firmly; protect from frost **Surface preparation** Surfaces must be sound, clean and dry. Sand lightly along the grain of the timber; do not use wet abrasive paper at this stage as this could cause staining later on if used on dry timber **Application** Apply an initial coat of the varnish by brush. The initial milky-white appearance will disappear to a clear, virtually invisible film as the varnish dries. Leave to dry for approximately one hour under good drying conditions then lightly sand along the grain to remove any raised fibres. Apply as many coats as required to fill the grain (usually three coats), allowing 30 minutes between coats. Rubbing down can then be carried out with wet abrasive paper, using water as the lubricant. Rinse the surface and allow to dry **Restrictions** As quick-drying varnish is water-based, it should not be applied when the ambient temperature is below 5°C or in conditions of high humidity. For clear wood treatments, it is essential to take all possible precautions against contamination by iron, any trace of which can cause unsightly stains. Do not use wire wool for rubbing down
Quick-drying floor varnish *A high-quality, low odour, fast-drying varnish; water-based*	**Uses** Suitable for all bare and pre-treated interior timber floors **Special properties** Durable and fast-drying **Colour range** Clear gloss and clear satin **Pack sizes** 2.5 and 5 litres **Spreading rate** Approximately 18 square metres per litre, depending on the nature and porosity of the timber

	Drying time Under normal conditions, touch-dry in one hour; can be re-coated in two to four hours
	Equipment cleaner Water
	Storage Replace lid firmly; protect from frost
	Surface preparation Ensure surface is sound, clean and dry. Rub down previously varnished or stained surfaces with fine wet abrasive paper and mild soapy water, then thoroughly rinse and allow to dry. Do not prepare the surface with wire wool
	Application Stir well before use and apply evenly with a brush or roller along the grain. Use only a glass or plastic container to hold the varnish and avoid contact with ferrous metals while wet. On new surfaces, the first coat should be thinned with up to 10% clean water, followed by at least two further coats of undiluted varnish. Avoid contact with alcohol and harsh chemicals. Do not apply when air or surface temperatures are below 5°C. Conditions of high humidity will prolong the drying time

Table 12.3 Wood stain

| Protective wood stain

A specially formulated protective wood stain made from UV light-absorbing pigments and water-shedding resins; air-drying and solvent-based | **Uses** A decorative and protective treatment for new and old bare timber surfaces (both softwood and hardwood) in interior and exterior locations. Ideal for timber cladding, window frames, doors, fences and sheds. Not suitable for use on painted or varnished timber

Special properties Very easy to apply, protects timber from rot and attack from other wood-destroying organisms, resists blistering and peeling, a fresh coat does not require removal of the old coat

Colour range A variety of wood tones

Pack sizes 750 ml, 2.5 litres and 5 litres

Spreading rate Approximately 15 square metres per litre, depending on the porosity of the timber

Drying time Under normal conditions, touch-dry in two to four hours; can be re-coated after 16 to 24 hours

Equipment cleaner White spirit or turpentine substitute

Storage Replace lid firmly; store away from heat and flame

Surface preparation Ensure timber is sound, clean and dry (the moisture content should be less than 20%). Old paint or varnish should be stripped off and grey, weathered timber should be sanded until clean and bright. Bare softwood should be treated with a preservative and then allowed to dry. Some hardwoods, such as teak, have a naturally occurring oiliness which must be cleaned off with white spirit and the surface left to dry

Application Apply two coats of protective wood stain with a brush, allowing overnight drying between coats |
| High-build wood stain

A highly durable, microporous, translucent, semi-gloss finish; air-drying and solvent-based | **Uses** The flexible, microporous properties of high-build wood stain make it particularly suitable for the protection and decoration of exterior timber surfaces. Ideal for window frames, sills, doors, cladding and other high-grade exterior wooden surfaces

Special properties Highly flexible film withstands normal changes in timber without cracking or loss of adhesion, reduced risk of blistering and flaking

Colour range A variety of wood tones

Pack sizes 750 ml, 2.5 litres and 5 litres

Spreading rate Approximately 15 square metres per litre, depending on the porosity of the timber |

	Drying time Under normal conditions, touch-dry in four to six hours; can be re-coated after 24 hours
	Equipment cleaner White spirit or turpentine substitute
	Storage Replace lid firmly; store away from heat and flame
	Surface preparation Same as for protective wood stain
	Application Same as for protective wood stain

Table 12.4 Sealers and preparatory coatings

Knotting solution	Uses Applied to knots, resin patches and stains on timber surfaces, knotting solution seals timber ready for paint or varnish application
Generally formed from a solution of shellac (the resin of the Lac insect) and methylated spirits; air-drying and solvent-based	**Special properties** Fast-drying due to the methylated spirit content, suitable for use beneath a wide range of coatings including alkyds, chlorinated rubber and acrylics (but not alcohol-based coatings), available as aluminium-pigmented or titanium-pigmented varieties for use on smoke- and water-damaged surfaces
	Colour range Clear (unless pigmented variety)
	Pack sizes 250 ml to 1 litre
	Spreading rate Approximately 10 square metres per litre
	Drying time Under normal conditions, touch-dry in five to ten minutes; can be re-coated after 30 minutes
	Equipment cleaner Mineralised methylated spirit
	Storage Replace lid firmly; store away from heat and flame
	Surface preparation Ensure that the surface is sound, clean and dry. Rub down surface with abrasive paper in order to provide a good key
	Application Shake tin well before use. Apply a full coat with the minimum of brush work. If a second coat is required it can be applied after 30 minutes, but brushing must be kept to a minimum in order to avoid any working-up of the underlying film.
Universal preservative	Uses Can be applied to new softwood that has not yet been treated with a preservative. Also suitable as a pre-treatment coating for weathered timber surfaces, providing that the underlying wood is still sound
A clear fluid made from a blend of fungicide and alkyd resins mixed in a penetrative mineral solvent; air-drying and solvent-based	**Special properties** Contains fungicide
	Colour range Clear
	Pack sizes 1 litre, 2.5 litres and 5 litres
	Spreading rate Approximately 10 to 12 square metres per litre, depending on the porosity of the timber
	Drying time Under normal conditions, approximately 16 to 24 hours
	Equipment cleaner White spirit or turpentine
	Storage Replace lid firmly; store away from heat and flame
	Surface preparation Ensure that the surface is sound, clean and dry

	Application Stir well before use and apply one generous coat with a brush, paying particular attention to the end grain and joints. If any drill holes or cuts are present in the timber, re-treat them with the preservative after drying
Red oxide primer *An anti-corrosive priming paint for metal surfaces made from zinc phosphate and red oxide pigments in an alkyd medium; air-drying and solvent-based*	**Uses** For priming iron and steel surfaces **Special properties** Contains no added lead or chromate pigments, provides excellent adhesion **Colour range** Red **Pack sizes** 2.5 litres and 5 litres **Spreading rate** Approximately 11 square metres per litre, depending on the surface to be treated **Drying time** Under normal conditions, touch-dry in four to six hours; hard-dry and can be re-coated after 16 to 24 hours **Equipment cleaner** White spirit or turpentine substitute **Storage** Replace lid firmly; store away from heat and flame **Surface preparation** Ensure surface is sound, clean and dry. Remove rust or millscale and any loose or defective paint, stripping to the bare surface if necessary **Application** Stir thoroughly before use. To ensure the best results, the brush should be fully loaded. Do not thin

chapter 13

Applying paint and creating special effects

OVERVIEW

Paint can be applied to a surface in a variety of different ways. Each method of paint application has its advantages and disadvantages and should be chosen according to the type of surface, the type of paint and the finished effect that is desired. The way paint and gilding is applied to a surface can also produce some interesting and decorative finishes. Special effects such as texture, pattern and the illusion of a different surface can all be created by a skilled decorator and the contents of their toolbox.

This chapter will cover the following topics:

- Getting started
- Applying paint using various pieces of equipment
- Creating special effects with paint
- Gilding.

These topics can be found in the following modules:

CC 2002K	CC 2020K	CC 2022K
CC 2002S	CC 2020S	CC 2022S
CC 2024K	CC 2019K	
CC 2024S	CC 2019S	

Getting started

Opening a tin of paint and decanting

You may think that there is not much to opening a tin of paint and **decanting** it into a work pot. However, if you follow a few golden rules at the very beginning of a painting job, you will find that the rest of the job is much easier.

- It is always best to work from a work pot and not the stock pot. This is because a full stock pot will be heavy and difficult to manage. In addition, if a stock pot is knocked over, you will lose a lot of paint.

- Gently dust the stock pot before you open it. This will greatly reduce the amount of dust and debris that gets into the paint.

- Most paints require a thorough stir before use, but always check the manufacturer's instructions first, just in case they advise different treatment of the paint.

- Decant paint *slowly* from the back of the stock pot into a work pot. By pouring from the back of the tin, the front is kept clean, which will help it to be quickly identified when it is on a shelf.

- Only pour enough paint into the work pot to work from (usually to the height of the bristles on a paint brush).

- Keep a paint brush or cloth handy when decanting the paint, ready to wipe up any spills from the stock pot.

Remember the golden rules when decanting paint

Applying paint using various pieces of equipment

Brush application

Applying paint with a brush is not as popular as it used to be and is now often replaced with roller application. In order to achieve a high-quality finish with brush application, the following three actions should be followed:

1. Working in the brush and getting a dip.

2. Cutting in.

3. Laying off.

Working in the brush and getting a dip

Working in the brush means dipping the brush into the paint and then gently rubbing the brush against the inside of the work pot until all the bristles are evenly coated with paint. If you were to simply dip the brush into the paint and then start painting, you would only have paint on the outer bristles of the brush. After you have worked in the brush, you can scrape the brush against the top of the work pot in order to get it back into shape.

Remember

Make sure your work area is properly protected before starting any paint job. Putting up 'wet paint' signs is a very good idea

Working in a brush ensures that all of the bristles are coated with paint

Getting a dip will ensure that paint stays on the brush until you apply it to the surface

Remember

Don't scrape the brush on the edge of the work pot to remove excess paint. The only time you should do this is when you need to empty the brush of paint, for example when preparing to wash it out

Getting a dip means applying paint to the brush, ready to begin painting. Get a dip by dipping the brush into the paint and then tapping alternate sides of the brush on to a dry area of the inside of the work pot. This action locks the paint into the bristles, stopping it from dripping or spilling during the transfer from work pot to surface.

Cutting in

Cutting in is the action of applying paint to one surface while keeping paint off an adjoining surface; for example, when painting a wall, keeping paint off the ceiling, or when painting the putty in a window, keeping paint off the glass.

Cutting in is normally done first so that the paint is applied in sections small enough to handle (i.e. just enough to keep the edge of the applied paint wet). A dip of paint can then be applied in a vertical (up and down) motion. The paint can then be crossed, which means moving the paint in a sideways motion with the brush in order to spread it evenly.

Cutting in gives a clean and straight line

Laying off

Laying off is done at the end of the paint application process and prevents misses and runs and ensures the paint is evenly spread. It is an action that the painter must perform in order to achieve the best possible finish. As the brush is brought down the surface, a small 'roll' of paint forms in front of the bristles. If the brush is not lifted off the surface by moving it back in the opposite direction, a run or sag will form. Figures 13.1 to 13.3 show the procedure for laying off.

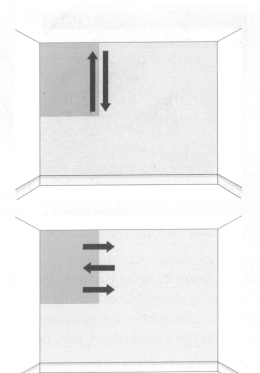

Figure 13.1 Step 1 Move the brush in a vertical motion (up and down)

Figure 13.2 Step 2 Move the brush in a horizontal motion (side to side)

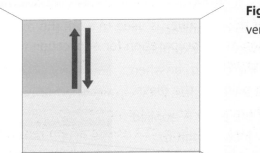

Figure 13.3 Step 3 Move the brush in a vertical motion (up and down)

Laying off emulsion paint requires a slightly different brush movement. The brush should be moved across the surface in an arcing motion so that it doesn't run or sag.

Roller application

Rollers come in various shapes and sizes to suit different surfaces and requirements. Table 13.1 shows examples of different roller types available, along with their purpose.

Laying off emulsion paint should be done with an arcing motion

Roller type	Purpose
Large	Covering large surface areas
Small	Covering small surface areas
Curved	Covering curved or rounded surfaces, such as pipes
Small and thin with a long handle	Covering surfaces behind radiators and other difficult-to-reach areas
Long pile	Creating rough, textured paint finishes
Short pile	Creating smooth, untextured paint finishes

Table 13.1 Roller types and their purposes

Remember

Use a roller when painting a large, open surface area. Rollers really prove their effectiveness when time is of the essence

Apply paint with a roller using a 'W' motion

Whichever type of roller you use, you will need a container in which to hold the paint. A roller tray or a scuttle has a deep end that holds the paint, while a shallow rough area of the container is used to work the roller against in preparation for application to the surface.

The roller should be dipped into the paint and then repeatedly rolled against the rough part of the container. The rolling action removes excess paint from the roller, ensuring that the right amount of paint is applied to the surface. When painting a surface using a roller, use a 'W' motion. Laying off with a roller should be done in a vertical movement, which, if done well, will ensure that no lines are left on the surface.

Did you know?

If specifications state that a roller finish is not acceptable, a brush can be used to lay off. This is done by using only the very tip of a brush in order to remove any bubbles or 'orange peel' effect left by the roller

Paint pad application

Paint pads have a short pile, usually mohair, attached to a cushion of foam. Paint pads can be used to apply all types of paint, whether water-based or oil-based. There are lots of different sizes available for different types of job, even pads small enough to cut in a sash window. The paint pad head is usually removable for easy cleaning.

Paint pads are available in a variety of sizes and shapes

Paint mitten application

As the name suggests, paint mittens are worn on the hand. The palm-side of the mitten is covered in sheepskin and is the part of the mitten used to apply the paint. Mitten application of paint is not the most accurate method, however it can be effective when painting around pipes and railings.

Spray application

When paint is applied to a surface with a sprayer, the stream of paint that flows from the nozzle is broken up and **atomised**. The main advantage of this method of application is that a relatively smooth film of paint can be applied very quickly.

The process of spray painting is very complex and is normally undertaken only by specialists. However, any decorator may get the occasional job when a spray finish is required, such as multi-colour finishes or metallic paint finishes on radiators.

A paint sprayer is ideal for large jobs

Dipping

Dipping involves immersing an object in a container of paint and then lifting it out to dry. This technique is mainly used in an industrial setting because it is a quick method of coating intricate surfaces in paint, ensuring that all nooks and crannies are fully covered, even the inside of tubes and pipes. Dipping results in little paint waste as any excess paint drops back into the container.

Creating special effects with paint

In this section, we will look at some of the many special paint effects that can be created by a decorator. Table 13.2 briefly details the surface preparation that will be required to create certain special effects.

Special effect	Preparation required
Broken colours (effects that produce a multi-coloured finish)	• A clean and hard surface with no brush marks, indents or nibs • Good quality undercoat such as oil-based eggshell
Graining	• An oil- and grease-free surface • The surface should be rubbed down between coats to provide a good key • To provide the background colour for the grain effect, an eggshell paint (normally oil-based) should be applied first and stippled to remove brush marks. A second coat should be applied in the same manner and left to dry thoroughly
Marbling	• Same as preparation for graining • The correct choice of background colour and the type of marbling to be imitated are essential parts of the effect

Table 13.2 Surface preparation for special paint effects

Graining

Imitating wood grain on inexpensive or non-timber surfaces has been carried out for centuries. Creating this type of special effect requires a high level of skill, as well as some artistic ability. We will now look at how an imitation mahogany finish can be achieved, although the basic principles are similar for other types of wood graining.

Graining procedure

- Apply mahogany **scumble** to the ground coat (it should be a deep red).

- Apply the graining colour in one direction, creating a straight grain.

- Using a flogger and beating from bottom to top, work up the grain. The flogger simulates the pore marks in wood.

- Apply some Van Dyke brown with a touch of black colouring.

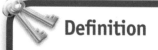

Preparation for graining involves creating a clean, brush mark-free surface with a good key

- Using a mottler, dip into the mixed Van Dyke brown and, using a half scrub with a sideways motion, move it down the length of work to be grained. This will give the impression of dark and light streaks.

- Soften the work with a badger softener.

- Finally, use a smaller mottler to distress the darker markings by half dragging and dabbing in short strokes down the wall.

- The straight grain marks you have just applied should be almost at right angles to the heavier streaks. When the graining effect is dry, the surface must be varnished to enhance and protect the effect.

Applying scumble to surface

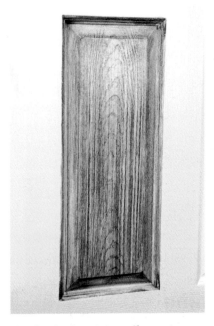

The finished graining effect

Dragging and combing

Dragging and combing are decorative effects usually associated with graining, but they are created with paint colours and glazes, rather than graining colours. When used with broken colour, dragging and combing produces a stylised version of the grain effect. An oil-based ground coat colour is best.

It is possible to produce many patterns by dragging and combing, including a straight timber grain, raw silk and even woven cotton combing effects.

A comb can be used to create a simple paint effect, as shown here, or more intricate patterns with practice

Step 1 Apply the glaze sparingly to the surface, laying off vertically

Step 2 Drag a brush through the glaze to create uneven lines. The ground coat should show through just enough to create a two-tone effect

Step 3 The finished dragging paint effect

Marbling

Many decorators will use a standard technique when creating this special effect, while others with a more artistic flare will create their own original designs for each job.

Vert de mer

The following procedure describes how to create a marble effect called 'vert de mer', which is a black and green marble originating from Northern Italy. Vert de mer marbling is a pleasing yet dramatic marble with a variety of interesting features.

Step 1 Apply an oil-based black eggshell ground coat, ensuring an indentation- and brush mark-free finish

Step 2 When the ground coat is dry, apply a thin layer of **glip** (two parts turpentine to one part linseed oil, adding 10 per cent **driers** to finish the mixture)

Step 3 Apply dark green paint to the ground coat

Step 4 Apply pale green paint to the surface while the dark green coat is still wet

Step 5 Stipple with a hog hair stippler. This will blend the two shades of green, losing the sharp edges of the colours

Step 6 Distress the surface with a plastic bag, exposing the ground colour

Step 7 Apply white spirit to the surface by flicking it onto the surface from a paint brush. This will open up the colours

Step 8 Mix a white eggshell paint and create fine lines on the surface using a feather or sable writer. This is done by dipping the tip of the feather in the paint and then slowly dragging it across the surface, twisting it as you drag

Step 9 Soften the white lines using a dry brush. Protect the paint effect with a layer of varnish

Carrera marble

Another marble effect is 'carerra marble', which unlike vert de mer is mostly pure white in colour with no visible veining. The beauty of replicating this marble is that you can create many different fantasy marbles from it: the less pure carerra marble has often got traces of yellow, green and blue to it, so there are many ways to 'create' it.

Carrera marble finish

Before you start, prepare your surface correctly and apply the required ground coat: white eggshell if done in an oil-based ground, or white emulsion if done in a water-based ground.

1. If using an oil-based coating, wipe a layer of glip over the surface of the prepared ground. If using a water-based coating, apply a fine mist of water over the surface of the prepared ground.

2. Mix three tones of grey transparent glaze, and apply these to the surface, creating a cloud formation (without creating an obvious texture).

3. Soften the effect with either a hog hair or badger hair softener, blending in all directions, and leave to dry.

4. Apply a tonally deeper grey to the surface in rounded lines, soften from one edge only, and leave to dry.

5. Mix a deeper grey and apply it to the surface again, softening it again, and leave to dry.

6. Add fine lines to represent veining, remembering to soften again, and leave to dry.

7. Apply a coat of clear varnish to protect your finished marble.

Rag rolling

Rag rolling is a broken colour effect created by applying colour to a surface with a brush or roller and then lifting the colour off with the rag, exposing some of the background colour. 'Ragging on' is the name given to the action of applying the colour to a ground coat using a rag or cloth. 'Ragging off' is the name given to the action of lifting off some of the colour and creates a different effect. The rag used should be **lint**-free and bunched up in the hand during paint application. A chamois leather roller (Duet® type) or even rolled up paper or plastic bags can be used instead of a rag and will create a softer or sharper effect.

Procedure for ragging on

- Mix up a coloured glaze and pour into a work pot.
- Bunch up a rag and dip it into the coloured glaze, making sure the rag is completely saturated.
- Wring out the rag and roll it into a loose cylinder, twisting it slightly.
- Apply the paint by rolling the rag across small sections of the surface in random directions to create a rag rolled finish.

Procedure for ragging off

- Apply a coloured glaze to the surface, removing any brush marks with a hog hair stippler.
- Bunch up a rag and roll it across the surface in different directions then lift the rag off of the surface. This will remove coloured glaze from the surface.
- Clean off the rag and repeat the process, remembering to alter the direction of the rag as it is rolling across the surface. This will prevent the finished effect from looking uniform.

A rag rolling paint effect can be more interesting than solid colour

Definition

Lint – tiny, fuzzy fibres of material

Safety tip

Paint-soaked rags should be opened out and allowed to dry before disposal – wet rags are a fire risk

Did you know?

A natural sponge is the soft and fibrous skeleton of a marine animal

Sponging

Sponging is quite simply creating a broken colour effect by applying and removing paint with a sponge. Either a natural or synthetic sponge can be used.

Sponging procedure

- Apply a coloured eggshell or thinned gloss paint and allow to dry completely.

- Decant the paint to be sponged into a tray. Load the sponge with colour by dipping it into the paint and squeezing out excess paint.

- Apply the colour to the base coat by gently dabbing with the sponge, ensuring you don't overload areas with paint.

Sponging is an easy way to create an interesting broken colour effect

- If desired, build up different layers of colour with the sponge, allowing each coat to dry thoroughly. Different types of sponge could also be used for each colour, giving the finished paint effect the appearance of depth and texture.

Stippling

Stippling is a way of creating a soft, suede-like appearance on a surface. Different colours can also be overlayed in order to create bands of colour. Water-based paints allow the decorator to apply a number of colours in one day, however the colour must be applied swiftly as the drying process will be rapid.

Stippling procedure

Step 1 Mix up a glaze consisting of colour turpentine and driers. Apply the glaze to the surface with a brush

Step 2 Use a hog hair stippler to stipple the glaze, ensuring no brush marks remain. The aim is to achieve a soft, even texture

Wiping and glazing

Wiping and glazing is a highlighting technique used on **relief surfaces**. A relief surface is one that has parts that are raised or projecting out from the background. Embossed wallpaper, ornate panels and mouldings are all examples of relief surfaces.

Wiping and glazing procedure

- Apply a ground coat to the surface and allow to dry.

- Apply a tinted glaze and stipple with a hoghair stippler to create an even blend with no light or dark patches.

- Immediately take a cloth or squeegee and wipe over the surface. The aim is to only remove the glaze from raised parts of the surface, leaving a two-tone effect.

Stencilling

Stencilling is a way of decorating a surface with a pattern or design using a cut-out template. A client may ask for stencil work because:

- it produces a unique paint effect on a surface. The position and colour of the pattern or design will be unique and tailored to the client's requirements

- it is quick and easy to repeat a pattern or design.

There are two kinds of stencil:

- Positive stencils – where a pattern is cut out and paint is applied over the openings, reproducing the pattern on the surface beneath (see photo)

- Negative stencils – the opposite of a positive stencil, whereby the background of a pattern is cut out.

Stencils can be made up of more than one part. These are known as multi-plate stencils. For example, a stencil of a flower design may be made up of three plates: the first for the

Wipe over the surface with a cloth to create a two-tone paint effect

A positive stencil

Remember

Dispose of soiled cloths in a way that complies with COSHH regulations

Remember

When creating a stencil, the pattern or design has to be held in place with 'ties'. Without ties, your design will simply fall out of the template so make sure you incorporate ties into your design

leaves and stem, the second for the first layer of petals and the third for the top layer of petals and flower centre. Multi-plate stencils are particularly useful when a pattern is made up of lots of colours or when it is very complex. When using multi-plate stencils, ensure that you match up the plates or your finished design will not look as it should. Lining up the plates with two pencil lines at right angles is the most effective method.

Stencil design

When applying stencils, careful consideration must be taken with the stencil design itself. As you will be pounding, dabbing or stippling the paint onto the design to create the picture, damage can occur such as broken ties or a twisted or buckled stencil. This could mean you have to make the stencil again, costing you time and effort to sort out and complete your task.

There is a range of materials that can be used to produce a stencil:

- acetate – a clear, flexible, sturdy sheet material that you can photocopy onto

- mylar – an inflexible polythene sheet

- cartridge paper – a thick paper, just like writing paper, which you can coat with linseed oil or knotting solution to strengthen it and make it waterproof: this is a cheaper alternative to normal stencil paper, and can be simply produced

Stencilling materials

- propriety paper – the most common stencil material used.

Positioning the stencil

Another important point you should consider is the positioning of your stencil. If you do not position it correctly, it could look lost or out of place. If you are repeating your stencil to create a design or theme, remember to space it out correctly.

There are a number of ways in which to correctly position the stencil. Here is the most common way:

1. Mark the area on the surface where the stencil is to go, then measure out the area of the surface.

2. Find the central point of where you want the stencil to go.

3. On your stencil, mark the centre points (registration marks) of the width and length of the design. To create the centre points, cut out a V on the stencil at each correct measurement with your stencil knife, making sure you follow the procedures for cutting so that you do not harm yourself.

4. Match the stencil centre points to the surface centre points you marked earlier.

Use a low-tack masking tape or spray adhesive to keep the stencil in position, but hold the stencil in place too, to keep it from moving. Remember to position your hand correctly so that you don't get paint all over it.

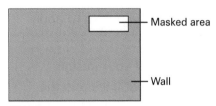

Step 1
Mask area of surface where stencil is to go.

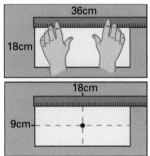

Step 2
Measure area of surface and mark the central point.

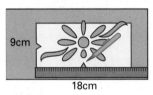

Step 3
Find the central point of the stencil. Cut a V on the stencil's length and width at the correct measurements.

Step 4
Align the centre points on the stencil and surface.

Figure 13.4 Marking up the wall and stencil for correct, even stencilling

Applying the paint

1. First, make sure you have enough paint colour mixed for the full job.

2. Have a clean stencil brush and palette/tray for your colour or colours, if you are applying more than one.

3. Get a clean sponge and a stencil brush or a 1" sash brush. Tape up the bristles; This will stop the bristles splaying.

4. Load up the tool you are going to use with paint from your palette.

5. Dab/stipple onto the palette to remove any excess paint. This will give you an even amount of paint on the tool, so that you can apply the paint to the stencil without any defects.

6. Apply the paint to the stencil in a stabbing motion, making sure you do not smudge or let paint creep under the stencil.

7. Once the stencil is complete, remove it from the surface carefully to avoid any smudging and tearing of the design (this is why a low-tack masking tape or spray adhesive is used).

Another way to apply a stencil design onto a surface is to place your stencil onto an overhead projector then, remembering to pick out your centre marks, project the design onto your surface.

Enlarging or reducing your design

Using an overhead projector, as above, enables you to reduce or enlarge your design. You would then use a small brush such as a fitch or lining brush to apply your colours to the design.

Another method is to take an enlarged or reduced photocopy of your design, then cut out the new stencil, remembering to cut out the straight lines and the small parts first. You can also draw out a grid onto your surface and then redraw your design onto the grid, free hand. This method is normally used for drawings of cartoon characters, etc. but it takes a lot more time. Alternatively, draw out a design or picture onto drawing paper, then chalk the back of the paper. Place the drawing into position, then draw over your design again. When you take the paper away, your design will be left in chalk on the surface, which you can then paint, using small brushes such as fitches.

Applying textured paint

Textured paint has been used for many years to provide a decorative finish to internal and external walls and ceilings. Textured paint can be made in two ways: it can be made from water-based or oil-based paint mixed with sand or other types of aggregates; or it can be made by mixing a powder (similar to Plaster of Paris) with water to create a thick, plastic-type coating which is applied to surfaces then painted, with water-based or oil-based paint.

Textured paint is sometimes referred to as 'plastic paint' because it is thick and can be manipulated into many different patterns and styles. The styles you can create include broken leather, swirl, broken swirl, bark, scroll, stipple and old plaster.

Textured paints can be made by mixing sand or powder into water- or oil-based paint.

These types of coating can last a lot longer than most traditional coatings, as they are harder wearing and offer durability and sheen to the surface being coated. They are also very good at sticking to a surface (adhesion), are flame retardant and do not encourage mould growth, so are ideal for coating up bathrooms, kitchens and outside building surfaces such as bricks and blocks.

The type with sand added to it comes ready-made, but you can create it yourself by mixing the colour and type of paint with sand or grit. This type of textured paint is usually used to create a non-slip floor paint. The second type (Plaster of Paris type) also comes ready-made, and again you can create it yourself, this time by mixing the powder with clean water. Take care when mixing either of these types of textured paint yourself, as you can easily create a cloud of powder or sand: make sure you are wearing a suitable dust mask. You can mix by hand or with an electric mixer to create your textured paint.

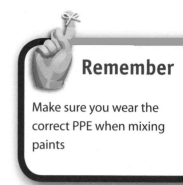

Remember

Make sure you wear the correct PPE when mixing paints

Plaster of Paris type

With the Plaster of Paris type, you apply the mixture to the surface with a brush or roller, then use a variety of tools to create the different finishes and patterns required:

- Stipple brush – for swirls, stipple, broken swirl and broken leather

- Texturing combs – for circles, fans, baskets and combinations of circle with fan, etc. Texturing combs also work well for producing patterns around light fittings, and can create decorative borders

- Pattern roller – for bark and other wood effects

- Lacing tool – to smooth the tips of denser, abstract wall texture patterns such as bark, swirl and broken leather. This tool is a blade that can remove high build-up of spikes, etc. created with the patterns above, making safer textures on walls and ceilings.

If you ever need to remove a textured pattern from a surface when decorating, you must:

- scrape the entire surface with a suitable scraper

- soak warm water into the texture with a sponge until you have saturated it

- carry on scraping until you get to the bottom surface.

Sand type

The second type of textured paint (sand added to water-based/oil-based paint) can also be applied to surfaces with either a brush or roller, although you will not normally create any patterns with this type of textured paint.

Textured paint and related tools

Gilding

Gilding is the application of gold or other metal leaf to a surface. The procedure has to be carried out with great care, both in terms of working practice and preparation of the surface.

There are two types of gilding:

1. Transfer leaf is when the leaf comes attached to a thin piece of tissue paper and is applied to a surface in the same way you would apply a transfer.

2. Loose leaf is a more skilled operation as the leaf is loose and applied either from a book of gold leaf or from a gilder's cushion.

A gilded surface

Did you know?

$23\frac{1}{2}$ carat and 24 carat gold leaf will not tarnish and does not need a protective coating

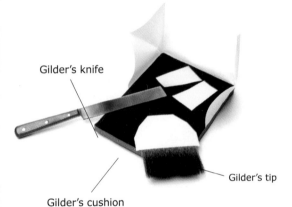

Gilder's knife

Gilder's tip

Gilder's cushion

Loose leaf may be applied from a gilder's cushion

Surface preparation

In order to ensure gold leaf only adheres to the parts of the surface you want it to adhere to, one of the following should be applied prior to gilding:

- Egg glair – The white of an egg is added to a litre of warm water and the mixture shaken to produce froth. The glair is then applied to the surface, followed by application of gold size (see Table 13.3 for more information on gold size). When the surface reaches the right level of tackiness, the gold leaf can be applied. Finally, the surface should be washed down with clean, warm water to remove all of the glair and any gold leaf that has not adhered.

- French chalk – This is a soft white chalk and is used in a similar way to egg glair.

Gold size

Gold size is an adhesive substance used as a **mordant** for gold leaf application. After applying gold size to a surface it must be left for a suitable length of time to reach the right level of tack (stickiness).

Gold size is available in two forms: oil gold size and Japan gold size. Table 13.3 gives some more details about each type.

Definition

Mordant
– a substance that provides a key

Gold size type	Uses	Drying time	Notes
Oil gold size	Suited to large metal or wooden surfaces. Not suitable for use with leaf other than gold	24 to 30 hours	Needs to be well brushed out to ensure no runs or snags. Ensure no dust settles on the surface
Japan gold size	Suited to lettering and ornamental work	Available with a ½-, 1-, 2-, 4-, and 8- hour drying time	Use Japan size when weather or dust is likely to affect surface

Table 13.3 Oil and Japan gold size

Did you know?

The block of chalk in a bicycle puncture repair kit is compressed French chalk

Transfer leaf application procedure

- Prepare the surface as described above and apply gold size.

- Wait until the surface has the right amount of tack and then begin to apply the transfer leaf. The leaf will be attached to a piece of waxed paper.

- Gently rub the waxed paper with some cotton wool, thus transferring the leaf onto the size. See Figure 13.5.

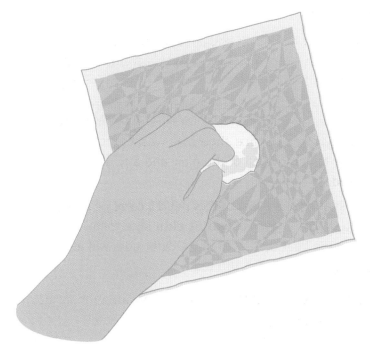

Gently rubbing the waxed paper with cotton wool transfers the gold leaf to the surface

Figure 13.5 Applying transfer leaf to a surface

Loose leaf application procedure

- Prepare the surface as described above and apply gold size.

- Wait until the surface has the right amount of tack and then begin to apply the loose leaf. The leaf can only be handled with a gilder's tip and cushion and the procedure will take time to perfect. In order to pick up the leaf, static or grease has to applied to the gilder's tip. The easiest way of achieving this is by rubbing the tip on your forehead. The tip can then be held to the cushion, whereby the loose leaf attaches to the tip.

- Gently brush off any excess gold leaf that has not adhered to the surface with a cotton wool pad.

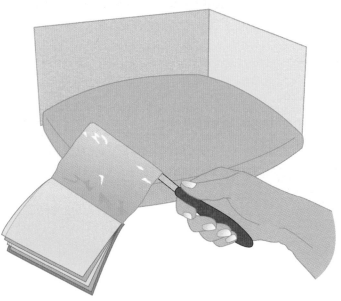

Lift the gold leaf from the book
and gently place it on the cushion

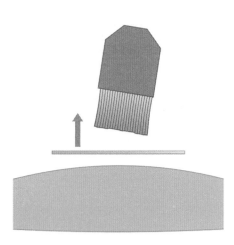

Create static on the glider's tip and use it to
pick up the leaf for application to the surface

Figure 13.6 Applying loose leaf to a surface

Definition

Rabbit skin size – a substance made from animal tissues, which is applied before a layer of varnish, as varnish alone will discolour the gold

When applying either transfer leaf or loose leaf that is not 23 carat or 24 carat gold, it will need to be protected with a layer of **rabbit skin size** followed by a layer of suitable varnish or lacquer. Leaf that is 23 or 24 carat gold will also benefit from a protective layer, shielding it from wear and tear.

Gilding defects

As you have already read, gilding needs lots of practice. During your training, you may discover some of the problems that can occur when gilding. Figure 13.7 details some of the gilding defects that can occur, along with their causes.

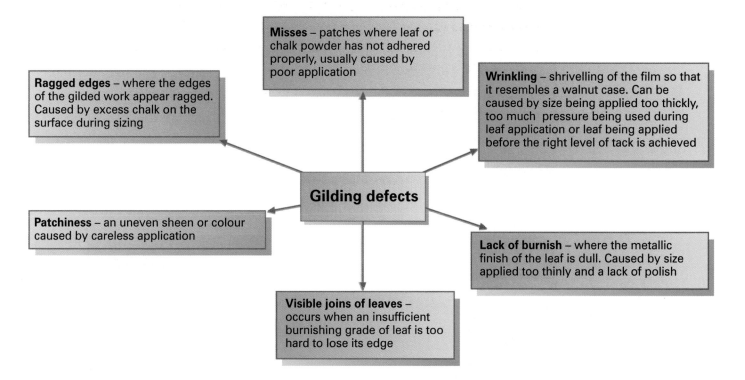

Misses – patches where leaf or chalk powder has not adhered properly, usually caused by poor application

Ragged edges – where the edges of the gilded work appear ragged. Caused by excess chalk on the surface during sizing

Wrinkling – shrivelling of the film so that it resembles a walnut case. Can be caused by size being applied too thickly, too much pressure being used during leaf application or leaf being applied before the right level of tack is achieved

Gilding defects

Patchiness – an uneven sheen or colour caused by careless application

Lack of burnish – where the metallic finish of the leaf is dull. Caused by size applied too thinly and a lack of polish

Visible joins of leaves – occurs when an insufficient burnishing grade of leaf is too hard to lose its edge

Figure 13.7 Gilding defects

FAQ

What does the term 'broken colour' mean?

A 'broken colour' paint effect is one that is created by layering paint colours and then breaking them up to reveal the underlying colours. This can be achieved by adding colour (for example, when sponging) or by taking off colour (for example, when ragging off). A broken colour paint effect can give a surface the appearance of shading and texture.

On the job: Applying an emulsion to a surface

Lynne is a second year apprentice and has just read a specification with regard to redecorating a domestic dwelling. The specification states that a roller finish is not acceptable for the emulsion finish on the wall areas. Lynne decides to apply the emulsion to the wall areas with a roller and then finish off with a brush to save time.

Do you think that Lynne has made a wise decision? How will she remove the effect left by the roller? Can you name the effect a roller leaves on a surface when emulsion has been applied?

Knowledge check

1. Why is it best to work from a work pot instead of a stock pot?

2. What is 'getting a dip' and what does this action do?

3. Briefly describe laying off.

4. If applying paint with a roller, what could you use to hold the paint?

5. When might a mitten be a good way of applying paint?

6. What is a broken colour effect?

7. What types of pattern can be achieved with dragging and combing?

8. Name two types of material that could be used instead of a rag to lift off colour during rag rolling.

9. What is a relief surface?

10. Name two types of stencil and describe how they differ.

11. What is egg glair and how would it be used?

12. How might wrinkling of gold leaf be caused?

chapter 14

Applying surface coverings

OVERVIEW

One way to change the look of a room is to apply a surface covering – wallpaper. The earliest wallpaper dates to around 1500 and was hand-painted and nailed to timber which was then fixed to walls. Printed wallpaper rolls first became available in 1841. Now there is a huge range of wall coverings to choose from – from basic wood pulp wallpapers to fabric wall coverings. A decorator may be asked to hang wallpaper on ceilings as well as walls in both domestic and commercial premises.

This chapter will cover the following topics:

- Wallpaper
- Preparing surfaces for papering
- Working out wallpaper quantities
- Wallpaper adhesives and papering equipment
- Preparing to apply surface coverings
- Application of surface coverings
- Types of surface covering
- Surface covering defects.

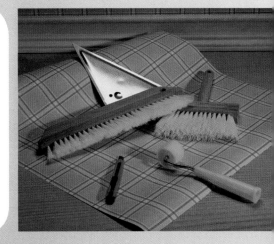

These topics can be found in the following modules:

CC 2002K	CC 2021K	CC 2024K
CC 2002S	CC 2021S	CC 2024S

Wallpaper

Wallpaper is one aspect of interior design. It is normally used to cover and decorate interior walls and ceilings of homes, offices, restaurants, doctors' surgeries, public houses (bars) and other buildings. Wallpaper can also be used as a centrepiece on a wall (wallpaper framed to look like a picture,) to decorate panels on interior doors, and to brighten up the interior of cupboards and recesses under stairwells.

Wallpaper emerged in the 1500s, but before that tapestries were being hung up in wealthier properties and cheaper woollen or canvas hangings in the homes of less well-off. This added colour to a room as well as providing an insulating layer between the stone walls and the interior of the room. These tapestries and the finer silks that were to follow were the forerunners of today's wallcoverings.

Tapestries were practical as well as stylish

Wallpaper has long had an important role in decorative schemes, as the choice of wallpaper can influence the choice of other furnishings in the room. For much of its history, wallpaper has been more than merely printed paper at an affordable price. It has been designed to imitate items such as tapestry, velvet, chintz, silk drapery, linen, wood, and masonry.

Wallpaper was first created by printing designs onto paper by hand, using the block method or stencilling. The blocks were made from seasoned hardwoods such as sycamore. A pattern was carved into a block, different coloured dyes were coated over the design, and the block was positioned on the paper then pressed down, leaving the design on the paper. Later, the blocks were mounted above a printing table, across which paper was drawn. After the blocks had been lowered onto the paper and the design printed, the paper was then pulled along for the print to be repeated. These days, screen-printing is used for speciality hand-printed wallpapers, although block printing can still be used in restoration work. Advances in technology led to machine printing – a much faster application of prints which can produce continuous rolls of wallpaper.

As well as wallpaper to cover wall areas, patterned borders and embossed friezes are produced to divide walls, frame interesting features or improve the proportions of a room. Many old houses and buildings were built with high ceilings, so their room walls looked very tall, dwarfing any furniture. Splitting up the wall area with borders and friezes can create a more balanced feel to the room.

Wallpapers imitating a range of other materials

Another wallpaper you may come across is 'ready pasted paper'. This is a modern vinyl wallpaper which has paste already applied to it. You need a trough of water to be able to hang this paper; the trough is usually provided with a batch of wallpaper. To apply this paper you immerse the required length into the water and leave for the recommended time, then fold as required, and then apply immediately to the surface. (Many decorators normally mix a thin solution of paste then apply to the paper as normal, then hang the paper as this gives a better grip to the paper and is easier to handle.)

Remember, wallpaper will only look good on a surface if that surface has been prepared properly and the paper been applied correctly.

Applying wallpaper

Wallpaper is applied to walls and ceilings as well as archways, columns, sloping ceilings, staircases/stairwells and dormer window reveals. It is vital that you have the right training before you hang any wallpaper, as it is a complex task.

Borders and friezes can help 'balance' a room

Tools and equipment for wallpapering

Here is a range of tools and equipment that will make sure you produce a quality finish, as long as you have been trained correctly.

Preparation tools

- Scraper – used to remove previous papers, loose paint
- Steam stripper – to soften existing wallpapers for easier removal from surfaces
- Filling knife – to fill any cracks, holes or surface defects
- Sanding block – to rub down any nibs or surface defects, and any filler you have used to repair cracks, holes, etc.
- Sponge and water – to soak wallpaper before removal.

Access equipment

- Stepladder – for high wall work

- Podium – for ceiling work

- Hop-up – for wall work

- Painter's trestle – same as a podium

Pre-papering tools

- Tape measure/folding rule – to measure area and wallpaper lengths/widths

- Pencil – to mark out start lines and mark wallpaper before cutting

- Plumb line and bob/chalk line – to mark vertical and horizontal lines before hanging wallpaper.

Paper hanging tools

- Pasting table – to paste paper correctly

- Pasting brush/roller/paste machine – to apply paste

- Paste bucket – to mix paste and to use throughout pasting paper

- Paper hanging brush(sweep) – to brush out air bubbles from underneath the paper when applying paper to walls

- Seam roller/felt roller/rubber roller – to seal edges of paper down when butting up papers together

- Trimming knife – to trim excess paper off

- Shears (wallpaper scissors) – to cut lengths and widths of wallpaper

- Straight edge – to mark lines on surfaces and wallpaper.

Papering round an archway

To paper around an archway, follow these steps:

- First paper the walls on both sides of the archway, allowing a 2 to 3 cm overlap at the perimeter of the arch.

- Next, make a series of small cuts (every 2 to 3 cm) in from the edge of the overlap – this is so you can fold the wallpaper onto the underside of the arch.

- Cut a strip of paper to fit the underside of the arch, leaving a few centimetres at each end of the length. Paste and apply to the underside of the arch. If you are using a patterned paper, cut two lengths for the underside of the arch and overlap them in the middle, then splice them through the middle to hide your joint.

> ### Remember
>
> Styles and fashions change over the years and you have got to be aware of this so you can advise customers properly. However, at the end of the day it's the customer's choice, and you should carry out their wishes

Later in the chapter, you will read more about papering walls, ceilings, window reveals and around obstacles.

Preparing surfaces for papering

The following general good practice should be followed when preparing a surface for wallpapering:

- Ensure the surface is sound, clean, dry and free from grease. Wallpaper will not stick to grease and dirt and it is also unhygienic to paper over dirty surfaces.

- Surfaces must be in good condition. Flaking paint should be rubbed down with medium abrasive sandpaper back to a firm surface, then sealed and filled. Powdery or crumbling surfaces should be painted with stabilising solution or PVA resin.

- Gloss or eggshell surfaces should be roughened with abrasive paper to provide a good key for the wallpaper paste.

- Prepared gloss surfaces can be covered with PVA adhesive to improve sticking.

- Any nail or screw heads must be primed with a metal primer to prevent rust staining.

We will now look at the preparation of some specific surfaces.

Painted surfaces

Preparing previously painted surfaces for wallpaper is very similar to the preparation required before applying paint. For further information, see Chapter 10 *Preparation of surfaces* page 197.

Sizing will prevent plaster absorbing water from paste

Bare plaster surfaces

Bare plaster surfaces should be **sized** with a purpose-made size or wallpaper adhesive or paste, such as cellulose paste or tub paste. Do not use starch paste to size plaster as this will flake when it dries, leaving an unsound surface.

Sizing is essential as it evens out the **porosity** of the bare plaster and prevents the water within wallpaper paste from being absorbed by the plaster. When this happens, known as 'snatch', the decorator will be unable to slide the wallpaper into position.

Definition

Sized – sealed

Porosity – the ability of a surface to allow water through

Some products, such as universal wall covering primer, are designed to allow the easy stripping of wallpaper when the room is next decorated. A thick coat of emulsion can also be used to size bare plaster.

New plaster must be allowed to dry out. Hard wall plaster may need up to six months to dry thoroughly before it is ready for wallpapering. Plasterboard that has been coated with board finish plaster (or skim) can be papered as soon as the plaster is visibly dry.

Plasterboard surfaces

If new plasterboard has been sized with a suitable adhesive or emulsion, the wallpaper will bond to the surface. However, removing the wallpaper at a later date could leave the paper surface of the plasterboard stripped or badly damaged (see Chapter 10 page 197). To avoid this, the surface should be sized with an oil-based primer, which will make the paper surface of the plasterboard waterproof and less likely to damage when paper is stripped from it. Alternatively, a wall covering primer can be used.

If removing wallpaper from the surface, all traces of old paste and small pieces of wallpaper should be removed by using water and a paste brush and scrubbing the surface. A Scotch-Brite® pad can also be used to do this. Finally, use a sponge and some clean water to rinse off the surface.

Working out wallpaper quantities

There are two main methods of calculating how much wallpaper you will require:

Method 1 Use a roll of wallpaper as a width guide to measure the number of full lengths required. Mark where the joints will appear along the wall or ceiling. Then measure the length of the ceiling or height of the wall to discover how many full lengths can be cut from one roll.

Method 2 Measure up a room or take dimensions from a drawing. Calculate the total surface area of the room, including windows and doors. Then work out the area of the offtakes (things that will not be papered, such as the doors and windows) and subtract this amount from the total surface area. This will give you the surface area that requires papering. Next, find out the surface area of a roll of wallpaper and divide it into the surface area. This will give you an idea of how many rolls of wallpaper you will need.

To ensure you get the right quantity of wallpaper, you will need to allow for wastage. This is usually 15–20 per cent depending on the type of pattern, shape and height of the room. To be on the safe side, a decorator should work on 20 per cent wastage.

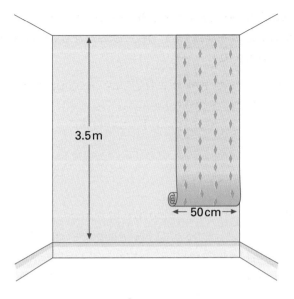

Method 1 – use the width of a roll of wallpaper and measure the height of the wall

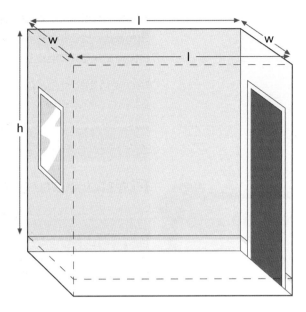

Method 2 – calculate the total surface area of the room and then subtract the offtakes (e.g. doors and windows)

Figure 14.1 Working out wallpaper quantities

Wallpaper adhesives and papering equipment

There are three main types of wallpaper adhesive. They each have a different moisture content (low, medium and high) and you will need to choose the right one for the job.

Adhesives are available in:

- ready-mixed tubs, in heavy-, medium- or light-grades
- sachets or boxes of powder which require water to be added.

Adhesives are also available for use with very specific wall coverings.

Ready-mixed adhesive

Ready-mixed tub adhesives have a very low moisture content. They contain a chemical called PVA, which improves the adhesive property of the paste (how well it sticks). Some tub adhesives are very thick and must be diluted before use.

Did you know?

Most modern adhesives contain a fungicide to prevent mould growth

Ready-mixed tub adhesive

289

Advantages	Disadvantages
Very good adhesive properties. Ideal for use with vinyl and contract vinyl such as Muraspec®	Expensive
Can be used to size surfaces	
Can be applied directly to wall surfaces to hang certain types of wall covering	
Contains a fungicide to prevent mould growth	
Does not rot and remains useable for a long time	

Table 14.1 Advantages and disadvantages of tub adhesive

Safety tip

Always wash your hands after using an adhesive that contains a fungicide

Adhesives that are mixed with water

Starch adhesive

Starch adhesive is also known as flour adhesive as wheat flour is its main ingredient. It has a medium moisture content and comes in powder form which needs to be mixed with water to produce a paste that is suitable for lightweight to heavyweight wood-pulp wallpapers.

Remember

Always check adhesive to see if it is still fresh

Advantages	Disadvantages
Good adhesive properties. Suitable for hanging heavy textured preparatory papers	More expensive than cellulose adhesive
Contains a fungicide so can be used with vinyl papers	May stain the face of the wallpaper
	Difficult to mix
	Adhesive will rot and so is only useable for one to two days

Table 14.2 Advantages and disadvantages of starch adhesive

Cellulose adhesive

Cellulose adhesive has the highest water content of any paste and comes in powder form which needs to be mixed with cold water before use. It is used with lightweight wallpapers such as lining papers and vinyls.

Advantages	Disadvantages
Inexpensive	Less adhesive than starch paste
Little risk of staining	Can cause paper to over-expand, resulting in wrinkling or mismatch
Easy to apply	If used on wallpaper that is unable to let water pass through it, such as vinyl, the water content in the adhesive may be prevented from drying out through the paper, leading to damage
Easy to mix	
Does not rot and can remain useable for a long time	
Contains a fungicide to prevent mould growth	

Table 14.3 Advantages and disadvantages of cellulose adhesive

Adhesives designed for specific wall coverings

- Border adhesive is ideal for applying vinyl on vinyl, for example when applying a border paper on top of another paper. It has strong adhesive properties.
- Lincrusta glue is a very strong adhesive with good bonding properties.
- Overlap adhesive is designed for bonding vinyl to vinyl. It can be used on vinyl to bond overlaps on internal/external angles and to apply border paper over vinyl.

Equipment

Equipment	Description	Dos and don'ts
Paste brush	A 175 mm flat brush makes a good paste brush	Choose a brush with synthetic bristles as these are not affected by mildew and can be left in paste for long periods of time
Pasteboard	Used for pasting wallpaper, arranging paper and for splitting lengths of paper	Keep clean and free from paste at all times as a dirty pasteboard will lead to a poor-quality papering job
Paste bucket	Used for mixing paste	Clean out after use and before mixing paste. If the sides of the bucket are thick with old paste, when mixing fresh paste the new paste may become lumpy
Plumb bob	A weight attached to a piece of string. Used to mark a vertical line (the plumb line) on to walls before hanging paper	You must be accurate when using a plumb bob because the measurements it provides act as a starting point for papering and the first line marked will affect every following length of paper

Table 14.4 Wallpapering equipment

A plumb bob must be used accurately

Marking a plumb line

- Mark your plumb line only once it stops swinging.

- Make sure that the string is hanging freely – check it isn't snagged on anything.

- Use only one eye to sight the plumb line and continue to use the same eye for every mark you make.

- When marking your pencil line against the string, do not overstretch but move your head to the pencil and keep your aiming eye level to the mark that you are about to make.

- If you need to move your hand down the string, make sure that it does not move by using alternate hands to position the string.

Preparing to apply surface coverings

Before hanging surface coverings, always read the manufacturer's instructions. These will contain all the information required to hang the wallpaper correctly, including soaking time, recommended paste and surface preparation required.

It is important to check the pattern and batch number of each roll of wallpaper before cutting any. If papers with different batch numbers are used on the same wall, you may be able to see a variation in colour. Once you have checked the batch numbers, the rolls of paper should be rolled out and the paper looked at in natural light as variations may still occur in some batches, known as shading. Look out for the international performance symbols shown in most wallpaper instructions which offer easy-to-understand information at a glance.

Before paper hanging, set up your site by laying down a dustsheet, mixing the paste, erecting the pasteboard and finding a box to put all the waste cuttings in. All wall-mounted fixtures and fittings, such as blinds, curtain rails and wall lights, should be removed. Any exposed wires should be individually taped up with insulation tape to prevent electric shock.

Electrical fittings must be switched off at the mains and removed from the wall by a trained person. The screws should be relocated in their holes, which avoids the problem of finding the screw holes once the wall is covered with paper. Cross slits can then be cut in the paper to allow the screws and cables through. Once you have set up your work area, you can then think about how you are going to wallpaper the room.

∼	Spongeable	Ready pasted	
≈	Washable	Paste-the-paper	
≋	Extra Washable	Paste-the-wall	
∼	Scrubbable	Free match	
☼	Moderate light fastness	Straight match	
☼	Good light fastness	Offset match	
	Strippable	$\frac{50}{25}$ cm Design repeat Distance offset	
	Peelable	Direction of hanging	
		Reverse alternate length	

Figure 14.2 International performance symbols

Time spent planning is important, because a well set-up room can save a lot of time and effort and can help you to use paper more economically. For example, before starting you should work out how to avoid the length of paper you are hanging from conflicting with any straight edges such as doorframes, window frames and internal or external corners. Remember that some wallpapers are very expensive, and the decorator is responsible for getting the preparation right.

The following golden rules should always be followed when preparing to apply surface coverings:

- Read the manufacturer's instructions supplied with each roll.
- Check each roll individually to ensure it is not damaged.

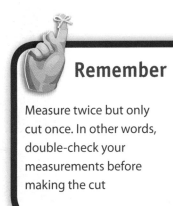

Remember

Measure twice but only cut once. In other words, double-check your measurements before making the cut

- Check that the batch numbers and shades are identical.

- Open the rolls to check the pattern and printing.

- Identify the pattern, for example **straight match** or **drop match** pattern.

- Check which way the paper should be applied. Some patterns are not easy to identify. If you are unsure, contact the client or the manufacturer.

Application of surface coverings

If you have identified the wallpaper as a straight match, then lengths of paper can be cut from one roll at a time. If the pattern is a drop match, you should cut your lengths from two rolls. This is because two lengths of a drop match patterned paper cut to the same size from the same roll cannot be used adjacent to each other on a wall because they would not match.

To cut lengths from two rolls:

- Place two rolls on the pasteboard.

- Match the pattern at the edge using the two rolls.

- Trim both top edges so that the waste is equal.

- Label one roll A and the other B using a pencil on the back of each length. Keep on marking them alternately until all lengths are cut.

- Keep the lengths in order when pasting and hanging.

When the first length of wallpaper has been measured and cut from the roll, it can be used as a template for the cutting of the other required lengths. After offering the first cut length up to the wall, check that there have not been any measuring errors. If not, all of the full lengths can then be cut.

You are now ready to start pasting the lengths.

A good pasting technique

Pasting procedure

1. Stand in front of the pasteboard and place the length of paper reverse side upwards.

2. Make a short overlap aligned with the furthest edge away from you.

3. Apply paste down the centre of the cut length.

4. Keep applying the paste from the centre to the furthest edge. Do not go from edge to centre because the paste will drop onto the face side of the paper.

5. Move the cut length to the nearest edge of the pasteboard and continue to work the paste brush from centre to edge, not from edge to centre.

Folding procedure

The paper should be allowed to soak before hanging, but to ensure **equal stretch** each length should have the same amount of soaking time. This can be done by working with two lengths at any one time, pasting one, then pasting the other before hanging the first length, and so on.

Now you are ready to fold a length of paper. How it is folded will depend on how long the length is or where it is to be hung.

● Two-lap fold – if the wallpaper is of normal room length, you should use a two-lap fold, making the top fold the longest fold. It should be roughly two-thirds to one-third (see Figure 14.3).

● Concertina fold – this series of small folds can be easily unfolded during the paper hanging process. The concertina fold is normally used for papering ceilings or for applying paper horizontally. It can also be used for folding very long lengths before vertical application.

Definition

Equal stretch – supple and pliable to the same degree

Remember

For the correct amount of soaking time, follow the manufacturer's instructions. Check that the paper is pliable (bends easily) before you use it

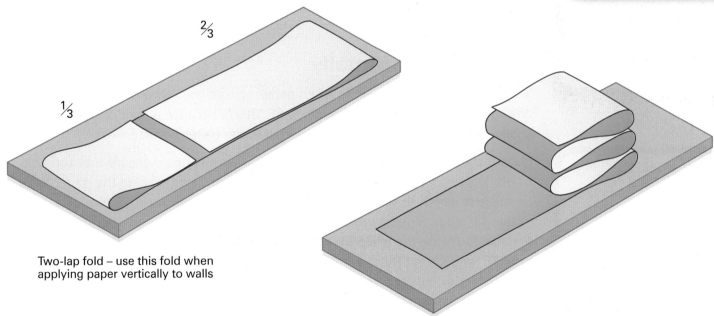

⅔

⅓

Two-lap fold – use this fold when applying paper vertically to walls

Concertina fold – use this fold when applying paper horizontally to walls or when papering ceilings

Figure 14.3 Types of wallpaper fold

Papering vertically

Take the first length of wallpaper and offer it up to the plumb line, with the longest fold opened and then place it on the wall. You should be able to slide the paper accurately towards the plumb line. Smooth the paper down with the brush, working from the centre towards the edges. When all the air is smoothed out, fold down the bottom fold and apply it to the wall as before.

Hanging paper vertically

Papering horizontally

When papering horizontally, or when papering a ceiling, always work away from any light source (for example, a window). This is because a light source will create shadows on the surface should an overlap in the paper occur.

Make a chalk line on the ceiling to work from, which should ensure that the first length is straight. Always use a concertina fold and after soaking the paper, offer up the first length to the ceiling against a line that allows for a 20 mm overlap at the wall edge. The concertina folds should be around 350 mm per fold. Apply one fold to the ceiling while supporting the unopened folds with a **decorator's crutch**. Smooth out the first fold. Then open one more fold and repeat the process – do not try to apply more than one fold at a time. When free of air pockets and creases, the paper should be trimmed out to both wall edges.

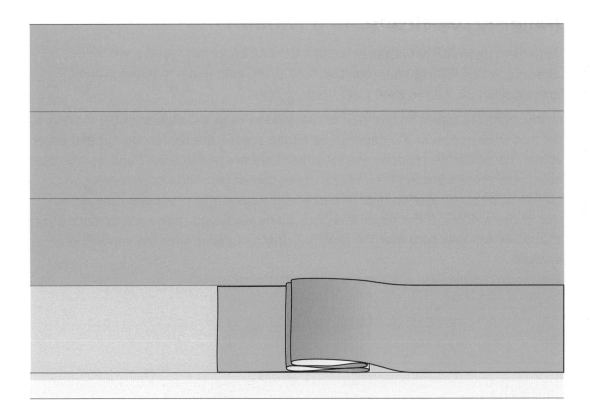

Figure 14.4 Papering horizontally

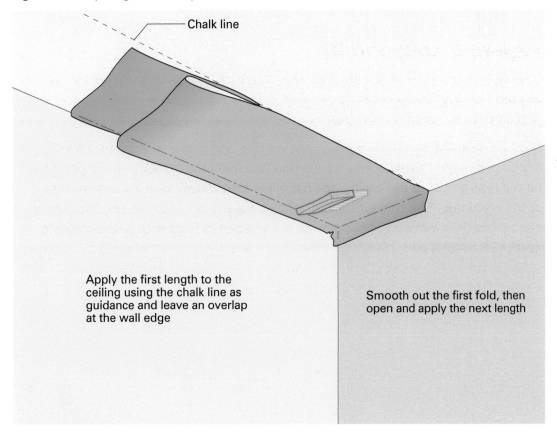

Chalk line

Apply the first length to the
ceiling using the chalk line as
guidance and leave an overlap
at the wall edge

Smooth out the first fold, then
open and apply the next length

Figure 14.5 Papering a ceiling

Remember

Prevent the edges of the wallpaper from curling by making sure you apply enough paste to the edge.

Hanging paper around a window

One of the most difficult areas in a room to hang paper is around a window. However, with a little practice and the right technique, hanging paper around features such as windows will soon become easy.

Firstly, hang the paper on one side of the window (see 1 in Figure 14.6), making a cut that allows some of the paper to be folded around the reveal. Next, hang paper above and below the window, ensuring that they are plumb (see 2 and 3). You can now patch the underside of the reveal in the corner (4). Allow approximately 10 mm of paper to overlap (see dotted lines). Repeat this process for the other side of the window. If the window is particularly wide, you may want to mark a plumb line to make sure that the next full length of paper after the window is straight.

Figure 14.6 Hanging paper around a window

Paper hanging a staircase

When applying paper to a staircase always start with the longest drop (length). After applying this first length, work from either side of it.

Table 14.5 gives some general golden rules you should follow when folding and pasting a surface covering.

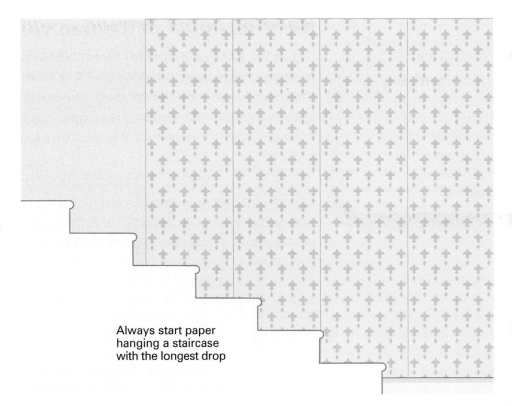

Always start paper hanging a staircase with the longest drop

Figure 14.7 Paper hanging a staircase

Do	Don't
Remove lumps from the paste	Leave areas of the covering unpasted
Remove any loose bristles from pasted lengths	Get paste on the pasteboard or the face side of the paper
Leave the top and bottom 50 mm of the length dry so it may be handled	Mix paste too thinly
Keep edges parallel (aligned) when folding	Place the paste bucket on the pasteboard
Keep all tools and equipment clean	Have an untidy work area
Check that you are using the right paste for the paper and its application	

Table 14.5 Dos and don'ts when folding and pasting

Centralising a patterned wallpaper

Figure 14.8 shows a chimney breast and alcoves of a room papered with a patterned wallpaper. The wallpaper has a set pattern and the pattern match is horizontally set – it does not drop. The wallpaper has been centralised – that means that the first length of wallpaper has been placed in the centre of the chimney breast. Notice how this creates a balanced effect.

Figure 14.8 Centralising patterned wallpaper on a chimney breast

Definition

Focal point – a place where your eyes will tend to look

The chimney breast is a **focal point** of a room and can be the place to start papering if the whole room is to be papered in the same patterned paper. If a room does not have a chimney breast, choose one wall of the room as the feature wall and start paper hanging from the centre of that wall to ensure that the pattern of the paper is centralised.

Back trimming

Back trimming, also known as double cutting, is a technique of cutting through two sheets of wallpaper to achieve a perfect joint. This method is used on 1-metre-wide vinyl to achieve a butt joint.

Types of surface covering

Basic wallpapers

Basic wallpapers are made from either:

- wood pulp
- vinyl.

Wood pulp papers

Wood-pulp papers can be used as preparatory papers or finish papers.

Preparatory papers are usually painted with emulsion to provide a finish or they can be used as a base underneath finish papers. The different types of preparatory papers include:

- plain, coloured and reinforced lining paper
- wood chip
- Anaglypta®.

Finish papers are available in a variety of patterns:

- standard
- washable
- **embossed**.

Definition

Embossed – decorated with designs that stand out from surface

Lining paper

Anaglypta® paper

Standard patterned wood-pulp paper

Vinyl wallpapers

There are three basic categories of vinyl paper:

- standard patterned vinyl
- sculptured vinyl
- blown vinyl, which can be either a patterned finish paper or a preparatory paper requiring painting.

Standard patterned vinyl paper

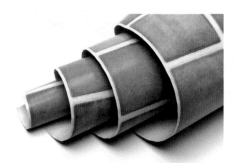

Sculptured vinyl paper

Patterned blown vinyl paper

Specialist surface coverings

Specialist coverings are those which are slightly different or unusual in some way from the standard papers already covered. They will probably only be used on particular jobs and in specific circumstances. Examples of specialist papers include:

- Cloth-backed vinyl – a paper that has a cotton backing and is textured to look like fabric. Usually used in high-traffic areas such as halls, corridors and public places.

- Lincrusta-Walton – a paper with a raised pattern or design that simulates carved plaster and wood. Usually used below dado rails, in pubs and restaurants and on staircases.

Cloth-backed vinyl paper

Lincrusta-Walton

Paper-backed Hessian

- Paper-backed Hessian – a fabric surface covering made from **jute**. Usually used as a decorative finish in offices and public buildings.

- Metal foil paper – a surface covering with a metal finish. Usually used as a very decorative covering on feature walls.

Metal foil paper

Definition

Jute – a rough fibre made from a tropical plant

For further information on wallpaper types, see Tables 14.6 and 14.7 on pages 308 and 310.

Surface covering defects

Figure 14.9 shows some common types of surface covering defects that can occur.

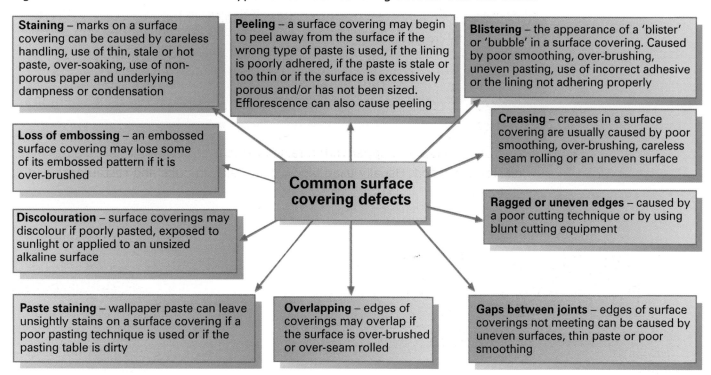

Staining – marks on a surface covering can be caused by careless handling, use of thin, stale or hot paste, over-soaking, use of non-porous paper and underlying dampness or condensation

Peeling – a surface covering may begin to peel away from the surface if the wrong type of paste is used, if the lining is poorly adhered, if the paste is stale or too thin or if the surface is excessively porous and/or has not been sized. Efflorescence can also cause peeling

Blistering – the appearance of a 'blister' or 'bubble' in a surface covering. Caused by poor smoothing, over-brushing, uneven pasting, use of incorrect adhesive or the lining not adhering properly

Loss of embossing – an embossed surface covering may lose some of its embossed pattern if it is over-brushed

Creasing – creases in a surface covering are usually caused by poor smoothing, over-brushing, careless seam rolling or an uneven surface

Discolouration – surface coverings may discolour if poorly pasted, exposed to sunlight or applied to an unsized alkaline surface

Common surface covering defects

Ragged or uneven edges – caused by a poor cutting technique or by using blunt cutting equipment

Paste staining – wallpaper paste can leave unsightly stains on a surface covering if a poor pasting technique is used or if the pasting table is dirty

Overlapping – edges of coverings may overlap if the surface is over-brushed or over-seam rolled

Gaps between joints – edges of surface coverings not meeting can be caused by uneven surfaces, thin paste or poor smoothing

Figure 14.9 Surface covering defects

FAQ

Nobody seems to have wallpaper in their house anymore – why do I have to learn how to hang it?

It is true that wallpaper isn't as popular as it once was, but as with many fashions and trends, the popularity of wallpaper will probably increase at some point during your career as a painter and decorator. When this happens, you will be glad you know how to hang it!

Why is wallpaper paste sometimes lumpy?

Because it hasn't been mixed up properly! Wallpaper paste should always be smooth. Make sure you read and follow the instructions on the packaging.

On the job: Mixing wallpaper paste

Phillip is at a client's house about to decorate a room in a new extension. The client has requested wallpaper and Phillip is getting his equipment ready to mix up some wallpaper paste. Phillip can't find his mixing stick and so he decides to mix up the paste using his hand.

Do you think Phillip has planned well for this job? What do you think of Phillip's idea to mix the paste by hand?

Knowledge check

1. Give two reasons why surface coverings should not be applied to greasy or dirty surfaces.

2. How should nail and screw heads be treated during surface preparation?

3. Why should starch paste not be used to size plaster surfaces before papering?

4. What can be applied to plasterboard prior to papering to protect it from damage when coverings are removed?

5. Briefly describe two methods of estimating the amount of paper that will be required for a job.

6. When might you use the following types of adhesive: border adhesive; Lincrusta glue; overlap adhesive?

7. Why is it important to check the batch numbers on rolls of wallpaper?

8. Name and describe two types of wallpaper folding technique. When would each be used?

9. What is 'centralising a wallpaper pattern'?

10. What is preparatory paper?

11. Name four types of specialist surface covering. In what circumstances might each be used?

12. Name four different types of common surface coating defect and explain how each may be caused.

Table 14.6 Basic types of wallpaper

Lining paper *A smooth preparatory paper available in a range of grades. Usually off-white, but brown and red lining papers are available as a base for coloured finish papers*	**Uses** As a base for finish papers of even porosity or as a base for painting. Masks minor surface defects and is especially suitable for well-prepared surfaces **Suitable wallpaper paste** Starch or cellulose **Preparation and hanging** Paste and allow paper to become supple before hanging. If used as a preparatory paper, it is usually hung horizontally to avoid the edges of the lining paper and finish paper falling in the same place **Other information** Available in 400, 600, 800 and 1000 grades in 200 mm and 555 mm wide single, double, triple or quad rolls
Non-woven lining paper *Made from cellulose and polyester fibre. Most common weight is 150 g*	**Uses** On surfaces that may move, such as tongue and grooved cladding or badly-cracked plaster **Suitable wallpaper paste** Starch or tub paste **Preparation and hanging** No need to soak. The wall can sometimes be pasted instead of the paper
Patterned pulp paper *A flat, standard wallpaper made from wood pulp, with a design printed on the surface. Many different qualities available ranging from simple machine-printed wallpaper to expensive hand-printed wallpaper*	**Uses** General living areas such as living rooms, bedrooms and staircases **Suitable wallpaper paste** Cellulose **Preparation and hanging** Check batch numbers and shade prior to hanging **Other information** Some patterned pulps have a coating of PVA varnish and are known as 'washables' because they can be sponged to remove stains
Anaglypta® textured paper *A brand name for an embossed paper made from wood pulp. A preparatory paper which requires painting*	**Uses** Ceilings and walls in domestic premises. Masks minor surface defects **Suitable wallpaper paste** Starch paste, cellulose (thick) **Preparation and hanging** Over-soaking, over-brushing joints and the use of seam rollers will flatten the embossed pattern. Always leave a hairline gap at the joints, which can later be flooded with paint to provide an invisible joint **Other information** Can be used as an alternative to blown vinyl (see below)

Vinyl paper *Made from a PVC (type of plastic) layer joined to a pulp backing paper. A very hard-wearing wallpaper*	**Uses** Domestic and commercial premises where there is heavy human traffic. Kitchens, bathrooms or areas where there is condensation **Suitable wallpaper paste** Cellulose can be used, but tub paste is a better choice. Overlap adhesive is required on overlaps. Ready-pasted paper is widely available **Preparation and hanging** Always read the manufacturer's instructions. Can be smoothed out with a smoothing brush or a caulking tool. Stanley knives and a straight edge can be used to speed up the trimming process **Other information** Can be sponged to remove marks and stains. Can be peeled off and is easy to strip
Blown vinyl paper *A textured layer of PVC-bonded paper. There are two basic types: a textured preparatory paper that can be used as an alternative to Anaglypta® and needs to be painted and a textured and coloured finish paper that can be used as an alternative to embossed, patterned pulp*	**Uses** Domestic and commercial premises. Not suitable in areas with heavy human traffic because the relief design can be easily damaged **Suitable wallpaper paste** Cellulose can be used, but tub paste is a better choice. Overlap adhesive is required on overlaps **Preparation and hanging** Apply with a smoothing brush. Avoid overlaps on internal/external angles by back trimming (double cutting)
Cloth-backed vinyl *Made of PVC on a cotton scrim backing. The vinyl is either printed with a pattern or self-coloured and textured to look like fabric*	**Trimming** Knife and steel straight edge. **Pasting** Use an adhesive containing a fungicide as the vinyl is water resistant and the paste will not be able to dry out through the material. Paste the cloth either with brush, roller or spread with filling knife. Paste the wall **Hanging** Fold and hang to a plumb line and butt all joints. Use the rounded edge of a plastic squeegee to smooth the material and smooth out all air from behind. Excess paste will be squeezed out at the edges, which must be immediately rinsed off. Paste the wall just beyond the width of material. Offer up the material dry and smooth down with squeegee. Paste the next section of wall and place the next length slightly overlapping the previous length before smoothing down. Place straight edge in line with the centre of the overlap and cut through the two thicknesses using a trimming knife and a 'first time cut'. Lift up the edges and take out the trimmings, then 'liven' the edges with paste and smooth down to a butt joint. Special tools are available for cutting through the overlaps that do not require a straight edge **Other information** Has a repeated pattern that the decorator may need to match. Available in 30 m x 1 m wide rolls and can be purchased by the metre

Table 14.7 Specialist surface coverings

Lincrusta-Walton	
Has a raised pattern or texture, which is created by rolling a putty-like substance onto a continuous reel of heavy cartridge paper. The putty is embossed onto the surface while the paper back remains flat. Textures commonly produced are hessian and wood in sheet and plank form. Requires painting after hanging	**Trimming** Knife and straight edge, undercut
	Pasting Use Lincrusta glue. Paste on the paper back
	Hanging Cut into lengths with a little in excess. Sponge several lengths of the paper backing with warm (not hot) water and leave to soak for 15–20 minutes, which will cause the paper to expand and will prevent blisters in the finished work. After soaking, sponge off any water and cut the expanded length to fit exactly. Apply Lincrusta glue to the backing. Hang with butt joints, smoothing down with a rubber roller using firm pressure and a vigorous action. When soaking and pasting, avoid sharp folds which may cause cracking of the surface. Lay lengths back-to-back when soaking which will help to retain moisture and achieve even expansion
	External angles must be turned by cutting through the putty on the face (but not through the paper) exactly on the angle and bending the paper back around the angle. Any gaps on the angle can be filled with stiff linseed oil putty. Internal angles must be cut to fit exactly
	Painting The surface is slightly oily and greasy and must be wiped off with white spirit before painting with oil-based paint (not emulsion)
	Other information Store rolls standing upright to avoid the weight cracking the face putty. Available in 1025 mm x 525 mm rolls; can also be supplied in panels and borders
Woven glass fibre	
White glass fibre woven into three textures: coarse, medium, fine. Generally used to reinforce cracked and imperfect surfaces and is then painted	**Trimming** Knife and straight edge. Trim on wall
	Pasting Use PVA reinforced paste or PVA adhesive (straight). Paste the wall
	Hanging Cut the lengths with 50 mm excess at top and bottom. Paste the wall evenly with a short pile paint roller, finishing a little short of the actual width of the glass fibre so that the edges of the first and second lengths overlap in a completely dry state. Hang the dry fabric and smooth down with a felt roller or plastic squeegee. Paste the second section of wall, again finishing a little short of the actual width. Cut through the overlap with a knife and straight edge, peeling away the two edges. Brush paste onto the 'missed' stripe of wall and press the two trimmed edges down as a perfect butt joint. If the wall is pasted to the full width of glass fibre then the edges will take in water and become too wet to obtain crisp, clean cutting, resulting in ragged joints
	Trim the fabric to parallel widths on the pasteboard. Paste the wall to the entire width of the fabric. Hang dry, trimmed fabric, smoothing down with a felt roller. Paste the next section of wall surface and hang the next length of dry, trimmed fabric with a butt joint. Continue with the next length using the same method
	Other information Available in 50 m x 1 m rolls and can be purchased by the metre

Paper-backed felt *Made from a thick blanket of dyed short wool fibres*	**Trimming** Knife and straight edge. The main problem is making a first cut. If a blunt knife or not enough pressure is used, a second cut can make the edges very ragged. A clean cut first time gives perfect butt joints **Pasting** Use stiff tub paste or PVA reinforced adhesive. Paste the paper back **Hanging** Very little soaking is required after pasting and folding the material. Hang to a plumb line with butt joints, smoothing down with a felt roller. Reverse alternate lengths to minimise the effect of any edge-to-edge shading. Angles can be turned in the normal way. If the fabric and paper are not too wet, cutting to top and bottom and around obstacles can be done with a template and knife. If paper-backed felt is too wet, either allow to dry off and then cut with a template and knife, or mark with template and chalk and then cut with scissors **Other information** Avoid getting paste on the cloth, which can damage it! Available in 50 m x 0.91 m rolls and can be purchased by the metre
Paper-backed hessian *Made of jute which can be dyed and then woven, or woven into cloth and then dyed. Laminated onto a paper back*	**Trimming** Knife and straight edge. The key to hanging hessian is clean first-time cutting when trimming the material. If a blunt knife or insufficient pressure is used and a second cut has to be taken, then the edges can become frayed. Two slightly frayed edges look very unsightly when butt jointed. Clean, first-time cutting hides the joint perfectly **Pasting** Use stiff tub paste or PVA reinforced paste. Paste the paper back **Hanging** Very little soaking is necessary after pasting and folding the material. Hang to a plumb line while smoothing down with a felt roller. Reverse alternate lengths to minimise the effect of any edge-to-edge shading Angles can be turned in the normal way. If the fabric and paper are not too wet, cutting to top and bottom and around obstacles can be done with a template and knife. If too wet, either allow to dry off before cutting, or mark with template and chalk and cut with scissors **Other information** Avoid getting paste on the cloth, which can damage it! Available in 50 m x 0.91 m rolls and can be purchased by the metre
Paper-backed laminated foils *A surface covering made from several thin layers, namely: paper (as the backing), a metal or mirror-like finish (foil) and a laminated top layer*	**Trimming** Knife and straight edge. Undercut slightly **Pasting** Some foils are straightforward laminates of tarnished metal leaves, or figured and engraved continuous sheets applied onto a paper backing. These present no problem when pasted and hung in the normal way except for a curling of the edges similar to cork veneer papers. See type 1 foils below. Other foils with burnished mirror-like backgrounds present many problems. The mirror-like background magnifies every tiny defect behind the foil so preparation must be perfect. If the foil backing is pasted, even the paste brush marks can damage the finish. Paste must be applied evenly to the wall with a short pile paint roller and the stipple effect allowed to flow out before offering up the dry material. See type 2 foils on the following page

	Type 1 foils: Paste the material
	Type 2 foils: Paste the wall once or twice with PVA adhesive (must contain a fungicide)
	Some highly reflective foils are also laminated to include a plastic membrane – these curl badly if pasted. Even when dry they are very stiff and the curl from the roll will not lie flat. Use a very sticky adhesive to hold this type of foil. This can be achieved by pasting the wall twice
	Hanging
	Type 1 foils: Fold down without creasing, then hang to a plumb line and butt all joints. Smooth down with felt or rubber roller. Cut to top and bottom and around obstacles in the normal way with scissors
	Type 2 foils: Paste the wall once or twice as necessary, allow stipple texture to flow out and hang the dry foil to a plumb line, then butt all joints. Smooth down with felt or rubber roller
	Cut to top and bottom and around obstacles with plastic template and knife. Remove any paste immediately from the surface after fixing with a soft sponge, and polish dry with a very soft cloth
	Other information Available in 7.31 m x 0.91 m rolls
Hand-printed papers *Many of today's hand prints are produced by silkscreen printing, and have large patterns*	**Trimming** Knife and steel straight edge. Undercut **Pasting** Use stiff tub paste and PVA reinforced pastes. Paste the paper **Hanging** Select a good top and centre the pattern on important features. Take care not to crease the folds after pasting. Most modern papers are printed with waterfast inks and will not smear, but there are still some delicate papers that will spoil if paste comes into contact with the face. Always smooth the paper with a felt roller to prevent polishing and breaking the edges. Avoid the use of a seam roller which will only tend to polish the joints. Cut at top and bottom and around obstacles in the normal way with scissors **Other information** Available in 10.05 m x 0.525 m rolls

chapter 15

High Volume Low Pressure spray application

OVERVIEW

High Volume Low Pressure (HVLP) spraying is a technological solution for applying large amounts of paint or coatings to surfaces. This method is far more efficient than other methods; you can spray large areas with the same colour or spray intricate surfaces such as mouldings and fancy plasterwork, with a lot less fuss. As a painter and decorator, you may need to use spray equipment at some point in your career.

This chapter will cover the following topics:

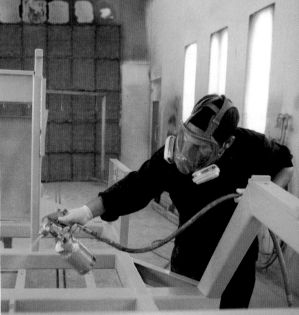

- Selecting and setting up equipment
- Health and safety when spraying
- Preparing areas for spraying
- Preparing and applying water-borne coatings
- Maintainence and storage of spraying equipment.

These topics can be found in the following modules:

CC 2002K	CC 2023K
CC 2002S	CC 2023S

Selecting and setting up equipment

There are various methods of applying paints and coatings to surfaces, as you will learn when becoming a decorator. A useful and efficient way is to spray paint. The High Volume Low Pressure (HVLP) method of applying paint is becoming more popular, as it gives a far better finish than a brush or roller. As the name suggests, this technology uses a high volume of air at low pressure (0.1 to 10 **PSI**) to **atomise** paint.

Advantages of HVLP

HVLP paint systems are light, mobile and easy to clean, and can greatly increase the speed of completing a job. As well as producing a high-quality finish, with no roller or brush marks, using HVLP reduces **overspray** (15 per cent of the paint or coating does not land on the surface), improves the transfer of coatings, and reduces the total volume of paint that is used. This in turn results in reduced emissions of two solvents found in paint:

- volatile organic compounds (VOCs), which are associated with the formation of smog and other air pollution, which adds to the problem of global warming

- hazardous air pollutants (HAPs), which are most associated with an increased risk of developing cancer.

Spray guns are designed to be easy to handle, and they need to be: the gun will be in your hand for five minutes, then put down, then it can be in your hands for hours at a time, so comfort is essential.

Spray guns

Like many spray guns, HVLP types have nozzles with large diameter openings, specially designed to atomise paint into a fine spray. The air nozzle, or air cap as it is sometimes known, is the most important part of the spray gun, as it forms the various spray patterns, directing the air into the paint stream to break it up into a fine mist.

Two types of spray gun are used in spraying: the bleeder gun, where only the fluid flow to the gun is controlled; and the non-bleeder gun, where both the air flow and the fluid flow to the gun are controlled by the use of a trigger. However, it should be

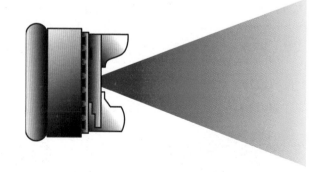

Figure 15.1 Paint being sprayed from tip of spray gun

An HVLP spray gun (electric)

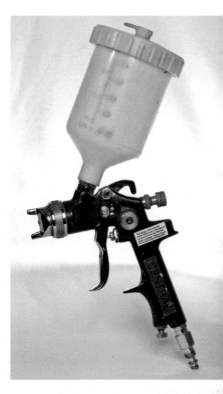

noted that a non-bleeder gun is used where air is stored in an air receiver, and a bleeder gun should be used where air is continuously pumped into the gun. Use of the correct type of spray gun will prevent damage and injury. The paint or coating is typically contained in a pressure vessel and fed to the spray gun using compressed air, usually supplied by a compressor. The compressor or motor drives air into the vessel or container to pressurise the paint. When the trigger is pulled, the paint or coating is released and atomised. The result is a gentle, controlled flow of paint with very little overspray.

A typical air-fed HVLP spray gun

Airless spraying systems

Airless spraying (high pressure) is very popular in the shipbuilding industry, with many painters carrying this skill over to the construction industry. Airless sprayers do not use compressed air to apply the paint: instead, the paint or coating is forced through the small tip opening of the gun at very high pressure to atomise it. A piston pump moves up – creating a vacuum to suck up the paint or coating into a chamber (the fluid section) – and then down to push the paint into a high-pressure hose and along to the gun.

An electric spray system

An air compressor

Piston-pump airless paint sprayers are the most versatile systems to use in this category as they can spray a variety of paint thicknesses. However, because of the high pressures used, these are also some of the most dangerous systems to operate.

Check the container or vessel that supplies the paint to the gun for any damage – this container is usually attached to the gun, with a pipe extending from the gun into the container, to feed the gun with paint/coating.

When you have checked all the equipment thoroughly and you have all the necessary PPE/RPE on, you are then ready to start your spraying job.

Types of spray gun

Air spray (conventional)

Paint is applied to the part by pneumatic fluid atomisation at higher air pressures. Air spray guns come in a variety of configurations: siphon feed, gravity feed, and pressure feed. This type of spray gun is most commonly used for industrial finishing.

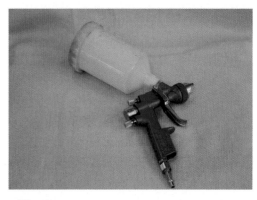

Air spray gun

- **Advantages** Complete pattern control. Finest atomisation. Good for high production rate applications.

- **Limitations** Uses more air. Creates the most fog. Low transfer efficiency.

HVLP

This is similar to the air spray gun in that it uses pneumatic fluid atomisation, except that HVLP uses a higher volume of air at a lower pressure. The lower pneumatic pressure allows for less overspray. HVLP spray guns come in a variety of styles: siphon feed, gravity feed, and pressure feed.

HVLP spray gun

- **Advantages** High transfer efficiency (65 per cent to 75 per cent). Sprays well into recesses and cavities.

- **Limitations** Uses a high volume of air. Atomisation not as fine as air spray guns.

Airless and air-assisted airless

Here atomisation is caused by the release of high-pressure fluid through a small opening. Airless atomisation can be assisted by air atomisation (air-assisted airless) to provide a finer finish and break up the tailing effect at the edge of the spray pattern. This method is most widely used by painting contractors, structural metal finishers and heavy equipment manufacturers.

Airless spray gun

- **Advantages** High fluid capability. Large patterns. Fastest spray application process. Low air consumption. Limited fog and bounce back – permits spraying into cavities.

- **Limitations** Potentially hazardous hydraulic injection. Higher rate of overspray due to high fluid output. Sharp patterns: difficult to blend. Expensive nozzles (tips). Coarse atomisation may flood surface or create runs. Equipment requires top maintenance.

Electrostatic

Electrostatic spray guns are most commonly used in spray painting factories or booths. With these guns, the material is atomised in the same way as conventional air (pneumatic), airless (fluid impingement), air-assisted airless or rotary guns. What is different is the way the paint is attracted to the surface. The particles of paint become electrically charged, and they are attracted to the surface to be painted, which has the opposite charge. The electricity may be turned off to permit normal spraying.

Did you know?

Many household items, like washing machines, are painted using electrostatic spray painting, each item is painted, then put in an oven to 'set' the paint

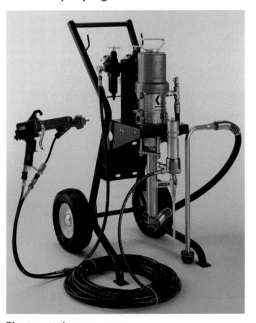

- **Advantages** A 'wrap around' effect: you can coat the back of the part while spraying from the front for example, you can coat both sides of a wire mesh fence by spraying from the front. Minimised overspray means material savings. Can be used with or without electrical charge.

- **Limitations** Some conductive materials require special equipment or paint reformulation. Parts must be conductive and able to be grounded. Difficult to penetrate cavities or recesses with power supply on.

Electrostatic spray gun

Health and safety when spraying

As a paint sprayer working in the painting and decorating industry, you face many dangers, but your training will help you to protect yourself from hazards. If you don't protect yourself, and you are involved in an accident, you will suffer immediate injury, as paint sprayers often face less obvious, more **insidious** hazards than conventional painters, which can result in death. These hazards are not always recognised until it is too late, so make sure you read the following section carefully.

Using the correct protection

The main hazard you will face as a paint sprayer comes from the fumes and mists given off during the application of paints/coatings. As well as the **PPE** you need to wear for all tasks as a painter and decorator, you will need to use RPE (respiratory protective equipment). RPE includes a variety of different spray masks.

- **Filter respirator** This is fitted with one or two disposable cartridge filters. It is important to select the correct type of filter to suit the nature of the hazard, and to replace filters as necessary. As with all masks, there are advantages and disadvantages with this type of mask (see the Table 15.1 on page 319).

- **Air-fed respirator** This comprises a full head set and regulator worn by the sprayer, which is connected to an air filtration unit. The filtration unit converts compressed air into clean, breathable air. The compressor must be situated well away from the work area.

- **Powered respirator** This has a battery-operated motor, which supplies the head set with filtered air. There are two types of powered respirator: one has a separate motor and filter away from the headset; the other has these items integrated into the helmet.

Checking your equipment

Once you have selected the correct spray painting equipment and necessary PPE and RPE, you need to check all components before you use them. This will prevent possible accidents to yourself and others, and will avoid problems with the job at hand.

You will need to check that there is an air supply to the spray gun, by checking the compressor/generator that supplies the air. The air is supplied to the gun via a hose, and within this air stream there is a region of low pressure. Check the hose for any damage, as this could cause a lack of pressure, causing problems when you apply the paint.

The gun has a trigger mechanism, which opens and closes a nozzle mounted in the gun. Around the nozzle, there are lots of holes through which air is expelled. You need to check both the nozzle and the trigger for any blockages or old paint/debris as this will also cause production problems.

Mask type	Advantages	Disadvantages
Filter respirator	• Cartridge filters can be selected to offer protection against toxic vapours and dust • Suitable when spraying some solvent-based coatings in well-ventilated areas • Can be worn with safety goggles	• Expensive compared to dust masks • Can become uncomfortable when worn for long periods • Not suitable for use in oxygen-deficient areas • Not suitable for use in confined spaces • Cartridge filters have a limited life and must be replaced regularly • Require hygienic maintenance (regular cleaning)
Air-fed respirator	• Effective against the most toxic carcinogenic /isocyanate two-pack paint coatings • Offers eye and respiratory protection • Protects against toxic dusts, gases and vapours • Particularly useful in confined spaces • Offers all-round vision	• Expensive to buy and maintain • Needs special training • Can be cumbersome and uncomfortable over long periods • Visors can be coated with spray mist • Needs a suitable compressor
Powered respirator	• Offers head, eye and respiratory protection • Protects against toxic dusts, gases and vapours • Particularly useful on demolition and refurbishment work • Offers all-round vision	• Expensive to buy and maintain (batteries, filters and visors) • Can be cumbersome and uncomfortable over long periods • Visors can be coated with spray mist

Table 15.1 RPE spray masks

Preparing areas for spraying

Speed and quality of finish are the main advantages of paint spraying, but one of the major disadvantages of this method is overspray. The HVLP system reduces this problem, but does not remove it. Overspray occurs because you cannot cut in effectively with a spray gun: there is always a degree of 'bounce back' of paint from the surface being sprayed.

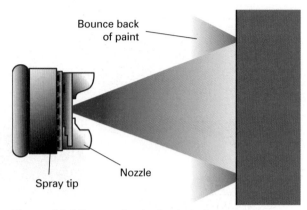

Figure 15.2 Bounce back of paint when spraying

Masking

Surrounding surfaces need to be protected from being damaged. The best way to protect any surface that does not need spraying is to cover it with masking materials. The main masking materials used while spraying are:

- polythene sheeting
- masking boards/spray shields
- dust sheets
- masking paper
- polythene rolls
- hardboard
- corrugated plastic
- cardboard
- polythene bags
- masking tape.

Figure 15.3 Masking light fittings and switches

Low-tack masking tape is used with most of the above items because it is good at securing the items to surfaces, but is also easy to remove during 'de-masking' (when you remove all masking materials after spraying). Masking tape is also ideal for masking up small items like electric sockets and light switches. This sort of tape is available in a variety of widths to suit different needs, the most common being 25 mm and 50 mm.

Polythene bags such as common plastic shopping bags are useful for protecting light fittings, wall lamps, etc. when secured with masking tape.

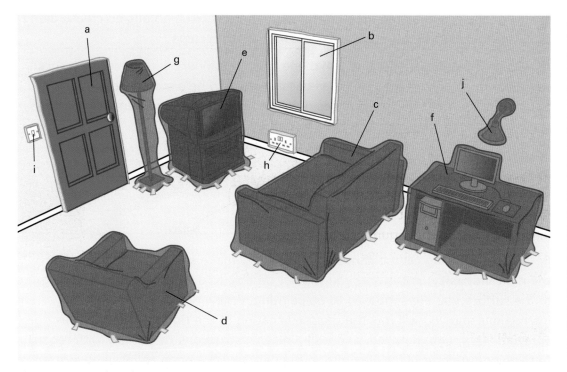

Figure 15.4 Masking larger items

a-b	Protect doors and windows with polythene or dust sheets and secure with making tape
c-g	Protect furniture and machinery with polythene or dust sheets and secure with masking tape
h-i	Mask electrical sockets and light switches with masking tape
j	Wrap light fixtures in polythene bags and secure with masking tape

Larger items such as doors, furniture and machinery are usually masked up with polythene sheets and dust sheets secured with masking tape. Rolls of polythene secured with tape are good for wrapping up tubular items.

When spraying walls and roof spaces in factories, warehouses and industrial premises, hardboard, corrugated plastic and cardboard secured with tape are ideal for protecting the floor areas. Windows, carpets, kitchen appliances and polished floors all need to be protected with masking paper and masking tape, sheeting and screening.

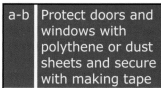

Did you know?

Masking paper comes in three different widths – 150 mm, 225 mm and 300 mm – and masking tape comes in 25 mm, 50 mm and 75 mm widths

Masking aids

Masking tape and masking paper can be used together in a masking machine, which allows you to mask up more quickly, saving time and money. There are two types of masking machine: a hand-held one and a static machine. Each type has a roller, which the masking tape is pushed onto, and a cutting blade for quick cutting action.

Masking boards and spray shields are sheets of springy aluminium which come in sizes of about 10" wide and lengths of 24", 36" and 48", reinforced along one edge, with an 18" handle fitted to the middle. These pieces of equipment are invaluable in big jobs where the use of

Figure 15.5 Spray shield

masking tape would be too time-consuming. There is often an angled crease along the length to allow better access of the spray fan in corners.

As well as using dustsheets and polythene to protect floors and furniture, you can use them to cordon off areas such as passageways to help stop dust and fumes reaching other areas of the premises. Remember to make sure that any openings are covered to prevent damage from overspray.

Preparing and applying water-borne coatings

Before any spraying can be carried out you must make sure that the paint is at the right **viscosity**: if it is not, you will not be able to apply the paint or coating to the surface you are supposed to be painting. Follow the manufacturer's instructions and you will mix the required coating to the right consistency for spraying. Thorough, detailed, and well-written instructions (especially with regard to thinning) are crucial for maximising the performance of an HVLP spray system, as everything that goes through an HVLP sprayer must be thinned properly. If you do not follow the instructions, you leave everything to chance. The result could be the paint or coating not spraying correctly, the gun clogging up and not working, or producing a sub-standard finish to the job.

Another important point to keep in mind is to make sure that, after you have correctly mixed the paint or coating, you should keep dirt and debris out of the paint. Small pieces of dirt or splinters of wood can easily become lodged in the tip of the gun, stopping it from spraying; dust stirred up by other trades working nearby could contaminate the paint and make it unusable. To prevent this from happening, it is a good idea to use a paint strainer. This piece of equipment allows you to strain a good quantity of the paint into a clean, dust-free container.

If you are not trained, are in a hurry or are using poorly maintained equipment, you may need to redo the job. In the end, you will spend more time and money preparing and painting the surface again. This could result in a bad reputation for yourself or the company you work for.

The spraying action

You must make sure you get the correct training before you try to complete a spraying task. Once trained, you should always follow these simple rules to achieve a perfect finish.

- Keep the distance between the gun and the surface as close as possible to the manufacturer's recommendation at all times.

- Move the spray gun parallel to the work, keeping the gun at a right angle.

- Overlap each successive stroke by 50 per cent.

- Trigger the spray gun at the beginning and end of each stroke, making sure that the gun is in motion before triggering. This will reduce overspray and runs.

- Optimise the fan size to suit the job/surface you are spraying.

It is important to keep the correct distance between the spray gun and the surface to be painted. If you place the gun too close to the surface, bounceback increases resulting in poor finish quality: the paint or coating could run and sag. If you have too much distance between the gun and the surface, it can result in overshoot and 'paint fog' – where not enough paint/coating hits the surface, creating more overspray.

When first spraying, many people arc the spray gun automatically. Don't let this action develop into a habit, as **arcing** the gun results in an uneven finish: the coating will be the right thickness in the middle of a stroke but starved of coating at the edges.

Tilting the spray gun causes similar faults to arcing – excessive overspray and an uneven or patchy finish.

Always hold the gun perpendicular to the surface, that is, square to the surface. The correct spraying speed allows a full wet coat of paint or coating to be applied to the surface without any defects. You should move the gun in a confident, flowing fashion, without hesitation.

Definition

Arcing – creating an arc, or a section of a circle; when spraying a surface, this is when you curve your wrist, and the gun, resulting in an uneven finish to the paint/ coating

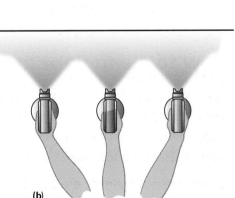

(a)　　　(b)

Figure 15.6 Incorrect (a) and correct (b) ways to hold the gun

Water-borne coatings

You can spray a variety of different paints and coatings using this system of application, but for this chapter we will concentrate on water-borne coatings. These coatings need to be thinned with water before you can spray them onto surfaces. Coatings that you can spray using the HVLP system include:

- acrylic primer/undercoat

- matt emulsion paint

- vinyl silk emulsion

- masonry paint (emulsion-based)

- moisture vapour permeable coating (water-thinned type)

- low odour eggshell finish (water-borne)

- emulsion varnish

- wood stain (water-borne).

Remember that correct preparation and correct training prevent poor-quality workmanship!

Maintaining and storage of spraying equipment

Having completely clean spray equipment is vital to trouble-free spraying. If you expect spray equipment to function when you use it, you must ensure that you look after it correctly, both during use and when the job is finished. If the spray gun, paint lines, paint containers, air lines or nozzles are dirty and badly maintained, it will affect the ease of application and the quality of workmanship. Poor care and maintenance can also damage equipment and cause it to break down, which will be costly to you or the company you work for.

How to clean your equipment

It is easiest to clean away the coatings that you have used immediately after application, while the coating is still wet. At this point, you can flush away any unwanted material from the equipment with water – something that is near impossible if you let the coating dry in the spray equipment.

You should clean your spray equipment as follows:

- When the job has been completed, empty any remaining paint/coating back into your main pot, making sure you have removed all traces of the coating from your spray container.

- Depending on which model of HVLP system you have used, spray or run a quantity of clean water through the system, until it is perfectly clear: if it is not, dried coatings can build up in the lines, possibly breaking away, contaminating fresh coatings and blocking the nozzle.

- Blow air through the paint lines after flushing them through to dry them out, then coil them up avoiding kinks and twists in the lines.

- Once the spray gun is free from coating/paint, remove the nozzle/air cap from the gun and clean it thoroughly again, paying particular attention to the holes in the cap.

- Store everything in a dry, clean area, ready for next use. Hang up the gun or lay it down in a drawer, preferably in its original packaging. Hang the paint lines up in a dry area on brackets or pegs.

- Place the compressor or generator in its correct storage area to avoid theft or damage.

Following these rules will help you complete a quality finish when spraying.

FAQ

Why do people spray paint rather than use brushes and rollers?

Spray painting gives a far superior finish, and is quicker and more cost-effective in the long run.

What sort of preparation do you need to do for spray painting?

Essentially, you need to do just the same as you would if you were brushing or rolling. You need to rub and brush down, wash down, fill, etc. as is required. The only difference may be that you will need to mask very carefully, as the mist from spray painting can spread a long way.

On the job: The paint sprayer

Rob is working on a new build site. He is a first-year apprentice and is proving to be a very quick learner. Rob's boss comes and tells him that when he has finished what he is doing, Rob is to go and get a paint sprayer and start a new job using this piece of equipment. Rob tells his boss that he has never used a paint sprayer before. Rob's boss says that the instructions are in the box and Rob should be able to work it out.

What do you think Rob should do? Do you think Rob's boss is right to ask Rob to carry out this task?

Knowledge check

1. Why is spraying becoming more popular?

2. What are 'VOCs'?

3. Name three types of spray gun.

4. What is the maximum pressure HVLP systems run at?

5. Name the main hazard spray painters face.

6. What does 'atomise' mean?

7. What is another name for the nozzle of the spray gun?

8. How is the spray gun operated?

9. What does RPE stand for?

10. Name an RPE mask.

11. What percentage of paint lands on a surface when spraying with an HVLP system?

12. Before spraying, why should you check the nozzle and trigger of the gun?

13. Give two advantages and two disadvantages with regard to an air-fed respirator.

14. Why should the paint or coating be at the right viscosity prior to spraying?

15. How can you stop dirt and debris contaminating the paint or coating before spraying?

16. Why should you keep the correct distance between a surface and a spray gun while spraying?

17. What is the best way to protect any surfaces that are not to be sprayed?

18. Describe a good way to protect a polished floor before spraying.

19. How can masking tape be used more easily to mask up areas?

20. Why should you avoid arcing the gun when spraying?

Technical Certificate: Module Codes

The technical certificate modules covered in each chapter are indicated on the chapter opener page by their code.

MODULE CODE	MODULE NAME
CC 1001K CC 1001S	Know how to carry out safe working practices Carry out safe working practices
CC 2002K CC 2002S	Knowledge of information, quantities and communicating with others 2 Information, quantities and communicating with others 2
CC 2003K CC 2003S	Knowledge of building methods and construction technology 2 Building methods and construction technology 2
CC 2019K CC 2019S	Know how to prepare surfaces 2 Prepare surfaces 2
CC 2020K CC 2020S	Know how to apply paint systems by brush and roller 2 Apply paint systems by brush and roller 2
CC 2021K CC 2021S	Know how to apply standard papers to walls and ceilings Apply standard papers to walls and ceilings
CC 2022K CC 2022S	Know how to produce specialist decorative finishes 2 Produce specialist decorative finishes 2
CC 2023K CC 2023S	Know how to apply paint systems using high volume low pressure (HVLP) spray equipment Apply paint systems using high volume low pressure (HVLP) spray equipment
CC 2024K CC 2024S	Know how to erect and dismantle access equipment and working platforms 2 Erect and dismantle access equipment and working platforms 2

Technical Certificate: Core Module Outcomes

This table outlines in detail the target outcomes for the core module training units and specifies in which chapter each outcome is met. The units that end in 'K' are particularly covered throughout the book, as they address the knowledge of certain criteria. This book will fully cover units that end in 'K' and will aid in the achievement of the units that end in 'S', which address the practical parts of the units.

For some outcomes, there are numerous instances throughout the book where sections or parts of the outcome are met. For example, health and safety is prevalent throughout the book in the form of safety tips, reminders and notes. These instances have not been indentified in this table.

MODULE	OUTCOME	CHAPTER
CC 1001K CC 1001S	1. Health and safety regulations	2 *Health and safety*
CC 1001K CC 1001S	2. Accident/first aid/emergency procedures and reporting	2 *Health and safety*
CC 1001K CC 1001S	3. Identify hazards	2 *Health and safety* Carried throughout book
CC 1001K CC 1001S	4. Health and hygiene	2 *Health and safety*
CC 1001K CC 1001S	5. Safe handling of materials and equipment	2 *Health and safety* 5 *Handling and storage of materials*
CC 1001K CC 1001S	6. Basic working platforms	3 *Working at height*
CC 1001K CC 1001S	7. Work with electricity	2 *Health and safety*
CC 1001K CC 1001S	8. PPE	2 *Health and safety* Carried throughout book
CC 1001K CC 1001S	9. Fire and emergency	2 *Health and safety*
CC 1001K CC 1001S	10. Signs and notices	2 *Health and safety*
CC 2002K CC 2002S	1. Interpret and produce building information	6 *Drawings*
CC 2002K CC 2002S	2. Estimate quantity of resources	7 *Numeracy*
CC 2002K CC 2002S	3. Communicate workplace requirements	1 *The construction industry*
CC 2003K CC 2003S	1. Principles behind walls, floors and roofs	4 *Principles of building*
CC 2003K CC 2003S	2. Principles behind internal work	4 *Principles of building* 5 *Handling and storage of materials*
CC 2003K CC 2003S	3. Materials storage	5 *Handling and storage of materials*

Technical Certificate: Painting and Decorating Module Outcomes

This table outlines the target outcomes for the certificate-specific module training units and specifies in which chapter each outcome is met. The units that end in 'K' are particularly covered throughout the book, as they address the knowledge of certain criteria. This book will fully cover units that end in 'K' and will aid in the achievement of the units that end in 'S', which address the practical parts of the units.

MODULE	OUTCOME	CHAPTER
CC 2019K CC 2019S	1. Preparation tools and equipment	5 *Handling and storage of materials* 8 *Tools and equipment* 3 *Working at height*
CC 2019K CC 2019S	2. Materials used to provide protection when preparing surfaces	9 *Site preparation*
CC 2019K CC 2019S	3. Surface defects and surfaces which need preparation	10 *Preparation of surfaces* 12 *Surface coatings*
CC 2020K CC 2020S	1. Tools and equipment used to apply paint systems	5 *Handling and storage of aterials* 3 *Working at height* 8 *Tools and equipment*
CC 2020K CC 2020S	2. Protection of areas prior to applying paint systems	9 *Site preparation*
CC 2020K CC 2020S	3. Prepare surfaces prior to applying surfaces	10 *Preparation of surfaces* 12 *Surface coatings*
CC 2020K CC 2020S	4. Apply paint systems by brush and roller	11 *Colour* 12 *Surface coatings* 13 *Applying paint and creating special effects*
CC 2020K CC 2020S	5. Measuring areas for paint amounts	6 *Drawings* 7 *Numeracy skills* 12 *Surface coatings* 13 *Applying paint and creating special effects*
CC 2021K CC 2021S	1. Tools and equipment used to apply standard papers to walls and ceilings	5 *Handling and storage of materials* 3 *Working at height* 8 *Tools and equipment*
CC 2021K CC 2021S	2. Protection of areas prior to hanging wall papers	9 *Site preparation*
CC 2021K CC 2021S	3. Preparation of surfaces prior to applying standard papers	10 *Preparation of surfaces*

CC 2021K CC 2021S	4. Applying standard papers to walls and ceilings	14 *Applying surface coverings*
CC 2021K CC 2021S	5. Measuring areas and surfaces for correct application of papers	6 *Drawings* 7 *Numeracy skills* 14 *Applying surface coverings*
CC 2022K CC 2022S	1. Specialist tools and equipment	5 *Handling and storage of materials* 3 *Working at height* 8 *Tools and equipment*
CC 2022K CC 2022S	2. Protection of areas prior to applying specialist decorative finishes	9 *Site preparation*
CC 2022K CC 2022S	3. Preparation of surfaces prior to applying specialist decorative finishes	10 *Preparation of surfaces*
CC 2022K CC 2022S	4. Applying specialist decorative finishes 5. Measuring areas and surfaces for correct application of specialist decorative finishes	13 *Applying paint and special effects* 11 *Colour* 6 *Drawings* 7 *Numeracy skills*
CC 2023K CC 2023S	1. Tools and equipment needed when applying coatings by (HVLP) spray equipment	8 *Tools and equipment* 5 *Handling and storage of materials* 3 *Working at height* 15 *High Volume Low Pressure spray application*
CC 2023K CC 2023S	2. Protection of areas/surfaces when spraying	9 *Site preparation* 15 *High Volume Low Pressure spray application*
CC 2023K CC 2023S	3. Preparation of surfaces prior to spraying	10 *Preparation of surfaces* 12 *Surface coatings* 15 *High Volume Low Pressure spray application*
CC 2023K CC 2023S	4. Measuring areas/surfaces prior to spraying for correct coating amounts	6 *Drawings* 7 *Numeracy skills*
CC 2023K CC 2023S	5. Applying coatings by spray application	11 *Colour* 12 *Surface coatings* 15 *High Volume Low Pressure spray application*
CC 2024K CC 2024S	1. Correct handling of materials	5 *Handling and storage of materials*
CC 2024K CC 2024S	2. Selecting access equipment	3 *Working at height*
CC 2024K CC 2024S	3. General safety considerations	3 *Working at height*

Glossary

abrading (abrasion)	to wear away by rubbing
adhere	stick
adhesive	glue
alkaline	having a pH greater than 7 (an acid has a pH of less than 7)
architrave	a decorative moulding, usually made from timber, that is fitted around door and window frames to hide the gap between the frame and the wall
arcing	creating an arc or a section of a circle
atomised	when a liquid is broken up into tiny droplets like a mist
banding	where brickwork has sections in slightly different shades
barrier cream	a cream used to protect the skin from damage or infection
bitumen	a heavy, semi-solid, brown-black substance also known as asphalt or tar
burnishing	polishing
carded scaffolder	someone who holds a recognised certificate showing competence in scaffold erection
combustion	burning or catching on fire
conservation	preservation of the environment and wildlife
contamination	when harmful chemicals or substances pollute something (e.g. water)
corroded	destroyed or damaged by a chemical reaction
corrosive	a substance that can damage things it comes into contact with (e.g. material, skin)
coving	a decorative moulding that is fitted at the top of a wall where it meets the ceiling

crawling board	a board or platform placed on roof joists which spread the weight of the worker allowing roof work to be carried out safely
damp proof course	a substance that is used to prevent damp from penetrating a building
decant	to pour liquid from one container to another
decorator's crutch	a rolled-up length of wallpaper or a piece of wood used to support a concertina fold
dermatitis	a skin condition whereby the affected area is red, itchy and sore
driers	a liquid chemical that promotes drying
drop match	a wallpaper pattern that is not repeated horizontally across the paper
durable	long-lasting
egress	an exit or way out
embossed	(wallpaper) decorated with designs that stand out from the surface
employer	the person or company you work for
enforced	making sure a law is obeyed
equal stretch	(of wallpaper lengths) supple and pliable to the same degree
filling	the bristles of a paint brush
fitch	a type of paintbrush used for painting areas difficult to reach with a standard paintbrush; also used for more detailed work
flush	when one surface is level and even with another surface
focal point	a place where your eyes will tend to look
hazard	a danger or risk

Health and Safety Executive (HSE)	the government organisation that enforces health and safety law in the UK		**porosity**	the ability of a surface to allow water through
induction	a formal introduction you will receive when you start any new job, where you will be shown around, shown where the toilets and canteen etc. are, and told what to do if there is a fire		**pot life**	the amount of time paint remains at a workable consistency
			PPE	personal protection equipment
			proactive	taking action *before* something happens (e.g. an accident)
			proportionately	in proportion to the size of something else
insidous	advancing without you realising it; treacherous		**prosecute**	to accuse someone of committing a crime, which usually results in being taken to court and, if found guilty, being punished
inverted	tipped and turned upside down			
jute	a rough fibre made from a tropical plant used in paper-backed Hessian wallpaper			
key	roughness on a surface provided to aid adhesion		**PSI**	per square inch, a measurement of pressure
Lincrusta-Walton	a wall-hanging with a relief pattern used to imitate wood panelling		**PVC**	polyvinyl chloride (a type of plastic)
			rabbit skin size	a substance made from animal tissues, which is applied before a later of varnish on a gilded surface
lint	tiny, fuzzy fibres of material			
LPG	liquefied petroleum gas			
manual handling	using the body to lift, carry or pull a load		**reactive**	taking action *after* something happens
mildew	a fungus that grows in damp conditions		**relief material**	a material that has a pattern that stands out from the background
millscale	a scale that forms on steel			
mnemonic	a pattern of letters or words formulated as an aid to memorise something		**relief surfaces**	a surface that has parts that are raised or projecting out from the background
mordant solution	a substance that provides a key		**rendering**	stone or brickwork coated with plaster
muster points	fire assembly points		**resin**	a natural or man-made material used as a binder in paint
noxious	harmful or poisonous			
overspray	paint that does not hit its intended surface, floating away and being wasted		**restoration**	returning a building to its original condition
			retard	dealy or slow
permeable	allowing liquids and gases to pass through		**rust**	a red or yellowish-brown coating of iron oxide
plant	industrial machinery		**sanitise**	to make something clean and free of germs
plaster skim	a thin layer of plaster that is put on to walls to give a smooth and even finish		**saponification**	a chemical reaction that makes soap and so foams up as a result
plumb bob	a weight attached to string or twine used to produce a vertical line			

scumble   a semi-transparent stain or glaze applied over a hard, dry ground coat

scuttle   a special container for paint used when painting from a ladder with a roller

shelf life   how long something will remain fit for purpose while being stored

size   seal

skinning   the formation of a skin on paint which occurs when the top layer dries out

skirting   a decorative moulding that is fitted at the bottom of a wall to hide the gap between the wall and the floor

spig   a very fine nail usied in glazing

spot prime   the application of primer (base coat) to small areas

stiles   the side pieces of a stepladder into which the steps are set

straight match   a wallpaper design that is repeated horizontally across the paper

symptom   a sign of illness or disease (e.g. difficulty breathing, a sore hand or a lump under the skin)

tie-rods   metal rods underneath the rungs of a ladder that give extra support to the rungs

toxic   poisonous

truss   prefabricated component of a roof which spreads the load of the roof over the outer walls and forms its shape

vibration white finger   a condition that can be caused by using vibrating machinery (usually for very long periods of time). The blood supply to the fingers is reduced which causes pain, tingling and sometimes spasms (shaking)

viscosity   the thickness of a liquid

vitrified   a material that has been converted into a glass-like substance via exposure to high temperatures

volatile   quick to evaporate (turn to gas)

Index

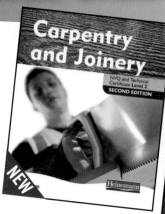

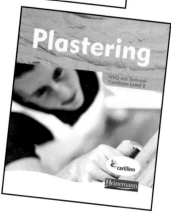